CABINETMAKING *The Professional Approach*

CABINETMAKING
The Professional Approach

Alan Peters

Stobart & Son Ltd
London

The choice lies with each one of us
as individuals, to build up or destroy.
So for the artist and craftsman he has
no enemy but time. Life is all too short
for learning his job and doing it well.
He cannot start too young nor live too long.

John Farleigh in *The Creative Craftsman*

Published 1984, reprinted 1986

ISBN 0 85442 024 X

Stobart & Son Ltd, 67–73 Worship Street, London, EC2A 2EL

Printed in Great Britain by A. Wheaton & Co. Ltd., Exeter

Preface

IT is now over twenty years since I set up my first workshop, and much has changed in that time. There is now a much greater public appreciation of creative craftsmanship in all fields, and it is no longer considered escapist to earn a living working largely with one's hands. The craft of furniture making in particular has been experiencing quite a renaissance these last few years, both here, in the USA, and throughout the English speaking world.

It is an exciting time to live and work and my motive in writing this book is partly the selfish one of stopping and taking stock of my own development, and partly I hope, to encourage all the young students and those not so young, who may be contemplating life as a professional woodworker. Hopefully, too, it may be of interest to the thousands of amateurs, who often have the ability plus the freedom from the economic restraints which can inhibit the professional, to produce work of a very high standard. My message to them is that simple designs, simple shapes, done well are just as true a test of craftsmanship as many of the elaborate designs that were popular in the past. For all too often they and students misguidedly seek the most difficult solution to the simplest problem and this is not the natural role of the craftsman.

This book is about cabinetmaking as I have experienced it. It is not intended, and I hope it does not read, as a criticism of others, for the whole strength of the craft today is that it is about individuals working in a way that is true and honest to them. If I have learnt anything these past twenty years, it is that there is no one right approach to either the design or the making of furniture.

Finally, I hope this book will also be of interest to all those people who, like me, love wood, love to feel it, stroke it, or just look at it, and who hate to see it abused or wasted.

Alan Peters,
Kentisbeare, 1984.

Dedication

At a time when 'the crafts' and the term 'fine craftsmanship' have come to mean so many different things, and when success in this field so often implies success first as an artist, designer or even entrepreneur, I feel it appropriate to dedicate this book to a man who would consider himself none of these things, but simply a maker. A man virtually unknown outside his own Hampshire village, but a man who for over 60 years now has made things both sensitively and superbly well, yet with a directness and economy of time and effort and a lack of undue fuss that most of us can only ever envy and admire.

Bert Upton was only 14 when he entered the workshop of Edward Barnsley in 1924, and for five years he went through the hard graft that an apprenticeship of that period entailed – tea boy, general dogsbody, long hours and weeks of moving and stacking timber, with the occasional reward of making his own piece from start to finish. At 19 he began the real task of learning to make furniture and joinery, and out of it all came a craftsman.

Not only do I owe this man a tremendous debt, but so too do all the pupils and apprentices who have come through the Barnsley workshops during the past fifty years. Today in Britain there is no shortage of people with bright ideas, no shortage of trained artists and designers, but so few craftsmen of his calibre. Equally at home working with machines or hand tools, he knows the merits and limitations of his materials, and has not suffered boredom during a lifetime of actually making things. Bert Upton, at 75 and in retirement since 1979, is still actively making because he cannot stop. We should not forget that this is what the crafts are primarily about.

Contents

Fig. 1   13th century oak chest. Collection of the V & A Museum, London.

One

The Cotswold School and the Birth of the Craft Furniture Movement

THE exciting upsurge in small craft workshops making quality creative furniture in recent years in Britain, the States, and throughout the English speaking world, has its origins in the ideals first expounded by the mid-nineteenth century pioneers of the British Arts and Crafts Movement, John Ruskin and William Morris. They too were disillusioned with industrialisation, which was more advanced here than elsewhere, and which they claimed diminished the dignity of labour to the point that men became mere cogs in a vast machine. Ruskin wrote way back in 1849 of one man no longer making a pin, but simply polishing the point whilst another made the head, and if that were true in the mid-nineteenth century, it became increasingly so over the years with more specialisation within industry and more recently with increased automation.

Thus today the need of many people is not just to have work and a reasonable standard of living from it, but to be able to derive satisfaction from the work they do, by exercising greater control over it and by having greater personal responsibility for the final product or service. And it was this need for a man to have pride and satisfaction in the work he did that was such a corner-stone of the Arts and Crafts Movement, rather than mere artistic or political considerations. It threw up men like Ernest Gimson and the Barnsley brothers

Fig. 2   Wm. Morris 'Sussex' armchair 1880

Fig. 3   Gimson cabinet c. 1891. Marquetry doors in palm, ebony and orangewood with silver handles

Fig. 4   Gimson ash ladder-back chair; 1896 onwards.

who formed what later became known as the Cotswold School of Furniture Making; on the other side of the Atlantic, Gustav Stickley also became influenced, and he in turn instigated the American equivalent with his Mission or Craftsman furniture; and in continental Europe too, these original ideas precipitated the Deutscher Werkbund in Germany in 1907, the Austrian equivalent in 1910, and greatly influenced Carl Malmsten in Stockholm.

Ernest Gimson was only a nineteen year old architectural student when he first met William Morris in 1884 but he quickly fell under the influence of both Morris' example and the writing of Ruskin. So, in 1893, after a preliminary attempt at designing and making furniture in London with Kenton & Co., he and his two close friends, Sidney and Ernest Barnsley, left their London architectural practices to go to the then quite remote area of the Cotswold Hills in Gloucestershire to work out their ideas for furniture making in a way which would give dignity back to the maker and at the same time establish some new tangible approach to furniture making.

Their ideas were broadly in keeping with the wider aims of the Arts and Crafts Movement, as were to be practised by C. R. Ashbee's Guild of Handicraft both in London and when re-established later at Chipping Campden also in the Cotswolds. They all believed strongly in a return to handwork as a means of achieving fulfilment for the maker and quality for the consumer, and that the workman should always be encouraged to give of his best, even if this meant a more expensive article.

Ernest Gimson and the Barnsley brothers interpreted the return to handwork far more literally than Ashbee's Guild, having no machines other than a treadle circular saw in their workshops, but in many other ways they were far more practical. They believed in honesty to materials and construction, in functionalism, and, in general, in simplicity of line with a minimum of decoration. They expressed a strong preference for native timber and largely ignored the colonial mahogany and rosewood so favoured for the previous 200 years. They also preferred their timber to be left as natural as possible and often finished straight from the cutting edge; scrubbed oak table tops and beeswaxed walnut replaced for them the current Victorian practice of staining and french polishing.

Many of these ideals were shared and became the foundation of a more general Modern Movement in architecture and design which had already drawn other architects into its orbit, such as Philip Webb, C.F.A. Voysey, W.R. Lethaby, E.W. Godwin and, later, C.R. Mackintosh and A.H. Mackmurdo, all architects cum furniture designers whose impact was on design thinking rather than on a reassessment of craftsmanship and cabinetmaking.

To fulfil their aims, Gimson and the Barnsleys largely ignored the golden age of furniture, the fashionable 18th century with its continental influences, and went back further, as Morris had done, to the Middle Ages for their inspiration, and they found it not so much in the furniture of that period but in the joinery construction of mediaeval houses and barns, which they felt represented a truly native tradition. They took the chamfer and through-jointing techniques of the wheelwright shown on the beautiful farm wagons and other tools of the field and incorporated them into their work. Following the example of William Morris with his Sussex chair, it was Gimson who sought out the few remaining country chairmakers who had been carrying on in a tradition of work untouched for centuries and revived interest in their work, the purest of structures, which are fortunately still being made today in the 1980's by such superb craftsmen as Neville Neal and his son in Warwickshire.

This was however more than a nostalgic harking back to the past, for, having stripped Victorian vulgarity to its bare bones, and conveniently forgetting the prevailing cabinetmaking techniques of cleverly hiding all forms and methods of construction, they proceeded to create over the next twenty years or so furniture that had its roots deep in British rural craft tradition but possessing also a freshness, honesty, and at times originality that has rarely been equalled in any craft furniture since.

They were no doubt influenced by their travels abroad, but they were also inspired by the idealism of Morris and by the practical examples of architects and designers such as

Philip Webb, Ford Madox Brown, C.F.A. Voysey and W.R. Lethaby. Gimson in particular seems to have been affected by the very strong and personal work of E.W. Godwin who began designing furniture in 1867 in what became known as the Anglo-Japanese manner. Godwin had made a great study of Japanese interiors, and his rectilinear design not only affected Gimson's earlier work but was also the forerunner of so much that was to come later both here and on the continent, inspiring men such as C.R. Mackintosh, who later shared his love for ebonised surfaces and adapted and softened his strong linear style. Godwin's influence can also be seen later in the work of Gerrit Rietveld and the de Stijl movement in Holland.

Fig. 5 E.W. Godwin's sideboard, c. 1867. Ebonised wood with silver plated handles and hinges.

But what makes Gimson and the Barnsley brothers so important, beyond their actual work and designs is the fact that they were the first of a new breed of furniture craftsmen and cabinetmakers, the creative craftsmen, the designer-makers. For, although there had always been excellent craftsmen, cabinetmakers and joiners, with skills and traditions handed down through many centuries, they were not themselves designers or by nature innovators. They worked more by instinct and according to tradition, and, unfortunately, their natural instinct for the rightness of things was being eroded by a furniture industry in Victorian times which could no longer afford their skills, or, if it could, misapplied them in the execution of excessive decoration.

There had, of course, been the fashionable designers of the 18th century – Chippendale, Hepplewhite, Adam and Sheraton amongst others – whose designs were copied so widely that they became national styles, but all too often it fell to the country craftsman to put humility into those designs, and to create the more tasteful masterpieces most of us now prefer and cherish. Chippendale, as well as publishing his directory of designs, also ran his own workshops employing up to 200 people and production line methods, a conveyor belt system that was far removed from what was to happen in the Cotswold Hills in the early 1900's.

Fig. 6 C.F.A. Voysey, oak desk, 1896.

There, there were three well-educated, professional men who, as largely self-taught craftsmen, began the intellectual exercise of designing and making their own furniture in their own premises, with complete control of the whole process from drawing board to completion. They were not sidetracked, like many in the arts and crafts movement and later, into spending their days milking goats and living the simple life.

Apart from the change in attitude towards the use of machines, these workshops in the Cotswolds at the turn of the century are the very embodiment of what is now happening throughout Britain and the English speaking world. We have shops, like Gimson's at Daneway House, where the making is done by a small band of skilled craftsmen and trainees under the close direction of the master, who is the true creator of all that is produced although he himself may rarely touch a tool. We also have shops like Sidney Barnsley's, where the designer is the sole maker and refuses to relinquish any part of the making, however tedious, to others. And there are plenty of others in between, with perhaps one apprentice, or, quite common now, as in Gimson's and Barnsley's earlier years together at Pinbury, a group of craftsmen working together in shared premises yet producing independent work. Basically though, the motives are the same – to gain the fulfilment that industry and commerce cannot give, and to have complete control over the aesthetic and technical standard of what is made, and to stamp a little of the maker's personality on the furniture itself.

Ernest Gimson died when only 55 in 1919 and his by then quite famous Daneway House workshops were disbanded just a year later. So all in all it was a relatively short period of intense activity at Daneway from 1902 to 1919, particularly as World War 1 ate considerably into the last four years, but it did at one time rise to as many as 15 craftsmen and trainees. His period at Daneway followed on from the previous workshops shared with the Barnsleys at nearby Pinbury from 1893.

Fig. 7 C.F.A. Voysey, oak armchair with leather upholstery, c.1906

Throughout his life Gimson was very critical of business methods and commercialisation. He spoke of the sheer inability of businessmen to understand good work and believe in it. At a time when industry was devoting much of its time to producing inferior copies of the handwork of past ages, he desired that commercialisation might leave the arts and handcrafts alone. On this point he declared:

"Let machinery be honest and make its own machine-buildings and its own machine-furniture, let it make chairs and tables of stamped aluminium if it likes. Why not?"

All he asked was that it might then use its own wits and not degrade the work of past craftsmen. He saw no distinction between the arts and the crafts, and he had no time for art which did not minister to some human need.

His attitude to his own workmen was always the same; he watched for their interests and was constantly planning and encouraging them to do their best. He felt deeply their need to satisfy their own self-pride and enthusiasm. Commenting on this once and its effect on the cost of the final article, he asked,

"What of the lifetime of the worker, is he to be constantly giving less than his best in order that someone may get a cheap article which may or may not interest him afterwards?" Work, he maintained, was far more than a means of livelihood. It could bring a man happiness or it could degrade and do more than make a man miserable.

Unlike Gimson, Sidney Barnsley continued from 1902 until his death in 1926, to construct all his furniture completely singlehanded and quite independently from the Daneway workshops. His brother Ernest meanwhile, upon dissolving his partnership with Gimson at Daneway as early as 1905, devoted the rest of his life chiefly to building and architecture, and in particular to the building of Rodmarton Manor in Gloucestershire.

Fig. 8   Gimson early oak wardrobe, with contructional details used as decoration.

Fig. 9   Gimson. Detail of floral decoration on an oak coffer.

Fig. 10   Gimson. Solid ebony cabinet decorated with mother of pearl and silver. Shown amongst 70 pieces in a one-man exhibition in 1908.

Figs 11, 12 & 13   Gimson's oak dresser c.1903, and chestnut sideboard c.1905, showing a simple peasant-like quality reminding me of the traditional work of Korea.

Fig. 14   Detail of metal fittings by Alfred Bucknell c.1903.

Fig. 15   Detail of butterfly joint on a Gimson table; the Cotswold School used this joint quite extensively.

Fig. 16   One of many variations of fielded panel work; this example in figured walnut.

Fig. 17   Detail of Sidney Barnsley's hayrack stretcher, c.1921.

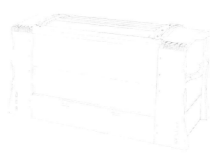

Fig. 18   Sidney Barnsley, oak chest with wrought iron hinges, c.1895. Note the protruding dovetails.

Fig. 19   Detail of oak table showing the influence of the wheelwright with rails whittled with drawknife and spokeshave. Sidney Barnsley c.1921.

There were disciples in the Cotswolds who carried on, namely Gordon Russell, who set up shop in neighbouring Broadway in 1915 and continued to make hand-made Cotswold-inspired furniture until 1926. Then he made the conscious decision to move over into mechanisation at Broadway as a means of pursuing the aims of Morris, Gimson and others in the wider field of industry, and thereby bringing good design and quality to a much larger and broader public.

Also, close by at Chalford, Peter Waals, Gimson's former foreman, and leading craftsman, set up his own workshop upon the death of Gimson employing many of his former colleagues at Daneway. He, like Ashbee's Guild of Handicraft at Chipping Campden, was quite well mechanised by the standards of his day, possessing a power driven circular saw, planing machine, thicknesser, bandsaw and mortiser. His work until his death in 1935 was a gradual refinement and simplification of the Cotswold style, and he continued to serve many of Gimson's and the Barnsley's former clients.

It is ironical that during Gimson's working life he, like others in the Arts and Crafts Movement, was to be received far more enthusiastically abroad than in this country. Germany and Austria were the first to put Morris' and Gimson's ideals into practice, forming Arts and Crafts societies of their own, such as the Deutsche Werkbund in 1907, whose exponents made regular visits to this country and its art and craft exhibitions. There was in both these countries in the earlier years of this century a greater willingness for art, craft and industry to work together than was evident in Britain, with the result that the work of the Austrian Werkbund in particular showed a vitality and a modern approach to furniture design that could not be matched anywhere else on the continent. The Deutsche Werkbund was also very influential in German art school training and this eventually led to the formation of the Bauhaus in 1919.

Daneway House at its prime became a scene of pilgrimage for many other people throughout Europe, and Gimson's work was in continental museums long before it was ever included in a British one.

One such important visitor was Carl Malmsten from Stockholm, who became in later years the Edward Barnsley of Sweden, standing almost alone for the dignity of handwork and the craft approach to furniture making at a time when the Swedish furniture scene had swung solely to industrial production, unlike its neighbour Denmark, who made quite a valuable export of its craft based furniture in the fifties.

Amongst Carl Malmsten's many pupils and trainees in Stockholm was James Krenov who despite a lifetime in Sweden and the United States still displays in his work many of the ideals and constructional details of those early Cotswold workshops.

Fig. 20   Ambrose Heal early chest of drawers in unpolished quartersawn oak. c.1900.

Fig. 21   Gordon Russell, early 1920's fine cabinet in cherry with all the hallmarks of the Cotswold School.

Fig. 22   Peter Waals, 1921 cabinet in English Walnut, closely following the Cotswold tradition.

In the USA, the Arts and Crafts movement, as applied to furniture, took off in a different way. Gustav Stickley, the father of the movement, was heavily influenced by the writings of Ruskin and Morris and the work of C.F.A. Voysey, but he interpreted their teaching much more literally than his British counterparts. Here, although Gimson and the Barnsleys often wished to, they could not make furniture that was inexpensive enough to reach any but the more fortunate sections of society. Stickley on the other hand, created furniture so simple and, basic at times almost to the point of crudity, that was made in substantial numbers and reached a sizeable portion of the American lower middle class.

Known as Mission or Craftsman furniture, it was copied and reproduced with no hang-ups about machinery as experienced in the Cotswolds, with the result that it became a considerable industry, albeit a craft based one, but one not averse to the latest production and marketing techniques. However, much of the furniture produced lacked the grace and charm of the earlier Shaker designs, and in world terms the Cotswold craftsmen, pursuing their more selfish aims of self-fulfilment and excellence left far more for posterity to cherish and study.

Although the Cotswold School under the influence of Gimson, Russell, two generations of Barnsleys, and Ashbee was by far the most dominant factor in the rise of the creative cabinetmaker in Britain, it was not the sole one. Besides the many architects cum designers, like Voysey, Godwin and Mackintosh, who made a great impact on design thinking, although they were not practising craftsmen involved in running workshop premises, there was also Ambrose Heal.

Almost alone of these furniture pioneers, Ambrose Heal was not an architect. He in fact served a cabinetmaking apprenticeship before joining the family furniture business of Heal's in London, which, under him, quickly became an influence for good design. He was both an excellent craftsman and designer, and his designs of the early 1900's were far ahead of their time, for although there was a strong similarity in the wide use of natural unpolished oak, his work was generally more refined and less crafted than the majority of the Cotswold pieces of that period. He eventually became involved with Gordon Russell in the formation of the Design and Industries Association, the forerunner of the Design Council, and continued till 1932 to design for the family firm pieces for one-off hand work as well as machine production.

Important, too, was Romney Green (1872 – 1945). He, unlike Russell and Heal, remained throughout his life totally committed to hand skills and craft workshops, and he was responsible for training another generation of craftsmen who, followed in turn by Edward Barnsley, kept the whole ideal alive through the difficult pre and post Second World War days. Green, not himself an architect but the brother of one, trained with Charles Spooner, an arts and crafts pioneer of the old Hammersmith Group of craftsmen in west London, under whose influence Edward Barnsley was later to come at the London Central School of Arts and Crafts.

Green established his first workshop close by at Chiswick, a far cry from the rolling hills of the Cotswolds, although his work was influenced by Gimson whom he visited in 1904. In the early 1920's he moved to Christchurch on the south coast in Hampshire, and, despite the general depression of the period, his shop expanded to ten craftsmen and trainees, including Eric Sharpe from 1921–29, Stanley Davies and Robin Nance, all of whom later established themselves as prominent craftsmen in their own right. Eric Sharpe stayed in the vicinity at Winchester whilst Stanley Davies worked at Windermere in the Lake District and Robin Nance moved down to St Ives in Cornwall.

Like practically all the craftsmen of this period, Romney Green worked solely to commission. He used virtually no machinery in his shop but he did contract out some of the heavy planing and sawing to a nearby joinery firm. His designs were not that distinctive from those of the rest of the Cotswold School, but his pupil Eric Sharpe did achieve a more personalised style in which carving played a significant role. However, he wrote and broadcast quite frequently on the crafts, exhibited widely, and did much to demonstrate and promote the relevance of craft workshops, using hand skills and concentrating on quality, bringing these ideas through well into the 1940's.

        *   *   *

There is difficulty in assessing the work of the Cotswold School since they, like most of us working today and indeed like the whole arts and crafts movement of that time, were full of contradictions. Courting the very wealthy for most of the time, and living the quite comfortable life of the Victorian country gentleman, their work generally never touched the lives of ordinary people even within their own locality, with the notable exception of their work for Sapperton Village Hall. Yet it was the common man and artefacts for them that was the corner-stone of their own personal philosophies and that of Morris who inspired them. They professed a desire for simplicity, humility and an absence of decoration in their work; but many of their pieces were far from simple, some being quite intricate and extensively decorated, whilst many others displayed sheer unadulterated luxury in their abundant use of prime figured walnut and the extensive number of man hours required to make them. All were, without doubt, functional items of furniture, but perhaps they were simply substituting one form of luxury for another; admittedly, more tasteful and less sophisticated, but nevertheless still a luxury. For many of these pieces simply could not be made economically in any craft workshop today, even with our large range of equipment, without each piece running into thousands of pounds, and they compare unfavourably with the stark simplicity of the work of Ambrose Heal in London. So, just as two present day visitors to Moscow could each return with a different impression of their visit, depending on their individual prejudices and expectations, one could also very easily build up two very distinct collections of their work which would tell two quite different stories. First, the commonplace furniture of the ladderback chairs and towel holders of the arts and crafts mythology, and secondly, the state furniture, as William Morris referred to it, that commanded much of their time and effort.

This is not to diminish their valuable contribution, but rather to question some of that mythology that has grown up around them. There is nothing wrong in craftsmen supplying luxury goods. Craftsmen have always done so, often needing in the past such rich patrons as the church and the aristocracy to bring out their best, whilst other craftsmen simply got on with supplying man's everyday needs. But it must be admitted that it was chiefly the former that the Cotswold School was about, and, as a result, their final contribution was actually much greater than that of Gustav Stickley in the States, who was more concerned with meeting the requirements of the common man.

Gimson and the Barnsleys had a choice of action that is denied most people working today. They were not, throughout their lives, too worried about money and paying the electricity bills. Although they were by no means wealthy and they ran their workshops in a business like way, they could, for example, afford private education for their children. One can assume, therefore, that the decisions they made as to the commissions they undertook and the work they concentrated on were governed more by choice than by economic necessity. It is this tyranny of economic necessity which is the excuse for many of us today when suffering lapses in integrity or direction. The Cotswold School was free to choose, and in the main, despite its ideals, it did not choose to make furniture of a truly commonplace kind.

Although Walter Gropius, founder of the Bauhaus and a leading advocate of the modern movement, gave full credit to the influence that Ruskin, Morris and the British Arts and Crafts Movement had on his own development, this acknowledgement was not generally shared. For many years whilst the Modern Movement reigned supreme and concrete machines for living and working were filling all our cities, Morris and the handcraftsmen were rather ridiculed as being sentimental and irrelevant, or worse, in some circles, as being detrimental to progress. Now, however, in the 1980's, as much of the Modern Movement itself is now in question; the interest in Morris, Gimson and the other pioneers of the Crafts movement, and indeed the crafts themselves, has never been stronger. Many more people now accept that society cannot exist on efficiency alone, and that, misguided as they might have been in their condemnation of machinery, this error was greatly exaggerated, and their main message is as relevant today as it was in the late 1800's.

PIONEERS OF THE CRAFT FURNITURE MOVEMENT

1819–1900	John Ruskin	Wrote *Seven Lamps of Architecture, The Stones of Venice* and other works which influenced Morris.
1834–1896	William Morris	Architect, painter, writer and craftsman.
1831–1915	Philip Webb	Architect and designer; built The Redhouse for William Morris in 1859.
1833–1886	E.W. Godwin	Architect and designer in Anglo-Japanese style.
1857–1942	Gustav Stickley	Born in Wisconsin, USA; established Mission furniture.
1857–1941	C.F.A. Voysey	Architect and furniture designer; exerted a great influence on design.
1857–1931	W.R. Lethaby	Architect and designer; first principal of London Central School of Arts and Crafts.
1861		William Morris formed his company, Morris, Marshall & Faulkner, to produce and sell well-designed furniture, wallpaper and other

		furnishings in Oxford Street, London.
1863–1942	C.R. Ashbee	Founder of the Guild of Handicraft at Whitechapel, London in 1888.
1863–1926	Ernest Barnsley	Born in Birmingham.
1864–1919	Ernest Gimson	Born in Leicester, son of an engineering craftsman.
1865–1926	Sidney Barnsley	Younger brother of Ernest.
1865–1937	Peter Waals	Born in Holland; became Gimson's foreman.
1868–1928	Charles Rennie Mackintosh	Architect and furniture designer; designed the Glasgow School of Art at the age of 28.
1872–1945	A. Romney Green	Teacher and craftsman.
1872–1959	Ambrose Heal	Designer, craftsman and furniture retailer.
1882–1949	Geoffrey Lupton	Builder and furniture maker.
1884		Whilst lecturing in Leicester, William Morris met Gimson and encouraged him to continue his architectural studies in London.
1884		The Art Workers Guild formed in London.
1886		Ernest Barnsley & Gimson met as students in the office of the London based church architect, John Sedding. Through Ernest Barnsley, Gimson also became a close friend of his brother, Sidney, an architectural student in the office of Norman Shaw. In London the three men became involved in the societies and groups which heralded the development of the Arts and Crafts Movement.
1887		Ernest Barnsley returned to Birmingham and set up his own architectural practice.
1888	Carl Malmsten	Born in Stockholm, Sweden.
1888		Arts and Crafts Exhibition Society formed by William Morris.
1889–1890		Sidney Barnsley made two trips to Greece with Robert Weir Schultz to study Byzantine architecture. On his return he received his first architectural commission for a church at Lower Kingswood, Surrey, which was completed in 1892 in a decorative interpretation of the Byzantine style.
		Gimson travelled widely in England and Europe. He began designing for two crafts, decorative plaster work and chair making. He acquired the technical skills from the plaster workers Messrs. Whitcombe & Priestley and the Herefordshire chairmaker Philip Clissett.
1890–1892		Five young architects, Ernest Gimson, Sidney Barnsley, William Lethaby, Mervyn Macartney & Reginald Blomfield, set up Kenton & Co., in London, to produce well-made furniture of good design. Professional cabinetmakers were hired to carry out their designs and the architects learnt cabinetmaking from them.
1892–1980	Gordon Russell	Born in London; moved to Cotswolds at the age of 12.
1893		Gimson & Sidney Barnsley left London for the country in order to get closer to the roots of architecture and the crafts. They persuaded Ernest Barnsley to join them, and chose the Cotswold Hills in Gloucestershire.
1893		Ambrose Heal, after a cabinetmaking apprenticeship, joined the family firm in London and set Heals on a new path as pioneers in retailing modern design.
1893–1901		Geoffrey Lupton was pupil at Bedales School, Petersfield; became Head Boy.

1894		Ernest Barnsley and his family moved into Pinbury Park, an Elizabethan farmhouse near Cirencester, Glos., whilst the two bachelors occupied adjacent cottages. They wanted to live like country folk, baking their own bread, making cider and keeping livestock. The practical difficulties in this for a group of city dwellers were overcome when Gimson's cousin who had been brought up on a farm in Lincolnshire joined them. She and Sidney Barnsley were later married. The outbuildings at Pinbury Park were converted into a joint workshop for the three men.
1900	Edward Barnsley	Born at Pinbury, the son of Sidney Barnsley.
1901		Gimson and Ernest Barnsley entered into partnership and hired cabinetmakers, based in Cirencester, to execute their designs. Peter Waals was appointed as foreman/cabinetmaker, whilst Harry Davoll, Ernest Smith and Percy Burchett formed the original team of craftsmen.
1902		The three men moved to the nearby village of Sapperton where they each built their own home. Gimson and Ernest Barnsley leased Daneway House as showrooms for their furniture and converted its outbuildings into workshops. Sidney Barnsley continued to work independently; he was one of the few Arts and Crafts designers to make all his own work.
1902		C. R. Ashbee's Guild of Handicrafts moves to Chipping Campden, Glos., a migration involving 150 people.
1903		A smithy was established as part of the Daneway workshops. Gimson also went into partnership with Edward Gardiner to produce turned ladder back chairs at the Daneway sawmill.
c. 1905		The partnership between Gimson and Ernest Barnsley was dissolved. The latter gave up furniture making to concentrate on his architectural work, whilst the Daneway workshops expanded and flourished under Gimson's direction.
1905–1906		Geoffrey Lupton trained with Ernest Gimson at Daneway House.
1907		Deutsche Werkbund established in Germany with the aim of selecting the best representatives of art, craft, trade and industry to work together to produce high quality in industrial work.
1908		Geoffrey Lupton built the Froxfield Workshops, near Petersfield, Hants., only two miles from Bedales School.
1909		Ernest Barnsley began work on Rodmarton Manor, Glos., a major architectural venture which was to absorb the rest of his career.
1910		Austrian Werkbund set up on similar lines to the German group.
1910–1917		Edward Barnsley attended Bedales School.
1913		Swiss Werkbund set up.
1915		Gordon Russell set up workshops at Broadway, Worcestershire.
1919		Ernest Gimson died, 12th August; buried at Sapperton Church.

1919	Peter Waals set up his own workshop at Chalford taking many of Gimson's craftsmen with him.
1919	Walter Gropius founded the state Bauhaus for the Weimar Republic. All students had to have completed a craft/trade apprenticeship before admission.
1919–1922	Edward Barnsley was a pupil with Geoffrey Lupton in Froxfield Workshops.
1923	Edward Barnsley took over Froxfield Workshops.
1924	Bert Upton joined Froxfield Workshops at the age of 14.
1925	Gordon Russell turned to mechanisation in order to "teach the machine manners".
1926	Ernest Barnsley died, 6th January.
1926	Sidney Barnsley died, 25th September; the two brothers were buried near Gimson at Sapperton.
1935–1937	Peter Waals became advisor on design and construction at Loughborough Teacher Training College.
1937–1965	Edward Barnsley succeeded Waals at Loughborough.

BIBLIOGRAPHY
Exhibition and other Catalogues

An Exhibition of Cotswold Craftsmanship	Cheltenham Art Festivals, 1951
Victorian and Edwardian Decorative Arts, Catalogue of an Exhibition	V & A Museum, H.M.S.O., 1952
The Furniture Designs of E. W. Godwin	Elizabeth Aslin, V & A. Museum, 1970
The Arts & Crafts Movement of America: (exhibition at Princeton, USA)	Princeton Univ. Press, 1972
The Arts & Crafts Movement, 1890–1930	Fine Art Society, London, 1973
Good Citizen's Furniture	Cheltenham Art Gallery and Museum, 1976
Ernest Gimson & the Cotswold Group of Craftsmen	Leics. Museums Publication. no. 14, 1978
The Designs of Gustav Stickley; 2 vols.	Reprinted Contemporary Catalogue, Dover Inc., New York 1980?
R. D. Russell – Marian Pepler	I.L.E.A., London, 1983

Books

Alexander, R.	*The Furniture & Joinery of Peter Waals;* Alcuin Press, Chipping Campden, 1930
Bavaro, J.J. & Mossman, T.L.	*The Furniture of Gustav Stickley;* Van Nostrand Reinhold, New York, 1982
Bradshaw, A.E.	*Handmade Woodwork of the 20th Century;* John Murray, London, 1962
Campbell, Joan.	*The German Werkbund;* Princeton Univ. Press, USA, 1978
Comino, Mary.	*Gimson and the Barnsleys;* Evans, London, 1980
Farleigh, John (ed).	*Fifteen Craftsmen on their Crafts* (article on The Cotswold School by Eric Sharpe); Sylvan Press, London, 1945

Jewson, Norman.	*By Chance I Did Rove;* Roundwood Press, Warks; 1973
Joel, David.	*Adventures of British Furniture;* Ernest Benn, 1953
Kurt, Rowland.	*A History of the Modern Movement;* Van Nostrand Reinhold Co., New York, 1973
Lambourne, Lionel.	*Utopian Craftsmen: The Arts and Crafts Movement from the Cotswolds to Chicago;* Astragel Books, 1980
Lethaby, W; Powell, A; Griggs, F.	*Ernest Gimson, his Life and Work;* Shakespeare Head Press, Stratford on Avon, 1924
MacCarthy, Fiona.	*The Simple Life;* Lund Humphries, London, 1981
Naylor, Gillian.	*The Arts & Crafts Movement;* Studio Vista, 1971
Pevsner, Nikolaus.	*Pioneers of Modern Design;* Penguin, 1960
Ruskin, John.	*The Seven Lamps of Architecture;* Dent, Everymans Library
Ruskin, John.	*The Stones of Venice;* Faber, reprinted 1981
Russell, Gordon.	*The Things We See, No. 3;* Penguin, 1947
	Designer's Trade; George Allen & Unwin, 1968
Thompson, Paul.	*The Work of William Morris;* Heinemann, London, 1967

Films

Against the Grain	An Arts Council of Great Britain film on the Cotswold School of Furniture Makers; 1983. Can be hired from: Arts Council Film Library, Concorde Films, 201 Felixstowe Road, Ipswich, Suffolk IP3 9BJ
The Furniture of Gimson and the Barnsleys	The Design Council, 1979, comprising 12 colour slides and booklet. May be purchased from The Design Council, 28 Haymarket, London SW1Y 4SU.

Places of Interest

Westminster Cathedral	Victoria Street, London. St. Andrew's chapel, choir stalls in ebony by Ernest Gimson.
Rodmarton Manor	Near Cirencester, Glos. Designed by Ernest Barnsley, 1909–1929. Built with traditional materials and superb craftsmanship. All furnishings by the Cotswold School including Ernest & Sidney Barnsley and Peter Waals. Small chapel of particular interest. Not normally open to the public, but undoubtedly the finest example of the work of the Arts & Crafts Movement and in particular the Cotswold School.
Bedales School	Near Petersfield, Hants. Assembly Hall by Gimson, 1910–1911. Library designed by Gimson and built by Geoffrey Lupton and the Froxfield workshops under the supervision of Sidney Barnsley. Completed in 1920. Not normally open to the public.

Collections of Furniture of the Cotswold School

Cheltenham Museum & Art Gallery, Clarence Street, Cheltenham, Glos.
Leicestershire Museum and Art Gallery, Leicester.
The Crafts Study Centre, Holburne of Menstrie Museum, University of Bath, Great Pulteney Street, Bath.
20th century furniture collection, Victoria & Albert Museum, S. Kensington, London.
Arlington Mill, Bibury Glos.
The William Morris Gallery, Water House, Lloyd Park, Forest Rd., Walthamstow, London E17. Contains work by Morris, Voysey, Gimson, Sidney Barnsley, and a room devoted to A.H. Mackmurdo.
Geffrye Museum, Kingsland Road, London E2. One room devoted to C.F.A. Voysey, 1857–1941, which also contains one piece by Ernest Gimson. 1930's room also contains work of Gordon Russell Ltd., 1933–1936.

THE RISE OF THE FROXFIELD WORKSHOPS

The early death of Gimson in 1919 and the closing down of Daneway House, followed only seven years later by·the deaths of both Sidney and Ernest Barnsley, was a cruel blow to the development of craft furniture making in Britain. For, although there were excellent craftsmen, among them Peter Waals and other former employees of Gimson, working out their lives making Gimson-inspired furniture in the Cotswolds, in reality the spark and impetus for creation had been extinguished far too early. Then, Gordon Russell's decision to expand from a craft workshop in 1926 to a thriving factory employing 120 men by 1929–30, and Ambrose Heal's growing concern with production furniture, welcome as they were in the wider context of design appreciation and education within industry, left the field of craft furniture making sadly depleted of creative talent.

Fortunately, however, another centre of craft activity was developing from 1908 which was to give support to those remaining in the Cotswolds and was eventually to become the new focal point for training and quality. Again, a beautiful and unspoilt part of England was to become an inspiration for creative work. The counties of Hampshire, Surrey and Sussex meet in a charming embrace and one of the prettiest spots in this area is the parish of Steep, near Petersfield, a few miles inside the Hampshire border.

It was here in 1900 that the new Bedales School was built. Founded in 1893 by J.H. Badley at Haywards Heath in Sussex, it moved to Steep in search of more space. The school was based largely on the theories of Rousseau that education should be close to nature and that whenever possible the children should learn by doing. The arts and crafts were naturally one of the main courses of study here and attracted many followers of Ruskin and Morris. Thus, over the years, many people interested in the crafts made their homes in the surrounding area, some in order to be near their children attending the school, others who so fell in love with the district whilst pupils that they returned in later years to set up business there. Two well-known examples of the latter are the bookbinder Roger Powell and Edward Barnsley.

Another such pupil of Bedales was Geoffrey Lupton. Here was a man who might well have become a second Gimson, so closely do his characteristics conform to those of his master. After working as a pupil with Gimson at Daneway House, he decided to come back to the district of his schooling and attempt to repeat what Gimson had done at Sapperton. To the north west of Bedales School is a long line of beech and yew clad hangers which afford, once one has reached the top, a splendid view of the Petersfield valley and the South Downs beyond. It was here, 700 feet above sea level in the scattered parish of Froxfield that he began to build from scratch a business of quality building and furniture making.

The workshop, the adjoining cottage and the timber stores were a clever piece of building, for the site dropped away steeply on one side and lacked any made up road or water supply. He built them strong, with heavy walls and sturdy oak beams to keep out the strong winds that frequently swept across that exposed hill top, and even the guttering was made on site in oak.

Gradually the pattern of Pinbury and Sapperton was repeated. Cottages for the workmen were built close by; local labour was increasingly being employed; and with Steve Mustoe from Sapperton to look after the metal fittings, and an excellent foreman, Bill Berry, the little colony began in earnest to design and build houses and furniture of distinction in the true arts and crafts manner.

In 1910 Lupton built the Great Hall at Bedales School to Gimson's design using only local oak and handmade bricks and tiles. Later in 1919 Gimson completed the drawings for a war memorial library for the school just prior to his death. The supervision of the work, therefore, had to be undertaken by Sidney Barnsley and once again Lupton was engaged to do the building and the oak furnishing.

From time to time Lupton took on pupils in his workshop in much the same way as Gimson had done. One such was Sidney Barnsley's own son, Edward, who, after his

*Fig. 23   Author's sketch of the Great Hall, Bedales School, designed
by Ernest Gimson and built by the Froxfield Workshops, c.1910.*

*Fig. 24   Detail of pew ends in
the Great Hall, Bedales School.*

Figs 25 & 26   Interior of Bedales School library, built around 1920 to Gimson's design by the Froxfield Workshop.

schooling at Bedales, now desired to learn the craft of his father, and so entered the
Froxfield workshops in 1919. He soon returned to Bedales not to study but to work and get
involved with Lupton and his craftsmen in all the hard graft that went into fashioning,
solely by hand, those giant oaks into that masterpiece of twentieth century arts and crafts
building that constitutes the interior of Bedales School library.

After three years Edward left Froxfield to study under Charles Spooner at the London
Central School of Arts and Crafts, but his period of study was quite short, for in 1923 he
returned suddenly to Froxfield because Lupton had decided to give it all up and take up
farming in South Africa. No-one is sure why he decided to do this; maybe Froxfield was
becoming too tame and he longed for the wider virgin lands of Africa. One thing, though, is
certain, there are many fine houses in the Petersfield area as well as the splendid work at
Bedales School which will long give him a place among those disciples of Ruskin and
Morris.

It was fortunate for the development of furniture making that Edward Barnsley, at the
young age of 23, stepped in and took over the workshop premises, with all the staff, and
settled down to the work he had to do to spread the idealism of his father, Gimson, Morris
and Ruskin. Geoffrey Lupton, in the meantime, returned to England from 1937–1946, and
then spent the last years of his life in Southern Rhodesia, where in died in 1949 very much
an unknown figure and link in the chain.

MY TRAINING AT FROXFIELD

I grew up in a small market town situated in the shadow of the South Downs and got hooked on wood at an early age. With the companionship of two dogs, I spent much of my childhood wandering on the hills and wooded hangers whittling away with a penknife making model aircraft.

This was the immediate post war period, when new toys were unavailable and model kits as we now know them were non-existent. So, by the age of 14 I had converted the cellar at home into a workshop and was supplying two local shops with wooden toys and aeroplanes on a sale or return basis.

Also, at about this time, I changed schools, and for the next two years came under the influence of a woodwork teacher of the old school; one who believed in good work and who could also do it. He encouraged me and helped to set those standards I was to need later.

My father was a precision engineer and design toolmaker, like my grandfather before him, so I came from a skilled artisan background. He was also an amateur water-colourist and a perfectionist by nature, and it was largely from him that I gained a deep love of the countryside, and learned of the immense pleasure to be had by just looking and seeing beauty in even the most unexpected things. From him also, I acquired the desire to do most things to the best of my ability, even if it were only sweeping the workshop more thoroughly than the fellow before.

I dwell on my childhood because it was an immensely happy one, for despite the war it was free of pressures from either home or school. It was also unsophisticated in every way – one outside lavatory up the short garden path and no running hot water in that small town cottage within a stone's throw of the market square. It also, I am sure, continues to influence my work and my thinking, for despite a desire to make things well, I still have a great dislike of opulence and ostentatious displays of wealth. In furniture, this is reflected in a dislike of excessive decoration or over-lavish use of expensive and rare materials. Likewise, I prefer buildings and interiors that depict some measure of austerity and humility, and furnishings that are quiet and peaceful.

But the greatest influence on my work is undoubtedly the 7½ years spent in the Froxfield workshops of Edward Barnsley. I was just 16 in January 1949 when as a nervous youngster I entered the workshops at the start of a five-year formal cabinetmaking apprenticeship. Not only was I fortunate in living only three miles away, and therefore having the chance as a local boy, but also I was fortunate to undergo it at the time that I did, for this was, truly, the end of an era. For in January 1949 the attitudes and techniques of furniture making were steeped deeply in the Cotswold tradition of the Arts and Crafts Movement, having remained largely unchanged since Geoffrey Lupton had built the workshops, complete with pit saw, exactly 40 years earlier.

Work started at 7 am, six days a week, and we worked a standard 50 hour week with no paid holidays. Far more to the point, we worked without electricity or any power tools or machinery. The workshop's sole equipment, beyond benches and hand tools, was one faithful treadle circular saw inherited from the Gimson workshops at Daneway House, and one hand operated mortise machine that was so inaccurate and clumsy that it was very rarely used.

I remember the oak sign outside which spoke of general building and joinery work as well as fine furniture making, for both Gimson and Geoffrey Lupton had been considerably involved in architectural work, although over the years at Froxfield this side of the business had largely lapsed in favour of fine furniture making.

In those days of my apprenticeship, we worked solely in solid timber, mostly home-grown and seasoned on the premises, with walnut, oak and chestnut being the most common. Laying down logs of timber for seasoning and trimming off the sap with an axe was a regular part of my duties. Huge boards of oak were converted by handsaws and hand planed into table tops, sideboards and bookcases, whilst chair legs in their dozens were cut by bow saws and shaped by hand, this being a workshop which honestly did produce hand made furniture.

The shop was comparatively small for the number employed, for there were around ten of us in all: four skilled craftsmen, led by Bert Upton the foreman; two apprentices; and around four or six pupils at any one time, plus 'the Governor', as Edward Barnsley was affectionately known.

Although the methods of making remained largely unchanged since the turn of the century, Edward Barnsley's designs had evolved since 1923 when he took over. From the somewhat heavy and solid appearance of his father's and Gimson's pieces, his work took on a more delicate and simple refinement by the late 1940's, very much in line with general design thinking at that time. However, the honesty of construction, with its wide use of through jointing, the unsophisticated surface finishing, and the emphasis on home-grown timbers, all these and other hallmarks of the Cotswold School were still very much in evidence. Most pieces made in oak, for example, were left finished from the cutting edge of the tools without a hint of glasspaper, and the applied finishes were usually of oil, turpentine or beeswax, or at most a light coat of sealer before waxing.

I still remember my first piece, an eight-sided bread board in quite a tough piece of English oak; a simple object, planed and chamfered by hand with chip carving around the

Fig. 27   Edward Barnsley with two of his apprentices and Mark Nicholas in the early 1980's. (Photo courtesy of Working Wood Magazine).

eight edges, very reminiscent of Sidney Barnsley's favourite decoration. It soon taxed my limited skill, but I graduated to my second piece, a stool in white walnut, and as long as I live I think I shall remember the heartache the day it was finished. It stood proudly on the bench awaiting the approval of Mr Upton, the foreman, when (and I cannot remember why) it crashed to the ground and was badly damaged. This was my first black day as a furniture maker, only one month after starting. There have, of course, been many others over the years – the gluing up that went wrong, the silly mistake I should never have made, or the sheer disappointment when a design or idea simply did not really come off – but probably the worst was when I realised whilst still an apprentice that I had just produced and fully mortised 24 right-hand rear chair legs and no left-hand ones on a batch of 12 chairs. Since these were in walnut, this represented quite an outlay in both time and materials. Bert Upton, as unflappable as ever, simply decided we would make two dozen chairs and hopefully sell the second dozen as well, which is just what did happen, but it was certainly not my happiest day.

Having survived that first trial month, I began over the next year or so to lose some of the awe that I experienced when watching the master craftsmen at work. Charlie Bray, for example, who was working in that same shop long before Edward Barnsley took over, and who eventually retired in 1959. Or George Taylor, an apprentice himself in the 1930's, working with a speed, dexterity, and organisation that I have tried desperately over the ensuing years to match. And then Oskar Dawson, regarded as a new boy for many years, despite the fact that he joined the workshop in 1947 with many years of skilled work and an apprenticeship already behind him. Overseeing all this of course, was Bert Upton (Mr Upton to me in those days). Born two miles away at Steep where he now lives in retirement, Bert started his apprenticeship at 14 with Edward Barnsley and, except for a brief wartime break, devoted his life to the workshop. He retired in 1979 after 50 years of working day in, day out, producing furniture which is renowned the world over for its quality, and yet he remains a man virtually unknown outside his own village. I very much salute this real craftsman, a man of incredible patience and mildness, who somehow managed to teach me and dozens of others most of what we know about furniture making without ever raising his voice in anger or exasperation, as well as making furniture himself. Not content with this, he has built himself two houses virtually single-handed in his spare time.

If it was Bert Upton who passed on the skills, it was certainly Edward Barnsley who passed on the idealism, that constant striving for aesthetic perfection, that sensitivity and feeling for wood, things not so easily taught or acquired. I have known days of work swept aside because it did not look absolutely right in the eyes of the Governor, despite the fact that the chances were the client would never have known the difference, nor even cared had they been told. We were working to our own standards, not theirs, although I did not always appreciate this until years later.

The workshop was an extremely happy and relaxed place to be in in those days, and I recall many a lunch time crouched over the coke stove talking over the world's problems; or warming my hands and scorching my hair on the pressure oil lamp whilst trying to see on a dark winter's afternoon, or playing cricket outside in the lane in the summer lunch times. Also, the views from the workshop were magnificent – at 700 ft, on a clear day one could see the whole line of the South Downs from Butser Hill in the west till they faded away 40 miles to the east towards Brighton.

I am still not sure whether there is any merit in cutting through a 4″ board of oak with a hand rip saw rather than the chain saw I now use, or in cutting out chair legs with a bow saw rather than an electric band saw, but I do know that it was an experience for which I shall be forever grateful, and in a strange way I regretted its passing.

But pass it did, and relatively rapidly once the decision to mechanise was taken. I was away at the time, for following my five year apprenticeship I left to do my National Service in the RAF, and for the next 12 months became far more involved in my sport of cycle racing and thought little of furniture making. After a year the RAF decided they could dispense with my services and I was medically discharged, and I soon became accustomed to my former habit of cycling daily up beautiful Stoner Hill from my home three miles away in the valley.

Things had changed, almost overnight it seemed. Electricity had arrived, and the peace of the rural workshop where time had previously stood still was frequently shattered now by the roar of the large planing machine that belched out shavings and dust all over the shop and over my bench in particular. It also, of course, completed what had been a day's work in an hour or less.

In later years, as more machines were installed, a special shop was built to house them and to contain their noise and dust, but I was away long before that, and my real memories are of the pre-machine era; of treadling that circular saw until the sweat dripped off me, and of the physical challenge and pleasure in planing a table top up by hand.

So happy was that shop, and so satisfying the work, that, but for fate, I could well have spent my lifetime there in the same way that Bert Upton, George Taylor and Oskar Dawson have, or Charlie Bray before them; set in such superb countryside as that corner of Hampshire, what better existence could one want? However, I had only been back about a year, and was beginning to learn to live with that planing machine, when the problem I had experienced in the RAF flared up again and I had to undergo a major operation. This meant several weeks in hospital and enforced rest, which was something quite foreign to me, and I spent the time questioning my life and how I was going to spend it. On reflection, I knew that I had enjoyed my year away from Froxfield, and I felt half inclined not to return. Then, unexpectedly, my mother died, and I knew that I wanted a change of direction. The result of this mixture of emotions was that I entered Shoreditch Training College in September 1957 for a two-year teacher training course. I must be honest and say that the prospect of becoming a school teacher did not fill me with any great excitement, but the thought of catching up on a very sketchy wartime education certainly did. I also secretly harboured the idea that I might one day graduate to lecturing, and long college holidays struck me as quite an attractive bonus to this way of life for, as now, there never seemed enough days in the week, or weeks in the year for all the things I wanted to do.

So, I left the Froxfield workshops, excited about the unknown but sad at leaving such good friends. The training that I had received there, although I did not always appreciate it at the time, had been very varied, and this was to stand me in good stead in later life. Right out in the country as we were, the workshop had to be in many ways self-supporting. Although we no longer accepted building work as a commission, if a new timber shed needed building, we built it; if the lovely old clay tiles came off the roof during a storm, we climbed up and put them back; and we reglazed and painted windows as a matter of course. My training had not only covered fine cabinetmaking but also many aspects of the building trade, giving me a versatility which was to prove very useful both at Grayshott and later with the more ambitious conversion of my present home and workshops at Kentisbeare.

BARNSLEY IN PERSPECTIVE

Looking back over 60 years' work by this great figure in English furniture, we see that it divides roughly into two thirty-year periods: the first, unmechanised and deeply rooted in the Cotswold School and yet at the forefront of current design trends; and the second, from around 1953, which coincided approximately with the arrival of electricity at Froxfield. Edward Barnsley, then in his early fifties, became increasingly influenced by the 18th century and Regency periods and his work took on a new sophistication. Rich Cuban mahogany, blackbean and rosewood, delicately relieved with fine lines of holly inlay, was worked into subtle curves and serpentines, and always immaculately finished – these became the new hallmarks of Barnsley furniture. But although it was inspired by 18th century work, by no stretch of the imagination could this be called reproduction work. He took that period simply as a springboard, developing a strong personal style easily recognised as the Barnsley school and quite distinct from the Cotswold school that preceded it. Helped by the increasing use of machinery, which made short work of complicated curves and serpentines, his work became the last word in cabinetmaking skills, surpassing that of any previous century, and it found a ready appreciation amongst a growing clientele and an interested public.

Only time will tell if this switch in emphasis in mid-stream was a step forwards or backwards. To a few, it is as though he had re-entered the establishment of fine English

*Fig. 28   Edward Barnsley.
1930's carver chair in oak.*

*Fig. 29   Edward Barnsley. 1940's
china cabinet in chestnut.*

*Fig. 30   Edward Barnsley, Rosewood with holly inlay;
one of many related pieces made during a period from late
1950's to early 1980's.*

*Fig. 31   Edward Barnsley. Oak bed ends with solid fielded
panels and simple drawknife chamfering. Late 1940's.*

*Fig. 32   Edward Barnsley designed chest of drawers in
Australian blackbean with holly inlay. Made by Alan Peters
1957.*

cabinet work as practised in the 18th and early 19th centuries, the establishment that his father and Gimson had been anxious to ignore. What cannot be denied is that for a period of 60 years the Barnsley workshop has reigned supreme, setting those standards of craftsmanship and idealism which, directly or indirectly, have been the inspiration and the touchstone for much of the craft furniture renaissance in Britain today.

Always a humble and unassuming man, he has never in those many years found it necessary to project any form of image, or court any organisation or media. His work, and that of his small team has had simply to speak for itself. With now over 7,000 individual Barnsley pieces scattered around the world one's mind boggles at the creative energy that can keep up this pace of activity for over 60 years.

It has taken me many years to fully understand Edward Barnsley's earlier objection to powered machines; why it was, when Ashbee's Guild of Handicraft had extensive power driven machinery at Chipping Campden in 1902, and Peter Waals likewise at Chalford in the 1930's, that the Froxfield workshops should have remained completely unmechanised until 1955. I had to have two visits to the Far East before I came back to my roots and fully appreciated the Gimson and Barnsley workshops and what they were trying to achieve.

There is a wonderful similarity between the traditional work of Korea and Japan and much of the early Cotswold School. The directness and honesty of construction and approach, with nothing contrived; the general lack of sophistication; the sheer joy and spontaneity that comes through into the finished work itself, which I believe is a direct result of contact with the materials at all stages with hand tools and hand skills. I now know what Edward Barnsley feared, and with some justification.

We cannot, and must not, put the clock back altogether, but some of you contemplating a lifetime as self-employed cabinetmakers might stop and ponder, before rushing out and mortgaging yourselves for thousands of pounds worth of the latest equipment, whether there might not be some other way, and still make a living.

For the amateur and semi-retired professional, where time is not of any great importance, you might ask why you should spend your leisure time and retirement endangering your health by working with noisy, dusty portable routers, planers, body grinders and spray guns for example, when hand tools are so much more relaxing, even if they do demand more skill.

Chronology

1908	Froxfield Workshops and adjoining cottage built by Geoffrey Lupton.
1910 – 1917	Edward Barnsley is a pupil at neighbouring Bedales School.
1910 – 1920	Bedales Assembly Hall and Library designed by Gimson and built by Lupton and the Froxfield workshops. The library, including the furniture, was finally completed under Sidney Barnsley's direction in 1920.
1919 – 1922	Edward Barnsley, a pupil-apprentice of Lupton, works on Bedales Library.
1922 – 1923	Edward Barnsley studies at London Central School of Arts & Crafts under Charles Spooner.
1923	Edward Barnsley takes over the Froxfield workshops.
1924	Bert Upton, aged 14, begins apprenticeship with Barnsley, under Walter Berry, Lupton's foreman, and Charles Bray, Barnsley's foreman until 1938.
1926	Barnsley works on a series of prestigious commissions including:–
1927	Ebony case for War Memorial Book for the House of Lords.
1929	Doors for Khartoum Cathedral.
1933	Furniture for St. John's College, Oxford.
1935	Furniture for eight studies at Charterhouse School.
1937	George Taylor, aged 14, begins his apprenticeship with Edward Barnsley.
1938	Barnsley appointed visiting advisor in Woodwork & Design at Loughborough Teacher Training College on the retirement of Peter Waals.
1938	Bert Upton takes over from Charles Bray as foreman.

1940 – 1945	All regular craftsmen and apprentices away in the services or working in munitions. Workshop continues with former pupil Oliver Morel from 1941 – 1945. Edward Barnsley was committed to a full-time teaching appointment.
1945	Workshop reverts to normal with Charles Bray, Bert Upton, George Taylor and Tom Barnet.
1945	Edward Barnsley receives CBE for services to furniture design and craftsmanship.
1946	Barnsley appointed as Advisor in Woodwork to the Rural Industries Bureau. Designs various items of furniture for their design catalogue for use in rural workshops.
1947	Oskar Dawson joins workshop staff as a skilled craftsman.
1948	Barnsley is a founder member of The British Crafts Centre at Hay Hill, London.
1949 – 1954	Alan Peters is apprenticed to Edward Barnsley.
1955 – 1957	Alan Peters returns to the Froxfield workshops.
1955	Electricity arrives at Froxfield.
1955 – 1956	Planing machine and electric saw installed.
1959	Charles Bray retires after 30 years' service.
1961	Machine shop and spray room built. (The workshop was to become fully mechanised by 1967).
1963	Designed and made boardroom and dining furniture for Courtaulds.
1965	Edward Barnsley retires from Loughborough College to devote all his energies to the workshop.
1976	Awarded a Civil Pension for his contribution to British Design and Craftsmanship.
1979	Bert Upton retires due to ill health after 50 years' service to the Froxfield workshops.
1980	The Edward Barnsley Educational Trust is formed to provide apprenticeship training.
1982	The only major retrospective exhibition of 60 years' work, held at the Fine Art Society, New Bond Street, London.
1984	Edward Barnsley and his wife Tania continue to run a thriving workshop ably assisted by George Taylor, although working only part-time now. Mark Nicholas, who entered as an apprentice himself from 1974 – 1979, takes day to day control of the workshop activities and assists in the training of apprentices.

BIBLIOGRAPHY

Books

No book has yet been written on the Froxfield workshops and Edward Barnsley, although one is in preparation, but the following publications have featured the work and workshops quite fully:

Bradshaw, A.E. Handmade Woodwork of the 20th Century, John Murray, London 1962
Comino, Mary. Gimson and the Barnsleys, Evans Bros. London 1980
Joel, David. Furniture Design Set Free, Dent, London 1969
Thomas, Helen. As it Was and World Without End, Faber 1972
     (references to work covering the earlier period of the workshops, especially in relation to Lupton)

Articles

Lowenstein, Harold. *Fine Woodworking*, May/June 1979
MacCarthy, Fiona. The Crafts Council, *Crafts*, Jan/Feb 1981
Thomas, Lavinia. *House & Gardens*, 1980
Arlott, John. 'An Artist Craftsman in Hampshire' *Hampshire County Magazine*, Feb 1968
Robertshaw, Ursula. 'Tradition in Furniture Making' *Illustrated London News*, June 1973
                    'Making Tomorrow's Antiques' *House & Gardens*, June 1974
Grant, R.W. 'Wonderful Furniture of a Commonplace Kind' *Woodworker*, August 1980
Cleaver, Idris. 'The Edward Barnsley Educational Trust' *Woodworker*, August 1980
Ridley, Samantha. 'Pioneers in the Edward Barnsley Trust' *Hampshire County Magazine*, September 1981
Bell, Lucy. article with 11 prominent photographs. *East Hampshire Post*, 3rd Feb, 1982
Curds, Polly. Review of Edward Barnsley's retrospective exhibition at The Fine Arts Society. *Woodworker*, April 1982

THE POST-WAR SCENE AND THE CRAFTS COUNCIL

The 1939–45 war temporarily decimated the craft workshops in much the same way as the First War had taken such a slice out of Gimson's career, and by 1948 there was really only one workshop which stood out as giving a clear lead and having anything profound to say. This was Edward Barnsley's shop, which quickly established itself after the war as the natural leader of the craft furniture movement in Britain, a position it was to maintain for many years. The most noteworthy of the other workshops in the 40's and 50's were those of Stanley Davies, Eric Sharpe and Robin Nance amongst a fair scattering of one man concerns, often ex-pupils of either Edward Barnsley or Romney Green, or exhibiting teachers, whose income came largely from teaching rather than from craftwork. There were also, of course, many other workshops up and down the country, and some very good cabinetmaking shops among them, which made a reasonably good living from a combination of being the small town undertaker, antique restorer, upholsterer, and generally producing reproduction antiques to order. But this has never been the real challenge in going self-employed; for the challenge that has defeated so many is to make furniture of quality, that speaks to us as a product both of our time and of ourselves as individuals.

So, although the late 1940's and 1950's saw quite a lot of people entering the creative furniture making field, most of them were professional people and high-ranking service personnel who were embarking on a second career, cushioned, as most exponents of the Arts and Crafts Movement had been, by a small private income, pension or by ancillary professional work.

Many of these people, such as Edward Baly in Devon, provided a great service to the crafts in general, as well as their own area of cabinetmaking, by bringing in an organising ability and vision. It was largely due to the efforts of Edward Baly that the Devon Guild of Craftsmen was founded in 1955, and, although this was not the first of the regional crafts guilds to be formed, it was the one on which most of the others were eventually modelled when county and regional guilds mushroomed in the 1970's.

But for most people in Britain, becoming a self-employed cabinetmaker, producing one's own work, had to remain a pipe dream for many more years because of financial problems. Workshop and design training had to be paid for, either in terms of a long, virtually unpaid apprenticeship, or, more commonly, in terms of a fee-paying period as a pupil with a master craftsman. Either way it was difficult to obtain and often unsatisfactory in that it lacked the vital element of design training. The nearest that most aspiring craftsmen got to that was a spattering of technique and inspiration whilst training as woodwork teachers, and as the course was only for two years and all embracing, it could only ever scratch the surface and whet the appetite. And if one were fortunate enough to have obtained the workshop training, the hard fact had to be faced that a living could not be made whilst attempting to live up to the high ideals of such people as Gimson and the Barnsley brothers. For not only did they enjoy a private income and a lucrative profession in architecture that they could turn to whenever the need arose, but it was also from within the ranks of the architectural profession that so many of their commissions came.

Unfortunately, long before the 1950's, architects in Britain had in the main lost interest in the crafts, so it was virtually impossible until the 1970's for a young person to seriously consider a career as a self-employed furniture maker without considerable parental backing, and even then the chances of success would have been slim, for as yet the public would not or could not pay the economic price for craftsmanship.

By the early 1980's the situation had changed. It had become possible to make a living, and the number of exponents, who were quite evenly dispersed throughout the country, grew rapidly from a trickle in the early seventies to a flood as the decade ended. There were several reasons for this. First, a fact that is very often overlooked by creative people working outside the industrial scene, it is the very success of mass production and modern technology in catering for man's everyday needs in the Western world that makes it possible for designer craftsmen to practise professionally. Year by year, if one excludes the unfortunate minority of unemployed, people earn more for fewer hours' work, and so, for the craftsman who is prepared to work more than 35 hours a week, to forgo the increasing number of Bank holidays, and to live modestly, it is easier today to survive, selling to a public that increasingly has more money at its disposal than it requires for mere survival.

Secondly, the breakthrough for the crafts is also the result of increased educational opportunities, particularly in art and design training, that were available by the 1960's. Previously, people had been able to buy their way into the leading art schools, but now they have to work in open competition to justify a place. It was this opening up and expansion of art and design courses to a much larger and broader cross-section of society that led to a new generation of artist craftsmen with design talent and a totally committed attitude who have been at the forefront of this latest craft boom in all media.

And finally there was the recognition by first the government and then the local authorities of the importance of the crafts in our society, and it not only became accepted that they should be supported, in the same way as art, music and literature have been, but also that there were strong economic advantages in having a flourishing self-employed section within the economy. Craftsmen constituted a group of highly self-motivated people, who, given a minimum of help and encouragement at the start of their careers, proved to be a good investment for public money at a time of growing unemployment costs which accompanied the decimation of so much of traditional industry. Thus it was that the Crafts Centre of Great Britain, formed in 1948, received an annual grant from the government of £5 000, a remarkable contrast to the budget of £1¾ million received by the present Crafts Council. Its budget is also topped up nationally by sympathetic regional Arts Associations and many local authorities which, in various ways, contribute to the general fund of public money now devoted to the promotion of British craftwork.

To discover why we in Britain were the first, and indeed still the biggest supporter in terms of public money for the crafts, we have to look back at all the early pioneers: men such as Edward Barnsley and John Farleigh who helped form the British Craft Centre; and Cyril Wood, OBE, who tirelessly led the first Crafts Council in the late 1960's with a government grant which rose from £5000 to £6000 a year. This sum scarcely paid the rent for the London offices, but that Council was to set the pattern for the government appointed body that was to come later, in 1971. This was initially called the Crafts Advisory Committee, and it came as a result of pressure being exerted by many people over many years on the government at all levels. Finally it was the foresight of the then Minister of the Arts, Lord Eccles, who gave it the last necessary push into reality.

Since 1971 the Crafts Advisory Committee, or the Crafts Council which it became, has got on with its mandate of promoting the work of the artist-craftsman in Britain, or, to be more correct, in England and Wales, as Scotland is administered separately, even though in practice many activities and facilities overlap.

It could be argued that the mandate was too narrow; that it should have embraced more areas of craftwork; that the Council has been too elitist in its areas of support; or that it has been more interested at times in the artist, full stop, than in the craftsman. Some, or none, of this quite wide criticism may be justified, but it must be admitted that it has been successful in promoting modern British craftsmanship both nationally and internationally. Our present level of craft activity, the quality of our best work, and the general organisation and administration of the crafts here is the envy of the rest of the world as they seek to emulate it. And it must not be overlooked that the general buoyancy, and the publicity that it has generated, have had profound repercussions for the unknown craftsman whittling away in his workshop who now has increasing prospects of success at making a reasonable living from his or her craft.

Two

Setting Up A Professional Shop

I set up my first workshop in August 1962 after a brief period of teaching. It was a small beginning in a rented corrugated iron shed which was part of a larger builder's yard. The lease was only for 12 months, such was the difficulty then in acquiring workshop premises in the Home Counties.

My initial experience is worth recounting here, for I think there may well be lessons for others in it. In that August I had some unique advantages. I had seven years workshop experience; a teacher's certificate – my insurance against failure; a period of design training followed by some drawing office experience; and an order book for about six months ahead. However, what I did not have was money, and my good friends, the banks, did not share my enthusiasm for good work, thus I was unable to raise any capital from that quarter.

Now, I must say that I do not consider there is any great merit in starting this way; I just had no choice. If I could have obtained a low interest loan of £5000 at that time I would have jumped at it, but I had no security beyond what I stood up in. So I started in that shed with one secondhand bandsaw, my sole machine. My bench, the most vital tool of all, I already had, plus the good kit of hand tools acquired as an apprentice.

I soon befriended a joiner in the nearby village who would plane and thickness my timber for me, and also, having no timber stocks such as I now enjoy, I would at times get my timber pre-cut to a liberal cutting list by an excellent firm in London who sent it all down neatly packaged. It was expensive, but it was the only way without interminable travelling. Of course, this situation could not continue for long; I badly needed equipment of my own, so I began to get it in bit by bit on hire purchase, but this was, in the main, after I had moved into my second workshop in nearby Grayshott twelve months later.

That first and bitter winter of 1962 was quite a nightmare. I had, many days, to walk the three miles over the hedge tops to a workshop that was cold and patched to keep out the snow and the wind. I vowed then that if I was going to make furniture for the rest of my life, then I was going to do it in warmth and comfort.

Laura, just fresh out of university, went out to teach for the first five years before the birth of our children, whilst I took some part-time teaching in order to obtain the hire purchase agreements for the machinery and later a bank loan to buy our first cottage.

During those earlier years I had one burning ambition, which was simply to get the business off the ground; to achieve what Gimson and the Barnsleys and many others had not been able to do at that time, which was to run a creative workshop working to my own

Fig. 33   Yew sideboard, 1962. My first commission.

Fig. 34   Simple bookcase in Parana pine with ebony inlay and wedges, 1966.

designs and to my quality, without resorting to teaching or any other source of income.

I did not consider myself an artist-craftsman, but a good furniture maker providing a design service. It seemed to me then, as it does now, that idealism and principles are nothing if the workshop cannot survive and grow; what is vital is that at the end of each year the shop is still there and has progressed in some way. One simply must balance the need for profit and money for development with the ultimate aims one has in mind. It was possible in 1962 to make a living from making furniture, and many did, by making reproduction antiques and undertaking repair work. But I knew of less than a handful of shops who were working to their own designs and doing work of any merit, and they were not finding it at all easy.

I badly needed money to finance the business, but I was determined and made a conscious decision that I would not touch reproduction work or repairs, which would have paid better, although I was not averse to tackling high quality joinery and built-in fitments, and my training in interior design was very useful here.

My first such job was to convert a London double decker bus into a mobile showroom for a firm of glass importers. Laura and I worked many times into the early hours of the morning gluing on fabrics and doing much of the repetitive work that a job of this nature entails. The result, in natural pine with handcut dovetails and attractive fabric surfaces was terrific. I cannot claim credit for the general design, as I was working in conjunction with a London architect, but it was an enjoyable and exciting job that paid the bills with some to spare, and, as important to me, I felt I had left my own personal stamp on that travelling bus.

Thus in these earlier years my work was a balance each year between one-off furniture commissions and the more profitable built-in fitments and interior work. I also did a little designing for an industrial firm in the locality and made their prototypes and exhibition models.

I think it worth saying here that interior fitments and joinery do not in any way imply inferior work. I made a good bookcase, or a good room-divider, and provided a personal design service – the difference was rather one of public attitudes, particularly in the sixties. I was competing directly with architects, interior designers and builders, but I was providing a quality and attention to detail that they could not match. Sadly, though, the same public that commissioned me, was less willing to spend that money on free-standing furniture which did not add directly to the value of their property.

Had there been the number of craft galleries, shops, fairs and exhibitions that there are now, I would probably have made a more serious attempt at batch production of some of my designs; as it was, I did a little, but it was mainly confined to small items such as bookends, lamps, stools and a few low tables and bookcases.

It took, in fact, eight years to totally realise my ambition, and it was a gradual rather than a sudden process. After five years we started a family and Laura stopped teaching; two years later I got rid of the last prop, one day a week teaching at Portsmouth College of Art. Since then we have never looked back. It was the final challenge, and by 1970 I had good, centrally heated workshops, a comfortable home, and we could even afford holidays. During that period, I was getting involved in more complete room schemes that at times included the entrance doors and panelling, as well as the free-standing furniture.

On the surface, much has changed in the twenty-odd years since that August in 1962. Workshop premises are now much easier to acquire; grants, low interest loans, government and local authority help and advice are now widely available. There are more opportunities to exhibit, more galleries and retail outlets through which to sell one's work, and a larger, more discerning public at one's feet. On the debit side, however, it is a much larger and more competitive field one is moving into.

Fig. 35   Bookshelves, vanitory unit, etc, in chestnut. Interior work done in 1965.

Fig. 36   Walnut entrance door, architraves and fitments, part of a complete room scheme including desk, seating, book storage etc. 1971/2.

Fig. 37   Room fitments in Burmese teak, c.1965.

Fig. 38　Bookends in ebony and sycamore, 1963 and still in regular production using coloured veneers.

Fig. 39　Inlaid cheeseboard and table lamp 1963. The cheeseboards have been in regular production ever since.

At its best, all the grants and assistance you might be successful in attracting, including the redundancy payment you may possess, will do no more than sustain you through the initial year or so. After that, you are out there on your own, battling it out with a growing number of like-minded people for a market that might, for all we know, become saturated overnight.

So first, you, the potential self-employed furniture maker, should ask yourself why you should succeed where so many other talented people have previously failed. I have experienced this past ten years a steady flow of students and mature people who have expressed a strong desire to become furniture makers, and my guess is that little more than a tenth ever get started, and even fewer survive the first five years.

So why is it that, with so much now going in our favour, so few break through with any measure of success? Many, of course, are ill-prepared by training and by nature for the very demanding life that requires of one individual to be so many things — from businessman to bench hand with a dozen more trades and professions in between. Many art school students in particular, have the ideas and the inspiration, but have neither the making experience nor the patience, nor stamina, to execute those ideas themselves, and so they move on to more lucrative fields.

It is here that we face the real problem, namely, making money. Although large sections of the population do now know about and admire good work and would like to possess it, they either honestly cannot, or do not, wish to pay for the hours that quality and individual work demands. We still live in a society that generally does not reward skill in the same way that it rewards enterprise, business acumen or academic achievement. It is a fact that most of us accept and learn to live with, but it does mean that most workshops producing anything of real value, operate on a financial knife edge with little room for error or miscalculation.

I have purposely not painted a rosy picture of furniture making as a living, as opposed to a very pleasant pastime, for it is not for the faint hearted, and the following is only a guide to the complexities of such a career. At the end of the day, you must realise that no-one owes you a living; you will have to create it for yourself by your own efforts and by the quality of the work you produce.

YOUR FIRST WORKSHOP

Most people setting up their first workshop have no clear understanding as to how they hope to see their business in five or ten years' time. I was no exception, but circumstances forced me to test the water very gently, and as the work grew, so my premises and equipment grew with it. There is something to be said for this cautious approach, particularly for those lacking financial security.

But if I had no clear idea of where my business would be in five years in terms of turnover, or even location, I did have a very clear understanding of my objectives. I knew the kind of work I wanted to do and what I would not do; I knew I wanted to employ from the word go; and I knew the eventual scale of the business I intended one day to run. And I do advise anyone contemplating life as a self-employed furniture maker to thrash-out thoroughly in their own minds what both their short term and their ultimate objectives are. Of course, circumstances can change over the years, but the people who succeed are those who have defined their aims and work towards them. This is not to say that one should not take advantage of opportunities as they arise, or have second thoughts on details. It is major changes of direction that can be so costly in terms of equipment and time.

To arrive at this sense of direction or set of objectives, you will need to ask yourself many questions, and the following may serve as a guide.

1. What kind of furniture do I want to make now and in ten years' time? Is it to be modern design or reproduction styles? Will it be basically one-off production or quantity batch production? Will it cover a wide range of furniture or will it concentrate on, say, chairs, or office furniture?

2. What kind of service do I hope to provide? Is it a design and making service, or solely a making service? If the latter, will it be for the general public, or for architects and other designers, and involve the contract furnishing field. Perhaps you will provide a repair and restoration service, or possibly a combination of any of these options.

3. How do I see my market? Is it going to be the wealthy; the professional class; or a mass market? And how do I intend to reach them?

4. Is my role to serve the local community, or do I aim to work on a national scale, or in exporting?

5. Do I wish to work on my own, or in partnership; to employ and train others, or simply share premises and costs with other like-minded people? (Or you could plan to work in one way initially as a stepping stone to something else.)

6. What kind of lifestyle do I hope to achieve? Is my chief objective to acquire and maintain that lifestyle and the profitability of the business that supports it? Or is it the quality and the development of my work and my standing within the profession which is the driving force? (This question has to be faced; you might conceivably achieve both, but it is pretty rare.)

LOCATION

The location of your workshop is crucial to your success, particularly in the earlier years and follows on from asking and answering questions such as those just stated. It is no use complaining of a public that does not come and visit you and buy your product if they can't find you, or if nobody ever visits that part of the country except in July and August.

If you are producing batch products for the retail market or mail order, remoteness from centres of population may not matter so much, but do stop and think what happens to that two-mile lane in a bad winter; and weigh up the costs of transporting your work around on a yearly basis.

The other important aspect concerning the location of premises, irrespective of the physical needs of running a successful business, is the grant aid that may be available. Simply by moving ten miles in one direction you could come into a development area, or move into the jurisdiction of a much more sympathetic local authority, or of a regional arts association more sympathetic to the crafts. My own second workshop at Grayshott for example, had a Surrey address which proved to be a useful business asset when dealing with London based clients. But the workshops were actually half a mile inside Hampshire, and that half mile saved me several hundreds of pounds in rates and insurance – even my car insurance was cheaper – and I dealt with a more sympathetic local authority and planning committee which did not see workshops as quite the threat to the rural environment of Hampshire as they did in Surrey at that time.

Of course, it is tempting to move into cheap accommodation, with cheap rates and rent, even subsidised in many instances now, but do remember that much of the aid available is to encourage people to go into areas where they would not normally go from choice for one reason or another. If, for example, you have to spend a great deal of your working life on the road looking for work and materials, the back of beyond may not prove such a bargain after all. So, do research your location thoroughly, always assuming that you have any choice. I personally now live and work down a narrow leafy lane in Devon with pleasant views out of the workshop windows; but, it is only a mile from the motorway junction; two miles from a main line Intercity train to London, just over two hours away; and my mail arrives at 6.30 each morning. This did not come by happy accident, but after a summer of weekend searches following a period of ten years perched on the edge of Surrey and the London area. And yet it has brought home to me the disadvantages of working in the country as opposed to a small town or large village such as Grayshott, the one I left. Now I have to get the car out almost daily and drive to the post office, my bank, my accountant, my solicitor, or even to buy a box of screws or a meal should I wish to; whereas previously I simply walked up the road and they were all there. Only little things, but they all add up to convenience and ease the running of a small business.

Whilst eyeing up that dream cottage and cowshed, ask yourself whether you will be able to obtain the materials you want easily; will you be able to get employees if you need them; are there good rail and road communications for you and your customers; can you get food easily if you are on your own, or will you have to spend precious hours cooking and shopping instead of working at your chosen craft; and could you get a plumber or an electrician easily in an emergency? If not, the dream could turn out to be a nightmare.

Living on the Job

From the point of view of saving money, living where you work has several advantages. For instance it can save on certain expenses like telephone and transport to work, and it can save on time because you can easily slip into the workshop after supper to put one more panel in the veneer press or to glue something up in preparation for the morning.

It also means that you are never free of the business unless you leave home! The telephone may ring at any time, day, night or weekend, and you are on the receiving end; people can call, "just on the off-chance" on a Sunday morning, just as you are relaxing in the garden or the bath.

Having had experience of both, for six years living approximately three miles away from the premises and for the last sixteen living on the job, I am still not sure which I prefer. Perhaps the best answer is to be tucked away half a mile up the road in an attempt to reap the advantages of proximity while retaining some degree of privacy.

Sharing Premises

This has considerable appeal particularly for those setting up with little capital, for, unlike a partnership, each individual has complete control over his own actions and products whilst still enjoying the advantages of shared overheads, facilities and companionship.

In the UK it is also helpful in avoiding registration for VAT, as each individual is still responsible for his or her own income and tax affairs, and it is easier for, say, four separate craftsmen to keep their respective turnovers below the VAT threshold than for a partnership or a craftsman who employs. Avoiding liability for VAT is quite an asset in such a labour intensive occupation as cabinetmaking, for, although it seems attractive to be able to claim back the VAT on material purchases, the registered craftsman also has to charge 15% extra as VAT on every hour of his labour, making his work less competitive.

Sharing premises is as successful as the human relationships which exist between those involved. It demands a lot of give and take, and it can be frustrating as one waits to take one's turn at a particular machine, but there are several examples in Britain today where this arrangement has worked most successfully over several years.

Workshop Premises

Although it is rarely attained, it is worth considering what constitutes an ideal workshop in terms of working comfort and maximum efficiency so that at least some of its characteristics can be incorporated in either new purpose-built premises or conversions.

Furniture makers are like farmers in two significant respects. Both require a heavy investment in equipment and buildings even though very few people are involved in the enterprise, and both are dependent on the weather, the farmer because it affects his livelihood outside, and the furniture maker because it affects his livelihood inside. A blistering hot dry summer might be paradise for the holiday maker but it can be a nightmare and ruinous for the furniture maker's timber stocks, furniture and working efficiency. Likewise, a heavy rainy season can equally bring its problems of high humidity, leaking roofs and rising damp; and snow not only finds its way under tiles and slates to get trapped in the roof space and lining and then drip on to whatever is stored beneath, but also gets driven into your timber stocks where it eventually melts and stains.

The ideal premises then, would keep cool in summer, keep out all the elements, provide good natural lighting and not be too costly to heat in winter. The solid stone barn with its high pitched roof has obvious advantages in summer but is very costly to heat in winter. If you choose, as I have done, to save on heat and put a second floor into part of the roof space, you then rob the ground floor of valuable roof light and air circulation. If the building is not constructed of stone, brick or concrete block, but of timber, clad with a variety of materials, unless the inner insulation is very effective you may find it difficult to keep cool in summer and you may face higher insurance premiums as well.

The best possible lighting in any workshop is natural daylight, the worst and most tiring is direct sunlight, and the problem is how to get the first without the second. The best solution is north-facing roof lights, which give very few shadows and cannot be bettered, coupled with windows facing north or east to avoid midday or afternoon sun. I cannot over-emphasise the dangers of bright sunlight coming through glass, for not only does it impair your ability to work efficiently but it can also positively damage furniture and timber. If south facing windows are unavoidable, fit them with blinds or curtains and ensure that these are closed at weekends or any other prolonged absences from the workshop. But however good the daylight, it will still have to be supplemented for winter and evening work by artificial light, and this is best supplied by a good batch of fluorescent tubes. It does not pay to be mean with these, for good work cannot be done in poor light; and even so there will be occasions when additional lighting in the form of anglepoise lamps will be necessary for bench-work and on machines such as the mortiser, pillar drill, overhead router or bandsaw.

In areas where machinery is to be installed a hard, solid flat floor is essential, and a cement screed laid on a concrete base is usually the answer here. If it is then given a couple of coats of industrial floor paint this will not only improve its appearance but also minimise dust problems. In bench-work areas and cabinetmaking shops concrete is unsuitable as it is tiring on the feet and unsympathetic to bent knees, dropped tools and furniture alike. An existing solid floor of this nature can be improved beyond all measure by insulating it with a combination of sheet polystyrene and inexpensive chipboard, finally sealed in the same way with industrial floor paint. The floor to my cabinet shop was done this way ten years ago and it has a slight spring to it that makes for comfort. I used second grade chipboard and now at last it requires a fresh coat of paint, but otherwise it is as good as the day I laid and screwed it down.

Finally, remembering the frequency with which it rains in Britain, two sets of double doors that enable you to drive your car or van into the workshop to load or unload in comfort and without letting out all the heat of the shop in the process is a valuable asset. Often this can be achieved by building an extension in front of the existing doors, a comparatively simple alteration which conserves heat and excludes wind and rain throughout the year as well as when loading.

Heating the Workshop

Elsewhere, when referring to timber and humidity control I have stressed the need for adequate heating, but here I stress it for its economic advantages. If you can work comfortably and efficiently inside your workshop, oblivious to the six inches of snow lying outside, you will be able to produce good work the year round and disregard any seasonal variations which might make your production less economic.

It is often considered desirable for woodworkers to consume their own wood waste as fuel. It always sounds attractive and appeals to our sense of economy and independence as well as to our concern for the world's dwindling resources of energy. The reality however, is that unless you are a fairly large concern with quite a large turnover of materials, you will never have enough for your needs without having to store the waste from the summer months and buy in extra supplies for the winter. In addition, there is the strong possibility that you will have to pay increased insurance premiums because of your solid fuel heating and the certainty that you will have to spend considerable time and energy in keeping the stoves or boiler clean and functioning.

For sheer convenience, nothing can beat a system that operates at the flick of a switch as and when you require it. Your personal preference and local availability will dictate which energy source you choose, but in my previous premises I used oil fired heating with very old heavy cast iron radiators discarded by the local hospital which were excellent as they retained the heat long after the power was turned off. For the past ten years, with the rise in the price of oil, I have used off-peak electric storage heaters. These are not ideal, because they cannot be instantly controlled in the same way as a boiler can, but generally they are quite effective and economical as they supply the greatest heat when we need it early in the morning, tapering off by late afternoon and evening.

WORKSHOP LAYOUT

It is difficult to lay down any fixed guide lines on this as so much depends on the size, nature and scope of your business. Basically though, the nearer your work is to batch and factory production, the closer your layout needs to reflect that of an efficient factory unit.

Materials should come in at one end, be processed in a logical sequence, and the products should be despatched efficiently at the other. The entire layout of each machine, bench and storage rack in relation to each other should reflect that efficient flow-line approach whilst complying with safety regulations.

However, if your main activity is working to commission, many other considerations may over-ride the simple pattern of the production line. You might find yourself using a spray gun as rarely as once in two months, for example, and this would influence your thinking as to the position of, or even the necessity for separate spraying facilities.

Again, if working on your own, you need not consider the noise of machinery conflicting with those quieter activities like designing on the drawing board or intricate cabinet work, and therefore your machines could be installed directly under your cabinet shop or drawing office on a lower floor, or simply partitioned off on the same floor to minimise the spread of dust. Such a layout as this would work perfectly well for the solo craftsman but it could be wearying and counter-productive in a shop where four people were attempting to work.

My own machine shop, or mill, is actually situated across the yard, at 90 degrees, from my cabinet shop, an arrangement which is inconvenient in wet weather. It would be easy, and on the face of it sensible, to cut an entrance through 18″ of stonework from one to the other. However, that inconvenient short walk saves a considerable expense on insurance each year, for machine shops are assessed as high fire risks and thus carry a higher premium than the adjoining stores, offices and cabinetmaking shop. The moment I break through that 18″ fire barrier, my whole premises would carry the same high risk assessment, but if I were engaged in serious batch production, the efficiency gained by so doing would simply have to over-ride the increase in overheads and noise levels.

So, although the layout of my workshop may be of interest, I strongly advise anyone setting up to really study what their own individual needs are in relation to the type of work they intend to pursue, and with this in mind, seek the advice of the technical advisors of rural or industrial workshop organizations, such as CoSIRA in England, who will be pleased to help.

THE SHOWROOM

Whether you work to commission or do batch production it is necessary to have examples of your work for people to see; pieces that will demonstrate the quality of the work you do and the *direction* in which you want to go. Besides getting these seen by a wider audience through exhibitions, it is also desirable to have an area set aside on your own premises where these pieces can be viewed alongside any other work which is awaiting delivery.

When I first set up in my tin shed, my workshop and situation was to some extent an embarrassment, so I always made a point of visiting prospective clients, relying on good photographs and smaller, portable items to demonstrate my range of work and its quality. This involved much time and many fruitless journeys, and it is so much better, particularly for that initial meeting, if the prospective client visits your premises to see what your work is really about. By being prepared to come, the client manifests the seriousness of his enquiry and is in turn able to reassure himself of your ability and reliability at first hand. Certainly you may get involved in a site visit later, but by that stage it is no longer such a gamble in terms of time. At all events, I am convinced that an hour or two spent face to face is far more rewarding and productive than numerous letters.

Therefore, I strongly advise setting up a reception and display area, a space where you can talk freely and comfortably and discuss any proposals with your work around you and, as far as is possible, away from the dust and noise. Maybe, as when I first moved to Devon, this could be an area in your house; or, as I have now, in the roof space of a barn with the workshop underneath. A second great advantage in doing this is that here *you* are in charge; you can display whatever you wish, in the way that *you* think does it justice, rather than at the whim of an exhibition designer or retailer.

Naturally, to do this well requires time and money, and this again is one of the advantages that can be derived from individuals sharing joint premises, although it could also lead to a conflict of interests if all the group shared the same craft. It does, of course, make for a more interesting and varied display if, for example, weavers' and potters' work can be shown alongside furniture, and you might consider either purchasing or having on loan the work of other craftsmen to complement your own.

RETAIL SELLING

It is very much a personal decision whether you extend this simple basic area for displaying your work into an active selling area, but if you should decide to do so, do ascertain whether your planning permission will allow it. It is really a question of whether you prefer to get on uninterrupted with your craft for most of the time, or whether the retail aspect also appeals to you. You may of course simply employ someone, perhaps a wife or husband, to take over this aspect, but whoever does it, your success will depend to a great extent on your ability to attract the passing seasonal tourist trade and this in turn will hinge on the nature of your product and the location of your premises – very few families return from their annual holiday at Southsea with a mahogany dining table on the roof rack!

Fig. 40   Display area in roof space.

Fig. 41   Cabinet shop cleaned up at the end of a day's work.

Three

Equipment

THE BENCH

THE most important piece of equipment for a cabinetmaker is his bench. It matters little whether you choose to devote valuable time to making it or to purchase it readymade as I have always done; what is important is the nature and quality of the bench and its day to day condition. Sadly, too many woodworkers are accustomed from childhood and from the school workshops to think only in terms of a very basic carpenter's bench, and consequently pupils and students have struggled along on benches on which I, for one, would have had great difficulty in producing anything worthwhile, let alone quality work.

So your first priority as a cabinetmaker must be a good cabinetmaker's bench with a sturdy tail vice that will grip securely any length of timber laid upon its surface, and I am sure that having once experienced working on this type of bench you wil wonder how you ever managed before. Then you need to treat your bench as a precious piece of equipment and care for it as you would the bed of your planer. It should be perfectly flat, and dressed periodically to ensure this; and its surface needs to be waxed so that any spillage of glue, for example, wil simply peel off. You cannot produce good quality work efficiently on benches such as those most of us are familiar with in education, with surfaces smothered in resin, paint, glue and metal filings, and with vices that do not grip accurately but bruise everything with which they come into contact. And if you must repair the lawn mower on its surface, or are using resin, protect it with a sheet of hardboard first, or better still, have other bench surfaces set aside for such activities.

The illustration shows what I consider to be the ideal cabinetmaker's bench, European in pattern and available in various lengths from 1.7m to 2.5m/5ft to 8ft. If you decide to make your own, do research the best height for you – all purchased benches appear to have been designed for midgets, or rather they are they are based on traditional patterns established when benches were used for chopping mortises and for hours of heavy hand planing. My four purchased benches sit more or less permanently on 150mm/6″ blocks to eliminate backache.

The fittings, including the bench dogs, for those making their own, are readily available from specialist suppliers, and the bench itself should ideally be made of prime beech, although sycamore and ash are quite good alternatives.

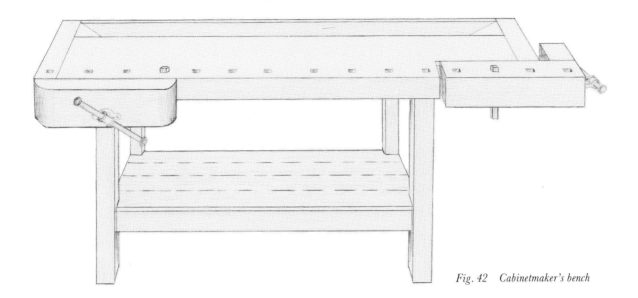

Fig. 42   Cabinetmaker's bench

HAND TOOLS

Visitors to my workshop are often pleasantly surprised to find that there are very few items in my tool kit that cannot be purchased from any good hardware store anywhere in the country. I do not believe there is any merit, beyond the enjoyment and satisfaction of doing it, in a professional spending days making his own wooden planes or gauges. Apart from a few old, secondhand wooden jack planes that I use for roughing out and shaping, I have happily used standard, fully adjustable metal planes for the past 30 years or more. I have often thought I would like to own a Norris smoothing plane, but I would only put it on a shelf in the house and admire it, for I am pretty convinced that my £20 scraper plane would do the job equally well, and I would hate to hide away such a beautiful object by having it in my tool kit. Although I do have a few favourites, like some of my chisels, (relics, as most of my tools are, of my apprenticeship days, only chisels show it when they are only a couple of inches long), I do not get over-excited over tools but look at them very much as aids to producing what to me is more important, the work itself.

There is quite a lot of sentimental rubbish talked about tools, and if some people like to collect them and cherish them as other people collect stamps or old silver then fine, but tools in themselves will not make you into a good cabinetmaker.

There is much enthusiasm at present for Japanese tools, and, whilst I am now completely sold on Japanese water stones, I do not in general find Japanese tools to my liking. Throughout the East I admired the superb joinery construction that I saw everywhere, but nowhere did I find the quality cabinet work that presently prevails in, say, Britain or Denmark. Japanese tools have evolved over centuries mainly for use by joiners and housebuilders working on the floor, not on the bench as we do, and most of the joinery construction of Japan and Korea is achieved in beautifully straight-grained cedar or cypress that cuts like cheese. It is only the Chinese, and to a lesser extent the Koreans, who have a strong cabinetmaking tradition of working in hardwoods, and they cut on the push stroke as we do, and their tools are closer to their European counterparts. So, although I have tried Japanese saws and chisels, I always come back to those tools of my apprenticeship and I cannot think of any saw that can match a good British dovetail saw.

I do have a few pet aversions in tools. I just cannot stand plastic handles in any shape, colour or form, or keyhole saws that bend the moment you insert them in the hole. (The Japanese have solved this one – theirs are superb and quite inexpensive.)

It is surprising now with the increased use of power tools and machinery, just how few tools one really needs as opposed to those early days of my apprenticeship. One could so easily spend a fortune on a beautiful kit of new tools only to find that 60 per cent of them stay in the tool box. So, for anyone who has not yet embarked on purchasing their handtools it would pay to relate them to those major decisions of what kind of furniture and what kind of workshop they wish to run, and what equipment they hope to use.

Fig. 43 Assistant craftsman Keith Newton working on an ebony display cabinet.

Fig. 44   The cabinet shop during the day.

My own workshop is very versatile in the wide range of furniture we make, and it might be useful for me to list only those tools that I now use and find indispensable given the equipment and machinery that I now have:

Setting out & Marking Tools

Roofing square   – invaluable for setting out on rough timber and for use as a large square.
Straight edges   – both metal and wood for the longer lengths.
Winding strips   – made in shop of mahogany, ebony and sycamore.
Squares   – engineering all metal pattern with both 3″ (76mm) and 12″ (305mm) sliding square.
Gauges   – one can never have too many, but I do not use cutting gauges; I cut both with and across the grain with one marking gauge filed to a chisel point.
Depth and profile gauge
Sliding bevels, calipers for the lathe, several pairs of dividers and trammel heads for setting out circles.
Plumb bob and spirit level for site work.

Planes

Wooden:
1 jack plane for fast removal of stock.
4 jack planes ground up for curved work.
1 smoothing plane with rounded iron for scrubbing off rough timber.

Metal: 1 No. 7 jointer used for practically every hand planing operation, however short the timber. I keep three spare irons and only sharpen when all four are dull.
1 No. 4 smoothing plane used only on site work.
1 No. 9½ block plane used only as a one-handed plane for working radii and chamfers.
1 scraper plane, which I find invaluable on difficult grain where I cannot use my large belt sander. This has replaced the flat metal scraper which I only use when ground for contours.
Shoulder and Bullnose planes
Side rebate planes – used occasionally, but I aim to fit all shoulders straight from the saw or machine.
Compass plane – used extensively for curved work following initial cuts on the bandsaw.
Spokeshaves – have a selection, but they are not used extensively due to drum sanding attachments on pillar drill. (I prefer wood to metal ones.)
Drawknife – used often for chamfer work and removing stock quickly in shaped work.

Saws

Rip, hand and panel – rarely used except on sitework.
Tenon saw – used as general purpose bench saw.
Dovetail saw – used extensively for all dovetailing and small shoulders.
Coping saw – used in dovetailing to remove waste.
Piercing saw – used in fine dovetailing to remove waste and for cutting letters, etc, to be inlaid.

Chisels

Set of boxwood handled bevelled edge from 1⁄16th to 1″ (approx. 1.5mm to 25mm)
2 long ½″ (12mm) paring chisels, one with cranked handle.
A few old firmer chisels for rough site work.
I now have no use for mortise chisels or heavy firmer chisels; where I cannot use the mortiser, I bore out the mortise and simply pare it down, or use a portable router.

Gouges and Carving Tools

I have a large selection, mainly secondhand, but this is due to my interest in using and developing carving on furniture. Probably 4 inner and 4 outer ground gouges would suffice for normal cabinet work.

Boring Tools

I do have a brace and set of bits but never seem to use them. All drilling is done whenever possible on the pillar drill or, failing this, with a portable, beautifully quiet cordless battery drill, which is also very useful as a production screwdriver.

A selection of screwdriver, hammers and mallets completes the kit; no doubt there are incidentals I have forgotten, but basically this is all I need today.

Buying Tools

When buying tools, quality is of the utmost importance. Cheap brands of tools, particularly chisels, are not worth buying. If buying new, go to a reputable hardware store or tool merchant who can advise you on the best makes and avoid the discount stores with their cheap products from Taiwan. 'Rogers' of Hitchin not only supply excellent tools but also produce a very informative catalogue which at £1-50 is very useful reading and can help you make intelligent choices.

I personally favour secondhand tools, although one needs some knowledge of what to look for and what to avoid. In this connection, the most excellent shop and collection of tools that I have ever discovered is at 'Old Woodworking Tools', Upper Street, Islington, London, N1. Many of the tools here are collectors' items. They are attractively arranged and just browsing here for a few hours can be quite an education.

You are, however, more likely to pick up a bargain on a market stall or in a junk shop, but this takes time and is more of a gamble. A word of advice – take a straight edge with you when purchasing metal planes and test the sole before you buy, as they can vary considerably!

Suppliers of Hand Tools

Great Britain

John Boddy Ltd.
Riverside Sawmills
Boroughbridge, Yorks, YO5 9LJ

Rogers
47 Walsworth Road
Hitchin
Herts, SG4 9SU

Parry's Tools
Old Street
London E2

Cecil Tyzack Ltd
79/81 Kingsland Road
London E2 8AG

Sargents Tools
62/64 Fleet Street
Swindon, Wilts.

Alec Tiranti Ltd
21 Goodge Place
London W1

North America

The Fine Tool Shops
20–28 Backus Avenue
Danbury, CT 06810

Frog Tool Co.
700 West Jackson Blvd.
Chicago, IL 60606

Garrett Wade Co.
302 Fifth Avenue
New York, NY 10001

Lee Valley Tools, Ltd.
857 Boyd Avenue
Ottawa, Ontario, Canada
K2A 2C9

Leichtung, Inc.
4944 Commerce Parkway
Cleveland, OH 44128

Woodcraft Supply Corp.
313 Montvale Avenue
Woburn, MA 01888

MACHINERY

My eagerness to install machinery might appear paradoxical, in view of my nostalgic feelings for my pre-machine age apprenticeship days, but I had no desire to live in poverty, and also I soon began to enjoy the challenge and scope for design that the machinery presented. During my time at the London Central School of Arts & Crafts, I had used, for instance, a large overhead pad sander of the type used frequently in industry before they were superseded by speed sanders. I had seen what it could do if operated well with a sensitive hand, and so we soon had one installed at Grayshott. That was in 1964, and it is still going strong in Devon today, having been built to last way back in 1928.

Despite some misgivings about the wider use of machinery and its implications for creative work, I know that I personally enjoy many of the machine operations. I like the speed with which the raw material can be transformed into workable sizes and components. I also like to exploit the potential for design that each new item of equipment I purchase throws up. Here I must stress that many of my designs of recent years would not have been logical, sensible or even conceived without the equipment I have at my fingertips.

Because I am chiefly engaged in working to commission, and therefore do much one-off work, machining takes up less than a fifth of my time and that of my assistants.

In order to have relative peace and quiet and a dust-free atmosphere for the remainder of our time, most of the machines are housed across the yard in a separate machine shop. Unfortunately, one item of equipment tends now to destroy this scheme, and that is the portable router. For years I resisted its intrusion into our quiet world of cabinetmaking, and never had one in the shop; eventually I relented, as its usefulness and versatility became all too apparent. I do have now an overhead table router in the machine shop, which relieves some of the problem, but the portable one still gets picked up, and shatters the eardrums, simply because it is so easy to operate on the work-piece itself, rather than taking the work to the machine. Frankly, I still hate it and wish it had not been invented, although I have the quietest one on the market. One of my next projects will be to develop an adjoining store into a sound proof area just to house this monster, and the work will just have to be carried in there and worked on. All this, of course, only becomes necessary when more than one person is using a workshop, for it is always the other guy's router which is irritating, not the one that you yourself are using.

The major decision one does have to make, however, on setting up and choosing equipment and machinery is whether you intend to concentrate on providing a service, the one-off shop, (whether it be reproduction, restoration or creative work, or working for other designers is immaterial), or whether it is a production workshop, producing in quantity either to your own or someone else's design. It is possible over the years to dabble a little in both, but I am convinced after 20 years that for success one must make this distinction and decide what your shop is really about. So important do I consider this that I have devoted two separate chapters to these very distinct areas of operation.

If working in the former, you may well survive for several years with very little machinery, and sub-contract work like veneering and planing quite successfully, although this may depend on the location of your workshop. Secondly, although grant aid may change one's view, secondhand machines are often quite adequate; in fact, it is often hard to justify installing expensive new equipment when most of it will be lying idle for much of the time. I have only recently replaced a secondhand panel saw that I purchased from a scrap merchant for £7.50 eighteen years ago with another secondhand machine.

In a one-off shop, it is far better, if space permits, to purchase a wide range of secondhand, separate machines rather than one expensive combination machine, which are nothing but a nuisance in a busy workshop. These are the items of equipment I have collected over the past twenty years, predominantly to assist me and my three assistants in providing a design and making service:

1) 3-screw veneer press – secondhand, 1966; sited in cabinet shop.
2) 10ft (3.05mm) pad or stroke sander, built in 1928, which I bought for £100 in 1966, and which is sited in the finishing area of cabinet shop.
3) 9″ (228mm) precision saw bench situated in cabinet shop – new
4) Floor mounted drill press with various sanding attachments – new, 1966; sited in cabinet shop
5) 10″ (254mm) diam. separate disc sander – new, 1968
6) Dust Collector for pad sander
7&8) Floor to ceiling timber racks – one to house 8′×4′ (2.44×1.22 m) sheets; one to store timber in constant use, ½″ (12 mm) oak and cedar for drawer making for example
9) Timber racks for oddments, arranged in species
10) Overhead router – secondhand
11) Woodturning lathe – secondhand
12) Planer grinder – secondhand
13) Spindle moulder – secondhand
14) 21″ × 9″ (534 × 228mm) thickness planer – purchased secondhand in 1966 for £25
15) Twin Dust Collector connected to both planers, spindle moulder and circular saw.

16)   15″ × 72″ (380 × 1830mm) surface planer – purchased secondhand in 1980 for £150
17)   Hollow chisel mortiser – secondhand
18)   12″ (305mm) sliding table panel saw with tilting arbor – secondhand
19)   18″ (456mm) bandsaw, new, replacing in 1981 my secondhand one bought in 1962
20)   Large Portable Dust Collector used on 9″ (228 mm) circular saw sanding disc, and as needed in the cabinet shop

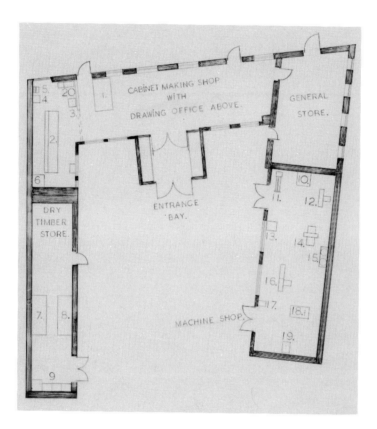

Fig. 45   Workshop layout.

Power Tools

Electric chainsaw – new
Portable cross-cut – new
Small portable router – new
Small jig saw – new
3″ (76mm) planer – new
Compressor and spray gun – secondhand.

I might add that all this, which includes two 5hp motors, operates off single phase electricity supply, 3 phase being too far away and therefore too expensive to install. It has never caused me any problem, except that it does limit me to secondhand equipment in many instances where the motors can simply be replaced by single phase.

Now all this secondhand equipment, that has cost me relatively little over the years, does need nursing along, but it is perfectly adequate until one starts thinking in terms of quantity production. Its weakness is readily apparent as soon as any quantity of repetitive work is undertaken, where accuracy from the machines is of the utmost importance, and where any one machine may be working solidly for many hours non-stop.

This is why the decision as to what your shop is really about is so important. It is pointless and expensive to install, for example, a new 36″ (915mm) planer if one is going to finish up making chairs or toast racks with a width of no more than 3″ or 4″ (76–100mm).

I am convinced that in cabinet work, as opposed to, say, country chair making, when quantity production is required one must not skimp on equipment. It must be sturdy, of the best make and preferably new, or at least comparatively so. Do-it-yourself toys and lightweight machines are fine for the amateur and useful in one-off shops, but they are completely unsuitable for any production work. Thus, anyone thinking in terms of batch production must allow for considerable outlay on equipment from the outset. A very useful, simply written book on wood machining for craftsmen is *Machine Woodworking Technology for Hand Woodworkers*, by F. E. Sherlock, Butterworth Publishers Ltd.

DUST EXTRACTION

For centuries cabinetmaking was a pretty healthy occupation. It provided constant, varied and quite strenuous exercise within the workshop and, with the reliance on hand tools, produced very little dust. In industry, this changed in the Victorian period with the growing use of machinery and the advent of mass production methods, after which one man could possibly spend his working life standing at one or two machines, inhaling the dust that came from them and being subjected to their continuous noise.

Over the years the furniture industry has come to recognise the danger to health that dust is, and the modern furniture factory takes most of it away at source, leaving noise as the major problem to be solved.

There has been much discussion and reports lately on the dangers of inhaling wood dust that can cause nasal cancer and respiratory problems. I think these findings have come as a shock to many of us who have spent our lives working in wood. We have long recognised the nuisance value of dust, but have generally felt that, since it is a natural organic material, some of it indeed even very sweet smelling, the health risk was not great, unlike the risks to which stone or slate workers were exposed. In my own shop, we simply stopped using those timbers that caused our noses to burn, eyes to run and severe coughing, and these were all timbers introduced comparatively recently into this country. The same problem does not appear to exist in the traditional home-grown hardwoods, and this is just one of the reasons why I work more and more in these timbers.

But, having said that, all dust is a nuisance; all of it, to a greater or lesser extent, is injurious to health and one of the biggest headaches for the cabinetmaker. The people most vulnerable today to this health hazard are not the wood machinists working in modern factories, but the craftsmen working away for ten hours or more a day in the confined space of a small workshop, or even the home hobbyist, spending all his leisure hours battened down in his basement workshop. If you include the dust of resin impregnated materials like chipboard, plywood and other particle boards and plastic laminates, add to it the fumes of modern wood finishes, solvents and some glues, add, also, heat and adequate insulation in winter, and the resulting atmosphere is quite removed from one's romantic vision of the healthy, country workshop, knee deep in sweet-smelling curly pine shavings, with pure fresh air whistling through the gaps in the walls and windows.

Twelve years ago, I personally became allergic to certain wood dusts, and my future as a furniture maker was thus in jeopardy. Following two nose operations and a long period without the senses of smell or taste, I had to tackle the problem of dust. This is why I now enjoy extensive space in Devon, with all my main machinery away across the yard in a separate shop, and why in the ensuing years I have spent more on dust extraction equipment than I have on the machinery itself. I have a 12ft (3.66 m) long stroke pad sander, and so efficient is the dust extraction for it that we never need to wear a mask when working it. I detest spending my working day wearing masks, goggles and ear muffs, and, like industry, I try to get this dust away at source.

I do implore all furniture makers to think very seriously about this problem and find the money for adequate extraction. Some of it is now compulsory by law if one employs, but the law does not seem to bother about the self-employed man who is perfectly at liberty to ruin his own health.

The other big health hazard, which is also related to the increased use of machinery and powered hand tools, is noise; and most wood machinists suffer in later life from loss of hearing. Noise is certainly a danger to be aware of and to guard against, but it is not such a hazard as dust for the small operator whose machinery is not constantly in use, and protection against it can largely be effected by the wearing of inexpensive ear muffs, especially when operating machines such as the router or thicknesser.

Installing A Dust Extraction System

Unlike wood machinery, it is a risky business, unless one has specialist knowledge, to buy secondhand dust extraction equipment, for each adequate dust extraction scheme should be tailor-make for the premises and its machinery. New and secondhand portable units, developed for the do-it-yourself market, can be bought, and they may be useful in some instances, on disc sanders for example, but generally they are greatly underpowered and they do not solve the real problem. So do research the market thoroughly here, for they are not cheap items, and in my own experience they have proved a waste of money.

As in so many other fields, it is advisable to call in the experts; firms that will survey your problem and produce a scheme aimed at solving it. Some will then supply and fit all equipment and ducting on site, whilst others will simply supply it with drawings for self-installation. It is an expert's job to know what power is needed; what diameter of ducting is necessary for each machine or area of the shop; to design the necessary hoods and the other purpose made items one may need. Naturally, a service like this does not come cheap, but I am convinced it is a necessarily incurred cost of running any cabinetmaking shop today where machinery is used to any great extent.

It is important for anyone setting up a new shop to get this installation planned and estimated for from the outset, rather than coming round to it eventually, five years later, with all the subsequent upheaval that it entails. It can then qualify for any setting up grants or tax concessions that may be available.

OTHER AREAS OF EQUIPMENT

Having solved your machinery and handtool problems, you will be unpleasantly surprised by how much support equipment you will require.

Assembly Equipment: I have made a sturdy bench with no vices, only a perfectly flat top, from 3″ (76mm) laminated ash, which I use purely for gluing up and assembly. It is not very wide, only about 18″ (456mm), so that I can cramp carcase work directly down to the bench to keep it perfectly flat and straight. This leaves your cabinetmaking bench free and undamaged by cramps, glue and panic.

Cramps: both sash and G varieties. These are hideously expensive and you will never seem to have enough. It is useful to have a few lightweight sash cramps, but in the main I would go for heavy duty tee-bar cramps. Liquidation sales can be a good source.

Fire-fighting Equipment: This is absolutely essential in such a high risk business, but it could be expensive if you take too much notice of the various reps' from the companies who manufacture extinguishers. Rather, seek advice from an impartial local fire inspector, or your insurance broker, but preferably the former. Much good fire-fighting equipment need not be that expensive – galvanised buckets, painted red and filled with sand is something we can all do; and I prefer asbestos blankets rather than fire extinguishers for early control of a fire spreading. You will still need extinguishers, but seek advice before purchasing.

Running hot water: essential if you choose to employ, but desirable even if you do not. It should if possible be sited within the workshop. We use an old-fashioned deep porcelain-type sink with an electric heating unit above, or you can tap it off the house supply. This is not just a luxury for washing hands and making tea, but a pretty essential installation, particularly in a shop such as mine where we use, almost exclusively, water solvent glues and undertake our own veneering, thus regularly needing to wash out rollers and brushes.

Sawing stools and Trestles: These of course can be made within the workshop. I use two types: the more conventional low sawing stools for supporting rough boards before setting and cutting out, and several pairs of lighter folding trestles that I use in conjunction with cheap hardboard doors to provide flat surfaces. These are simply set up around machines or workbenches whenever and wherever we require a temporary flat surface–which is all the time but in different places.

Storage cupboards: One can never have too many and they are well worth spending the time making. Wherever possible, fix them to the wall at a convenient height that does not restrict your floor space. We have purpose made wall cupboards for screws, hardware, abrasives and handtools, as well as for all the equipment, cutters etc. that go with the individual machines. Ensure that they have dust-excluding hinged doors, which can themselves also act as storage areas, two shallow shelves being better than one deep one.

It is, however, unsafe, and forbidden by Fire Regulations and Factory Acts, to store polishes, lacquers and other inflammables in quantity in the workshop itself. This can present a problem which we have overcome by using old freezers stored in an outhouse away from the shop and timber stores. These are ideal, as they are sealed, metal lined, and cost nothing; they could even stand in the open, away from the sun, and last for several years.

Four

Finance and Business Efficiency

COMPANY and general law naturally vary from country to country and the following text refers to English law. New statutes which may come into force after the publication of this book may, of course, alter or amend any situation or status. Readers from other countries should make the necessary enquiries for laws applicable to their region.

FORMS OF BUSINESS

Sole trader

If you are working on your own, for yourself, you are a sole trader. Your legal obligations are no different from those of any private citizen. You must not break the law and you must fulfil, where applicable, the requirements of the Inland Revenue (for Income Tax), the Customs and Excise (for VAT), and the Department of Health and Social Security. There is no legal separation of your private and working life.

This is a simple but risky existence. If your business were in financial difficulty you could be compelled to sell your house to pay your debts. The tax system, too, does not work in your favour as you are taxed each year on your income and profits, and should you make a loss in the following year, you cannot balance one against the other. You may also find it difficult to finance expansion of your business from one year to the next.

Partnership

A partnership (two or more people working together) can be an attractive proposition. It shares the cost of premises and equipment, may result in increased business for all parties, and can relieve the stresses of starting up a business by giving the opportunity for discussion and joint decision-making. Partners may have complementary skills, for example, where one makes the goods and the other sells them.

The disadvantage is that in a partnership you assume responsibility for not only your own but your partner's business errors; you may have to sell *your* house to pay for *his* lack of success.

A partnership has no special legal status, and for tax purposes the assessor will divide profits equally between the partners or in an agreed proportion. Anyone contemplating a partnership should think carefully what is involved and preferably have a clear-cut agreement drawn up by a solicitor, stating how the ownership, profits, and responsibility are to be divided. The agreement should also provide for an equitable method of ending the partnership, which might include an independent arbitrator in the event of disagreement afterwards. Where only one partner wishes to end the partnership, the agreement can require him to name a price for the half share (or proportion where more than two partners are involved), at which price the unwilling partner can choose to buy or sell.

Business Names

It is no longer necessary for sole trading businesses or partnerships to register a business name. Notes on the new simplified requirements are available from the Small Firms Service.

Limited Company

Forming a limited liability company has advantages and disadvantages. It removes the worry of losing your house and private possessions in the event of bankruptcy, since your business and private lives are legally separate. It gives added control over the use of money in financing expansion and balancing profits against losses. A limited company can more readily retain profits from one year to the next and (particularly in the first years of trading) plough back this money to expand. Generally speaking, company profits are taxed at a higher rate than personal income.

Running a limited company involves you in the preparation of audited accounts which are more detailed than the normal accounts for tax purposes and which you are legally required to file annually. This may involve considerable work and expense. *You should ask your accountant for advice on whether it is appropriate for you to form a limited company in your own particular circumstances.*

The legal requirements for a limited company are a minimum of one director and one other shareholder (this may be yourself and your spouse), and a minimum share capital of £100. This does not mean that £100 must be paid into the company initially; but should the company become bankrupt the amount that the creditors can demand from the shareholders is limited to a total of £100.

There are company registration agents who will set up a company for you for a fee of around £200; but you can obtain guidenotes on the procedure from the Registrar of Companies, Maindy Road, Cardiff, and if they are followed, the process is not difficult.

Taxation

As soon as you start your business you should inform your local Inspector of Taxes on Form 41G which is contained in the Inland Revenue's booklet 'Starting in Business'. This also gives full information on tax matters and is available free of charge from your local tax office.

As a self-employed person you will be assessed in one year on the profits shown in your accounts for the preceding one. Your profit is arrived at by taking all your earnings from your business and deducting your personal allowance, allowances and business expenditure. The assessed tax then has to be paid in two equal half-yearly instalments.

Value Added Tax (VAT)

You are legally required to register with your local VAT office of the Customs and Excise if your annual turnover is, or is likely to be, above the tax liability threshold of £18,700 (1984). The VAT General Guide Notice No 700, which is issued free by Customs and Excise Department, gives further information on this.

Once registered, you are in effect a tax collector on behalf of the government, and you will be legally obliged to charge and collect Value Added Tax at the present rate of 15% on top of your normal prices for both goods sold and fees and services rendered. On the credit side, you can deduct the VAT you yourself have paid on all your purchases that are connected with your business and the production of your goods and services. You will therefore be involved in more book-work than the non-registered trader, as VAT returns have to be sent to the Customs and Excise Department each quarter.

Employing

The decision to employ is a major one and should not be undertaken lightly by the self-employed cabinetmaker, for, from the moment you take on even a 16 year-old apprentice, in the eyes of the law you are running a factory and as such your workshop becomes subject to all the legislation laid down for the smooth running of industry and the safety of its employees.

A basic guide, *Employing People*, is available free from the Small Firms Division, John Islip Street, London, SW1P 4LN, or Freefone 2444; alternatively, you can obtain up-to-date information from your local employment office.

I am indebted to the Crafts Council for the use of some information from their publication *Setting up a workshop*.

NATIONAL INSURANCE

If you are self-employed for all or part of the time, and if you have employees, you must arrange payment of national insurance contributions. The class of contribution is determined by status and earnings and are obligatory, although in certain circumstances exemptions are made.

The Dept. of Health and Social Security issue a number of leaflets which explain these points in detail and the relevant ones are:
Employer's Guide to National Insurance Contributions
National Insurance Guide for the Self-Employed
Class 4 NI Contributions
Social Security Benefit Rates
National Insurance Contribution Rates
People with Small Earnings from Self-Employment
More than one job? Class 1 Contributions
NI Contributions for Employees
These are available from your local DHSS office.

Pensions

As a self-employed person you will only receive the basic state pension on your retirement, not the earnings-related part. If you want more than this you will have to make arrangements with a life assurance company. There is tax relief on payments towards a pension, subject to a maximum.

Signing On

If you are running your own workshop business you are technically ineligible for unemployment or supplementary benefits. However, some local offices have been willing to allow those starting up some flexibility and it may be worth going along and explaining that you are about to set up but will have no income for the initial period and ask their advice about continuing to draw benefit.

Insurance

Motor Insurance – Be sure to check that your car insurance covers all the activities for which you use the car. If you are running a business your car will almost inevitably be used for business purposes, and you must inform your insurers and ensure that your cover includes this.

Employer's Liability – If you employ others you are legally bound to take out this insurance and failure to do so would lead to prosecution.

Public Liability – If your workshop is visited by members of the public you should take out this insurance against any claims for injury or damage to third parties caused by alleged negligence.

Useful Booklets

So you want to start a Factory	Factory Inspectorate	Free
Starting in Business	H.M. Inspector of Taxes	Free
Taxation & the Smaller Business	CoSIRA	£1.00
VAT A General Guide	H.M. Customs & Excise	Free

THE NEED FOR PROFESSIONAL ADVISERS

The financial aspect of my work over the past 22 years has, I believe, been the least successful. The pursuit of good work often meant too many hours spent for the eventual price I was to obtain, and even today, the number of people who are prepared to pay the economic price for good work, in whatever field, is still quite small, although growing. We have become conditioned as a nation to accept mediocrity in so many things, and furniture is no exception, so that when we are faced with the real thing, we recognise it, admire it even, but find the price tag unacceptable. There is also the problem, as in all creative work, that some objects just have their price and value, and one simply has to ignore the hours spent in their making and put the exercise down to experience.

But in accepting this, and the fact that making money is not the motivating force that drives the craftsman, we should not forget that we have a duty to ourselves and to our families to carve out a reasonable living by conducting our affairs and our workshops in a business-like way. The work and its development will always remain the driving force, but, however good that work is, the world does not owe us a living and we have to create that for ourselves at the same time.

No-one setting up as a self-employed cabinetmaker should ever forget that he is in business just as much as any other individual selling tobacco or tea bags. Being supposedly creative is no excuse for not answering letters promptly, returning phone calls when promised, or delivering goods at the time and on the day agreed. Nor is it an excuse for not keeping accurate records of time and expenditure, keeping the books up to date, or generally running your workshop and small business as efficiently as possible given the nature of the work you do.

But although you may be self-employed, a sole trader even, directly employing no-one else, it is difficult to succeed without the help and advice of certain professional advisers who have a direct interest in both your survival and your ultimate success; people such as your bank manager, accountant, insurance broker, solicitor; your local CoSIRA organiser if you work in the country; and the technical reps' for the various products that you may use, from timber to wood finishes.

Bank Managers

It is quite probable that you will find yourself working with such people for many years, so it is important to choose the person who will be right for you. Take the bank manager first. As it is most unlikely that you will never require a loan, or overdraft facilities, or need to talk man to man at times over the various financial problems and choices that will confront you, it is obviously far better if you can discuss these with someone whom you know well and whose opinion you value and respect. Your chances of finding such an individual are far greater in a small country town that in a large city or suburban branch, where the staff is young, ambitious and constantly changing, and where, in consequence, your small problems are handled by a succession of assistant managers over the years.

Having found the right bank and manager, and you can always change if you find you have made a mistake, treat him as an equal, not someone to fear. Keep him well informed of all your future plans involving capital outlay, for he will be far more understanding about that large cheque which puts you badly in the red if he knows it is for a new van and materials and not for a luxury holiday. Invite him regularly to your premises and let him see what your work is about; show him, in passing, the growing timber stocks, the new machine, or the alterations and extensions you have just completed; give him copies of your accounts as they are completed each year; in short, hide nothing from this man because you need him and his support which can only grow from his confidence in you.

On a more humdrum level, do obtain regular monthly statements of your accounts and ask for the cheques back, since these are a more faithful record of transactions than scribbled cheque stubs, to cross check the statements when making up your books.

Accountants

Before you engage the services of an accountant, you should decide just what you want him to do for you. He can simply be someone who audits your annual accounts, or he might prepare them from the records and information you supply him and then deal directly with the tax authorities for you, and you may see him once a year or not at all as you wish. You may even choose to pass over to him such mundane matters as your VAT books and returns, as well as the normal business and sales books. On the other hand you may engage him more as a financial adviser, and consult him in common with your bank manager on every major development or expenditure you are planning. The choice is yours; the more he does for you the more he will charge, but his advice at the right time could be invaluable.

However, few accountants seem to understand what motivates the artist or the craftsman. They find it generally difficult to understand why we ever choose to pursue unprofitable work, and why we do not simply become realistic, and seek the highest return for our labour at all times. Why, for example, we consider forgoing a profitable contract for six fitted kitchens in favour of a one-off but exciting commission for a desk where the budget may be extremely tight.

So, over the years, I have looked for accountants who understand my reasons for being in business and who do their best for me within the restraints that I place upon my ability to make money. It pays to look around and to enquire from other craftsmen whom they use, and maybe even your local CoSIRA could help here. Of course you need to make money, every business does, but if you do not wish to rise to twenty employees this should be made clear to your accountant from the very start.

Insurance Brokers

Throughout your business life you will be inundated with people attempting to sell you insurance, and this will not be confined to representatives from the actual companies, but also all too often your financial advisers, even your friendly bank manager, will have an interest in insurance, with many banks running their own schemes.

Of course you will need insurance; indeed, if you employ, some of it is compulsory, but you might well consider if you are in your early twenties whether it is really worth parting with regular payments that you can ill-afford for such things as a retirement pension at sixty-five. Later in your career there will be tax advantages in doing this, but at a time when you need every penny you can get, first to live and then to invest in your workshop and business, it will pay you to question just what insurance is essential and to beware the smooth tongues of those who peddle it.

Following an unpleasant experience when my workshop went up in smoke eight years ago, and the subsequent bitter wrangle with the insurance company concerned which resulted not only in financial loss for me but also considerable depression and anger, I am now convinced that a reputable broker is a major asset. He will handle every aspect of insurance for you, and is there as a friendly, helpful and impartial voice at the end of the telephone. It is in his interest to shop around and find the most advantageous policies and companies for you, and in the event of a claim, it is likewise in his interest to get it settled with a minimum of fuss, because if he handles everything for you, from your private house down to you exhibition insurances, you become a valuable client to him over a period of years. Of course, he may well try and persuade you to insure more heavily, and he could be right, for it is obviously unwise to be under-insured, but at least his opinion is likely to be less biased than most.

As with all my business advisers, from bank managers to solicitors, I favour a personalised service and thus I chose a small family concern of insurance brokers who have been able to save me time, money and frustration over the years because they are familiar with the idiosyncrasies of my affairs. As a result, I now have every policy renewed on the same day, one annual bill for insurance, which makes book-keeping so much simpler. With these arrangements, whenever anyone enters my shop and mentions insurance I simply explain that everything is well taken care of by my brokers and politely show them the door. However, before you place such trust in the firm you have chosen, do take the trouble to ascertain that they are reputable brokers and not simply insurance agents representing two or three companies.

Solicitors

A solicitor is not someone you are going to need on a regular basis as you do your accountant or bank manager. He is, rather, an important figure hovering in the background with help and advice when required. As a sole trader you will probably use his services less than a limited company would, but either way, the general advice on choosing the right individual still applies.

His services will be sought when drawing up contracts and agreements, including private loan agreements and when purchasing or leasing premises; in fact, whenever your interests need to be protected or pursued with legal authority.

Other professional help

Again, much of this is never required on a regular basis, but it is still helpful and sensible to build up and maintain friendly relationships with such people as your local CoSIRA organiser and regional arts and crafts officer; your local VAT office, planning, building and fire inspectors, the water authority, and the technical representatives of the firms whose machinery and services you use. These people can keep you abreast of developments in your area, and their timely advice can often avoid costly mistakes.

It is equally important that you should get to know and trust your local plumber, engineer, builder and electrician, and that they in turn should become familiar with your premises and your equipment, for you never know when you will need these people to help you out in an emergency.

Honesty in Business

I do advise complete honesty in business, primarily for your own peace of mind, but also because you can hardly expect banks or any other organisation to be sympathetic to your application for a loan, for example, if, as far as they can ascertain from your books, your business is a financial disaster simply because you are conveniently 'forgetting' all those cash sales and payments and putting them under the mattress. So, don't make your advisers' jobs more difficult by plain dishonesty; you need a healthy turnover, so put all your payments into the bank even if you need to take it out again three days later. In this way at least the bank knows that money does come in. Leave it to your accountant to deal with the taxman; he will do it to your advantage, but legally.

You will doubtless also be approached from time to time to invoice goods for office use when they are obviously domestic; you will be asked to waive the VAT or Sales Tax, because that wad of notes tossed casually onto your bench is supposed to make you quiver with excitement. Do not succumb. If you wish to give someone a cash discount for prompt payment, that is up to you, and perfectly in order; conniving in tax avoidance is quite another thing, and as a legitimate trader you have a duty to uphold the law, not break it.

Likewise, treat cautiously those tempting offers of materials from people demanding cash not cheques, and offering no receipts. Tell them bluntly that the transactions will be recorded in your books, receipt or no receipt, for you cannot claim the expense against your income if there is not proof or record; and besides the moral obligation, you may well find that the price is not so cheap if the cost cannot be offset against your sales.

RAISING FINANCE

All too often craftsmen are reluctant to borrow and invest in their future. Many spend their lives working in cold, damp and badly lit premises with insufficient stocks of materials and inadequate equipment.

This reluctance to borrow stems from the fact that most craftsmen are cautious people who possess a strong desire to be independent and beholden to no-one, be it friends and relations or the more impersonal bank. This reluctance is further strengthened by the poor financial returns normally experienced by cabinetmakers, who look on any repayment of loans as too big a cross to bear.

I am convinced that this is an attitude that has to be reversed, for it is the poor working facilities, inadequate stocks of materials, etcetera, which contribute directly to the poor incomes experienced.

Unless you are wealthy, or prefer to run your business with one hand tied behind your back, you will need to raise money for any of the following reasons:
1) To improve your premises and working conditions.
2) To install better or extra machinery and equipment.
3) To purchase materials in bulk.
4) To provide working capital to finance a large order book or a particularly large commission. Once established, this is best achieved with floating overdraft facilities, where the upper limit can be raised from time to time as the need arises.
5) To finance a particular project, perhaps a one-man exhibition in a major town or abroad.

Not unnaturally, grants appear a more attractive proposition than loans, but the problem here is that they are generally one-off solutions, and all too often they need to be balanced by finance from other sources, which for most people means acquiring loans. For example, in certain rural areas CoSIRA will at present give a grant of 35% towards the cost of converting redundant farm buildings into workshop accommodation. This is extremely generous and helpful, but the individual is still left with the need to raise the remaining 65% from other sources.

Friends and relations

Private loans arranged with friends and relatives can be most beneficial to both parties, but they can also be fraught with danger unless a fully business-like agreement is entered into, possibly with the help of a solicitor if the sums are considerable.

The chief advantage of this method is that you can often agree on a lower rate of interest than you would have to pay a bank, which would still be attractive to the lender, because, unlike banks, nothing goes in administration. Secondly, borrowing in this way still leaves you free to approach the bank for other sources of finance, maybe overdraft facilities to provide working capital.

The danger is, however, that nothing undermines good friendships and happy relationships with close relatives more brutally than arguments and disputes over money, so you may prefer the impersonal face of a bank or institution.

Banks

The Department of Industry currently runs a loan guarantee scheme under which it guarantees to the bank 80% of a loan given to an approved small business. This naturally makes the banks more willing than they have been in the past to lend in cases where the security offered in exchange for the loan is not very great. Further information on this scheme can be obtained from your bank, and when you are ready a well thought-out and carefully costed proposal should be presented in writing for them to study.

You may well require assistance with this presentation if it is your first loan application, and here your accountant, or friends and relatives who are in business themselves will be able to help you. Useful information on the whole process of raising finance is available in greater detail in the following booklets, but do remember that whatever agency you decide to apply to, your presentation and forecast of your needs must be thorough.

Sources of Finance for the Smaller Company. Institute of Directors, 10 Belgrave Square, London
Starting a Manufacturing Business & Raising Finance. Small Firms Division, Dept. of Industry, Abell House, John Islep Street, London SW1P 4LN.
Loan Guarantees for Small Businesses. from banks, or Dept. of Industry regional offices.

GRANTS AND LOANS

The Crafts Council administers loans and grants for craftsmen in England and Wales. They are designed to assist craftspeople at various stages in their careers and are awarded mainly on the quality of work produced, although other considerations are also taken into account in accordance with the guidelines for each scheme.

Setting Up: Craftsmen who are about to set up a workshop or who have run one for less than two years may apply for an equipment grant of up to 50% of equipment costs, or a maintenance grant currently amounting to £1860 towards running the workshop in the first months of business. The maximum grant is for one year and is comparable to an undergraduate grant.

Workshop Assistant Scheme: Allows established craftspeople to take on a trainee and obtain help to provide a living wage usually for a year. In return, the employer is naturally expected to provide training in all aspects of the business.

Advanced Training Scheme: Art school graduates and others whose work has reached a sufficiently high standard and who intend to set up a workshop, or who are already pursuing a career as artists/craftspeople can apply for assistance to enable them to spend three to twelve months in one or more established workshops for intensive training and workshop experience. The maximum grant of £1860 can be used either for living expenses or as payment to the workshop.

Loan Scheme: This is available to craftsmen who have been in business for at least two years to help them finance workshop enlargement, improvement of facilities or purchase additional equipment. A true rate of interest is charged, payable over a five-year period.

   Applications for all of the above schemes should be made by the 10th of March, June, September or December.

Bursary Scheme is offered in alternate years to craftsmen who have been working for seven years or more to allow them to take a sabbatical or undertake a special project connected with their work. The final date for applications is 10th December in odd-numbered years only.

   Further details of all these schemes are availabe in the following three leaflets:
Grants and Loans
Guide to the Council's Information Services
List of Group Workshops

The Council for Small Industries in Rural Areas is the main agent within England of the **Development Commission**, which aims to encourage and support small rural businesses. CoSIRA can provide information, training and finance for workshops in rural areas. Capital Grants of up to 35% of the total cost of converting redundant buildings and loans towards buildings and/or equipment are available. Contact your local CoSIRA office or the Head Office for details.

The Welsh Arts Council's schemes do not duplicate those offered by the Crafts Council and Welsh craftspeople are eligible for both.
Special Projects: This scheme enables societies, organisations or craftspeople to apply for a grant/guarantee against loss for a project which may include exhibitions, demonstrations lecture fees, research or travel grants.
Special Awards: Awards up to the value of £1,000 are made to established craftspeople who wish to take time off, or who want to carry out a specific project, or who need materials to prepare new work.

Commission Aid Scheme: A grant of up to 50% and with an upper limit of £2,500 may be offered to support a private body or a company that wishes to commission an item from an artist or craftsperson which will be displayed permanently in an accessible place.

Craft Fellowships: A limited number of awards are made to young craftspeople to set up workshops in selected secondary schools for 18 weeks in the Spring term.

For more detailed information of any of these schemes contact: Craft Officer, WAC, Museum Place, Cardiff CF1 3NX. Telephone 0222 394711. Information and advice for small businesses in Wales can be obtained from The Welsh Development Agency (Small Business Section), Treforest Industrial Estate, Pontypridd CF37 5UT.

The Scottish Development Agency organises a comprehensive range of assistance for craftspeople who establish business on a full-time basis in Scotland with help chiefly directed towards the making, marketing and promotion of craftwork.

Craft Setting Up Scheme: Under this scheme newly established craftspeople may receive almost £2,000 paid over the year towards maintenance expenditure. In addition, 50% grants of up to £1,000 are available to purchase essential machinery, or for the renovation or purchase of workshop premises. The distribution of these grants is discretionary depending on quality of craftsmanship, originality of design and sound business proposals.

Workshop and Equipment Grant Scheme: Established craftspeople may receive a 50% grant towards the cost of an approved programme which may be designed to raise production standards and increase output, or to purchase equipment, or to repair workshop premises. The distribution of these grants is made according to the same principles as for the Setting Up Scheme.

Exhibition Grant Scheme: Grants to offset costs chiefly in printing and promotion incurred in mounting exhibitions are available.

Crafts Fellowships Scheme: Two awards of a maximum of £3,500 may be awarded each year to finance a specific research project which may include travel and lead to an exhibition. Applicants should have been established for at least five years and have shown outstanding achievement in their work.

Consultancy Scheme: Visits by experts can be arranged and subsidised to help sort out a technical problem.

Mid-Career Training Scheme: Scottish colleges of art run special courses to enable craftspeople to learn new technical skills and to stimulate design awareness.

Crafts Training Scheme: Funds are available for established craftspeople to offset wages, NHI or other expenses for a young trainee during the first two years of a three year contract.

For further information contact The Crafts Manager, Scottish Development Agency, 102 Telford Road, Edinburgh EH4 2NP. Telephone 031 343 1911.

The Local Enterprise Development Unit (LEDU) will assist small businesses within Northern Ireland with information and finance. Small capital grants are available through The Crafts Industry Scheme. For further details write to LEDU, Lamont House, Purdy's Lane, Belfast BT8 4TB. Telephone (0232 691031)

Local Enterprise Agencies, Enterprise Zones and other Council Agencies

Throughout the country there are many agencies which have the common aim of encouraging small businesses to set up in local areas. Some local councils have also developed policies aimed at assisting small businesses and the Government has set up a number of special zones which offer financial help and freedom from planning controls. You should contact your local council for details of any such help within your locality.

The Enterprise Allowance Scheme: Under this new government scheme to encourage people to start their own workshop businesses you can receive £40 a week for one year to supplement the receipts from your business if you meet the following conditions:

1) Be receiving unemployment benefit or supplementary benefit at the time of application.
2) Have been out of work for at least 13 weeks before your application.
3) Be able to show that you have at least £1,000 to invest in the business over the first twelve months.
4) Must be 18 years old or over.
5) Have no other employment while you are receiving the allowance and work full-time (at least 36 hours per week) in the business.
6) Have your proposed business approved by the Manpower Services Commission as suitable for public support. There will be no test of the likely success of the business.

Full details of this scheme are available from your local Job Centre.

BOOK-KEEPING, COSTING AND ESTIMATING

It is important not to look on book-keeping and business affairs as a chore but as an interesting and important aspect of self-employment. If in fact it is such a chore, then you would be far better advised to let the accountant handle it all.

I have always preferred to make up my own books in order to exercise greater day-to-day control over the business. My account books for example have many columns both for income and expenditure arranged to suit my purposes and not necessarily those of an accountant. I can then pick up very quickly what I have spent in any given period on, say, photography, or travelling expenses, and what income I have received from gallery and exhibition sales as opposed to commissioned work, and so on. As a result, with the help of previous years' accounts, I can readily and reasonably accurately assess how things are progressing, and whether or not I can really afford that new planing machine this year.

Do make up your accounts and VAT books each month, as one tends to forget details of transactions if they are left to quarterly sessions. Remember that each lost receipt, particularly if it is for a cash payment, is like throwing money down the drain. And do get the books to the accountant as soon as is physically possible after the close of your financial year. You are largely paying your accountant for an annual statement of your business prepared, not just for the taxman, but also for you, to get confirmation of how your business is doing. If, just because you have been too busy to complete the books and hand them over, it eventually arrives on your desk nine months after your business year ended, it is only history. (In this connection, business years do not have to start in April, and you will obtain speedier service if operating from another quarter in the year.)

There is an actual legal requirement to keep accounts, sales and VAT books, but there are also many other records which, although they are not compulsory, you should keep, in order to stay abreast of your affairs and to assist you in estimating, costing and assessing the viability of your enterprise at any particular time. You should have a permanent record of your main stocks of materials and constantly update them with materials consumed or replenished. In this way you can always value this asset without going through the laborious process of measuring it all up. Similarly, your stock lists of finished work, whether on sale or return or on exhibition, should be kept up to date. Both materials and finished work should be recorded at cost price without profit; the moment it is sold, it becomes a sale and is transferred to the sales book inclusive of profit. The value of your work in progress, another valuable aid in assessing the state of your business, can be arrived at simply by totalling up all the job sheets relating to every productive activity going on in your shop; both design work, stock and orders, and including all used materials. Besides having to do this annually for your yearly accounts, it is sensible to do it quarterly for your own predictions and forward planning. The job sheets should be made up weekly to enable you to keep an accurate record of all the materials and time involved in any particular job, and, possibly more importantly, to record the actual time spent on the various stages of construction, such as making and fitting four drawers. By doing this over a priod of years one builds up a good guide as to the time needed for the many differing processes that can go into the making of a piece of furniture. Thus, with the aid of an estimating sheet, on which are listed all the variations and processes possible, including those so mundane they are easily forgotten, one is able to build up a pretty accurate picture of the hours likely to be involved in the making of any piece of furniture. Examples of a Job Sheet and Estimating Sheet are shown reduced size on page 65.

Once the job has been completed, all the job sheets, cutting lists, drawings and correspondence are filed away under two reference numbers, the order and job number and the invoice number. This simple system, backed up with a card index file of clients for quick reference, has provided me with very accurate records of every job I have done during the past 22 years – invaluable when one is asked for a repeat ten years later!

Determining your costs

Some people try and charge as much as they can get away with while others charge the standard rate going for that particular job, but at some point you are going to be in a position of wondering whether you can afford to reduce your price in order to get work you may badly need, or whether you should be charging a little extra. This is when a complete breakdown of all your overheads should be done so that you can determine how much to charge for your overheads and time, which is usually worked out at an hourly rate.

The following example may be useful:

	£
Costs of running premises:	
Rates inc water	420-00
Rent	1,000-00
Heat	340-00
Light and Power	320-00
Telephone	280-00
Maintenance	240-00
Insurance	620-00
Costs of finance:	
Interest charged on bank or other loans	400-00
Costs of equipment:	
Rent	NIL.
Hire Purchase	NIL.
Depreciation of equipment	380-00
Repairs and Maintenance/Replacement of of cutters, blades etc.	240-00
Administrative Costs:	
Stationery and drawing materials	180-00
Postage	260-00
Publicity/Photography and Exhibitions	480-00
Travel and Motor expenses	1,200-00
Depreciation on vehicle	600-00
Fees to professional advisers and bodies	410-00
General bank charges	280-00
Secretarial expenses, photocopying	750-00
	8,400-00

Now all the figures should be available from your annual accounts using two or three years, not just one, in order to get a more balanced picture. If just starting out in business, you will have to attempt as accurate a forecast as possible.

Next you need to calculate what these fixed costs actually cost you per hour of workshop time and the following calculations can only ever be used as a guide as it revolves around actual production time, that is the time that can be charged out. This will vary on you as an individual and your willingness to leave paperwork, client visits and design thinking to evenings and weekends. Also, as to whether the non-productive activities of your business are shared over, say, five employees or none at all.

52 possible weeks of 40 hours each =		2080 hrs
Loss		
3 weeks annual holiday	3 × 40 hrs	= 112 hrs
9 days public holiday	9 × 8 hr day	= 72 hrs
2 weeks average sickness	2 × 40 hrs	= 80 hrs
20% (1 day in 5) unproductive		
or lost time	20%	= 416 hrs
		680 hrs
Total productive hours in one year		1400 hrs

Fixed costs £8400

Fixed costs per hour: 8400 ÷ 1400 hrs	£6.00 per hour	
Add 5% for current annual inflation	£0.30	
Hourly cost	£6.30	

Now you will begin to see the advantages of employing, for if you employ five people that figure of £6.30 per hour can be proportioned over five benches.

If working on your own you have to include it all before adding your hourly salary. If your proposed annual salary is £7000 – quite modest you might think – then your hourly charge must be;

Fixed costs per hour at	£6.30	
Salary at £7000 per annum = 7000 ÷ 1400		
production hours	£5.00	
Total	£11.30	Plus profit margin

What does become apparent is that if working on your own the fixed costs and overheads need to be kept to a minimum, for few could expect to charge these rates per hour. However, as a single, self-employed unit, you can spread these fixed costs by choosing to work much longer hours, and this is how most survive.

Here we come up against the difference between you, the self-employed and fully motivated individual, and your employees. For as dedicated and loyal as they may be they will not work for nothing, so their time and expense to you must always be calculated on that standard working week, which promises to get even shorter as the years go by.

So when employing you must find the true cost of that employment to include, employees insurance, any bonus payments, holidays, sickness, etc., and divide as before by the productive hours in the year. These might need to be calculated differently for the various individuals employed, because a foreman, for example, could be spending a lot of time on the supervision of trainees.

Estimating

This is never easy, but if you know just what you require per hour to run your business, and you know from your records how long various operations take to do, with the help of an estimating sheet, at least it will be not so much a gamble but a well thought-out, calculated risk. It is one area that should never be rushed or skimped, for it is pointless running an efficient workshop and working hard, if in fact your original price is wrong. *It is easier to gain or lose money at this crucial point than it is at any other stage of the making.*

This is where making pieces without a particular customer in mind is easier, in that you arrive at the price after the objects are made, and cost them on the actual time taken, but bearing in mind, also, their value in the market place. This figure can then be adjusted according to the size of the batch involved next time.

Commissioned work, however, puts you in a dilemma; for as often as not you have not made that piece before, and if you price it too high you could lose the order, too low, you could lose money.

If you are dealing with private individuals it is often possible to be a little flexible, provided this has previously been agreed, both on the price and on the amount of work involved in order to keep within an agreed figure. This flexibility should really only ever be minimal, *for there is no worse advertisement for the crafts than the person who, having given an estimate for £1000, then blatantly presents a bill for £2000.* Remember, it is not your client's fault if you gave the wrong figure in your estimate, but yours; and they have a perfect right to pay no more than they had been told to expect by you. Not many people will give you an open-ended cheque, and there is no reason why they should.

On the other hand, when dealing with local authorities, government bodies and large businesses, you will not be able to get away with an estimate, but will have to give a quotation, usually with a discount as well. This is a fixed price which cannot be raised under any circumstances unless specific clauses, such as inflation clauses, are included in the initial contract. In this type of situation you are usually completely in the dark as to the budget available, simply tendering for a service or contract in competition with others. It is you who fixes the budget or price, not them, based on their requirements, which can be quite detailed in the case of government and local authority bodies.

Your final figures no doubt will be clouded by how badly you need or desire this particular order, but the final price quoted should always include a percentage for unforeseen snags and a built-in discount. (In the case of government bodies it may be advisable to offer a discount for prompt payment, particularly if your cash-flow needs livening).

ALAN PETERS FURNITURE

CLIENT .... DATE OF ORDER .... ORDER No. ....

JOB .... DATE OF COMPLETION .... INVOICE No. ....

COSTS			£	p	DATE	TIME SHEET	WORK COMPLETED				
DESIGNING & SITE VISITS											
LABOUR ON CONSTRUCTION											
SUB-CONTRACT											
MATERIALS	£	p									
TOTAL											
PRODUCTION COSTS											
PROFIT											
AGENTS COMMISSION							HOURS @	£	p	£	p
TOTAL											
VAT or SALES TAX											
INVOICE PRICE											
DELIVERY											
SITE FIXING					TOTAL		TOTAL				

ALAN PETERS FURNITURE ESTIMATING SHEET

CLIENT .... ORDER No. ....

JOB .... INVOICE No. ....

COSTS	HOURS	£	p	MATERIALS	£	p
SITE VISITS						
SKETCH DESIGNS/ESTIMATES						
WORKING DRAWINGS						
FULL-SIZE MOCK-UP						
TEMPLATES/CUTTING LISTS						
SELECTING & CUTTING OUT TIMBER						
MACHINING TO SIZE						
SELECTING & LAYING VENEERS						
SETTING OUT ALL CONSTRUCTION						
CUTTING JOINTS						
LAMINATING JIGS						
LAMINATING						
SANDING PRIOR TO ASSEMBLY						
ASSEMBLY						
CLEANING UP AFTER ASSEMBLY						
DRAWER MAKING & FITTING				TOTAL		
DOOR MAKING & FITTING				SUB-CONTRACT		
FITTING HARDWARE						
FINAL CLEAN-UP/FINISHING						
UPHOLSTERY/LAYING LEATHER						
SUB-CONTRACT WORK						
MATERIALS USED						
PRODUCTION COSTS				TOTAL		

Figs 46 & 47 Example of Job Sheet and Example of Estimating Sheet.

In all your pricing you will learn to be realistic. Of course, it is right and proper that your hourly rate should equal that of your local garage, or your solicitor for that matter, but the hard truth is that no-one *has* to buy your furniture, whereas they do need to keep their cars on the road and use the services of solicitors from time to time. Those with little experience of actual making should beware of being too greedy, since there is no reason why customers should be expected to pay for lack of skill, experience, and on the job training; and just as it is important that amateurs and part-timers should not undercut the professionals, it is equally important not to destroy, by overcharging, the very market every one of us is trying to create.

LETTERHEADS AND BROCHURES

Your letterhead, business card or brochure is the first impression that many people receive of you, your work and the service you are offering, so it is worth taking the trouble to ensure that it is a good one. If you consider yourself a designer, then this should be reflected in all your printed material; if you pride yourself on the quality of your products, then this too should be reflected in the quality of the paper and printing used. If you wish to impress a potential buyer by your professionalism both as a craftsman and as a businessman, then scrappy pieces of paper with illegible hand-scrawled letters will not do; naturally, there will always be a place for the personal hand-written letter or post-card, but these are the exception rather than the rule.

Printing is relatively cheap but the preparation of the original artwork is expensive, so it is worth doing it yourself or finding a friendly graphic artist or student to do it for you. If you do it yourself, use Letraset on white A4 sized paper, and this will give you an adequate copy which any modern printer can use. David Plumb's book, *Design & Print Production Workbook* is useful here for those with no experience.

Using your letterhead notepaper as a basis you need six documents for your trading:
Order – for purchasing goods or raw materials. It should state the date, the quantity, the description of goods, price and delivery details.
Delivery Note – This accompanies goods whether despatched or delivered. It should state the customer's name, his order number, the quantity, price and description of the goods delivered. If you deliver personally, always get a signature on your copy.
Sale or Return Record – for recording work left on sale or return. This should be dated and state the retailer's name and the quantity, description and price of each item. Make sure that the retailer signs your copy.
Invoice – or request for payment. This should be sent separately from the goods when supplying a firm, but with private clients it can be handed over with the goods. It carries the same information as the delivery note or sale or return record, plus the number of that document, the total cost, any discounts, VAT and VAT number where applicable.
Credit Note – If goods are returned for any reason, make sure that you record it, for there may be a dispute at some later stage as to whether you delivered the goods or not. When the returned goods are received, send the customer a credit note stating his order number, quantity, type and price of each item and the reason for return. If and when the goods are replaced a fresh invoice is sent.
Statement – This is a reminder to the customer that they have not yet paid. It quotes any unpaid invoices, totals them and deducts any credit notes issued in the period.

In every case be sure to take a carbon copy and file it. Include a date (day posted) and number each category consecutively to assist in your book-keeping and to guard against loss. Do not start numbering at 1, as this has an amateur look. Start at 100 or 200 to make it appear you have been trading for some time.

Brochures

These are cheaper and more informative than parting with expensive photographs at every request. It is difficult to generalise as to what a brochure should do, beyond excite the recipient enough to make him want to find out more. It is useful to have a map showing your location, a brief summary of the service you are offering, and how the customer should set about acquiring that service or product.

I have mine printed on two qualities of paper: one to be used as an inexpensive handout at exhibitions, shows and fairs, and the other on top grade paper for more individual enquiries. I have also designed mine so that I can replace certain photographs at a later date with others of later work, and I can thus up-date it every two or three years without having to have the whole thing redesigned and set up.

Photography

Onc your work has left your workshop, especially if it has been commissioned, a photograph or transparency may be your only record of it as a finished piece as opposed to sketches and drawings of the design. You may on occasion be able to borrow a piece back for a special exhibition, and thus expose it to the public gaze, but more often than not your best and most valuable pieces will leave your workshop and never be seen again by anyone other than their owners and their circle of friends.

So it is important not only that these pieces are photographed but that they are photographed well; poor photographs showing distorted pieces against a muddled background are worse than useless. The importance of good quality photography cannot be over-emphasised. Selection for many exhibitions, or for indexes of national bodies or guilds is usually done initially from slides or photographs, and you are far more likely to get your work featured in a magazine or newspaper if the quality of the photography, irrespective of the quality of your work, is good.

However, furniture is not an easy subject, and even many professional photographers experience problems particularly with the larger pieces. It is really worth learning to do it yourself even though initially you may need to call in the experts. Learn all you can from them; take evening classes in the subject, and then don't be mean with film! It is far better to take 36 shots of one piece from every conceivable angle and permutation on the camera and throw away 33 later, than to take three special shots and find out a month later when the piece is no longer available that really they were not very good after all.

Generally speaking, furniture shoud be taken on a large format camera. 5″ × 4″ is ideal, but good results can be obtained using 2¼″ square or 120 film. It is advisable eventually for you to master the processing of at least black and white film yourself, as so much can be achieved even with a poor negative if one has the expertise and is prepared to give it patient and individual treatment.

In short, whenever possible I do recommend setting up your own photographic studio area and darkroom, because you, as the creator of any particular piece of furniture, know better than anyone else the merits and highlights of that piece. The challenge of recording it faithfully for posterity, for your own records, and for more immediate use in your advertising material perhaps, is one well worth accepting. You cannot simply rely on other people to take photographs for you. If you have work on display in an important exhibition, you are the one who should be able to supply good photographs for the press or anyone else, so have them printed and ready in good time for Press and Private Views instead of feebly trusting that the exhibition organisers will do this for you.

Five

Design – Thinking, Techniques and Inspiration

CRAFTSMANSHIP

THERE is a great need today to re-assess what we mean when we talk of quality and good craftsmanship when applied to craftsman-made furniture. It was John Ruskin who said,

"Man was not intended to work with the accuracy of tools, to be precise and perfect in all his actions. If you have that precision out of him, make his fingers measure degrees like cog-wheels, you must inhumanize him. All the energy of his spirit must be given to making cogs and compasses of himself. …You must either make a tool of the creature or a man of him, you cannot make both."

Ernest Gimson, for example, demanded a high degree of accuracy from his men, but it was an accuracy that did not rely on the micrometer or calipers but on hand and eye. Each curve looking and feeling right; each portion of a joint perfectly fitted to its mate; doors and drawers so constructed and fitted as to ensure a lifetime of trouble-free service; these to him were the signs of the true craftsman. We refer today to the superb workmanship of the Gimson era, but all of it showed a complete absence of fussiness which is now so widely associated with quality and good work. No effort was made to sand and polish the backs and bottoms of drawers, or the undersides of tables or chests – they came spontaneously from the planes and tools that made them.

Increasingly over the years I have become concerned by the growing tendency to 'preciousness' in much of our top craft furniture in Britain. Just as a painting can be ruined by being overworked, so too can a piece of furniture. It is as though we are in danger of becoming precision engineers in wood, rather than creative exponents of a live tactile material.

So strong is our obsession with surface finishing and the near worship of technical perfection and wizardry that it is in danger of becoming more important than the piece itself, and no amount of fine glasspaper, steel wool and fuss will mask a design that is in itself unsatisfactory.

Not only can this obsession lead to extremely expensive furniture being made, but it can also leave much of it soulless; lacking that spontaneity and freshness that those earlier Cotswold pieces possessed and that I was to admire constantly in Korea and Japan. I know this problem worries not only me, but has worried Edward Barnsley for a long time, and to judge by the recent flow of Cotswold inspired scrubbed oak furniture from John Makepeace's workshops, it also concerns him. It is not an easy question to resolve, for in a modern workshop we no longer execute everything by hand, but make wide use of machinery which by its very nature implants an engineering accuracy and approach into much of what we do.

I am equally disturbed by mock rusticity, not being over-enamoured with chairs and seats which resemble sheep hurdles, and adzed and gouged table tops seem to me to be incongruous when the board was previously sawn flat by machine anyway.

Just as with design, the solution must lie in knowing when to stop, and when not to just flaunt one's skill, patience and pride. But this decision on knowing when to cry enough can be made more difficult when the master craftsman employs others to implement his ideas. Where, in the larger workshops, the master craftsman tends to make less himself, entrusting the making to highly skilled craftsmen who rightly set their own standards of technical perfection and derive their personal satisfaction from doing every detail to the very best of their ability.

The danger here is that many may read this as a lowering of standards, which it is not; it is a deliberate definition of principle. Craftsmanship for me, as I learned in those early days at Froxfield, is about getting things right first time, as a matter of course, and then not fussing over it. Dovetails, to take one example, should be cut straight from the saw, and shoulders of tenons likewise; it should not be necessary to spend days fiddling and fussing because the original skill was not there. If one is making a small, intricate jewel casket, a precious object by any standards, then every detail should be as near perfect as man can achieve, but to apply those same standards to a 10 foot solid oak refectory table for a stone farmhouse, is no proof of craftsmanship at all, but rather, insensitivity.

There will always be, as Morris and many others have recognised since, a place for the item of furniture, or indeed any craftwork, produced with no consideration of time and cost; pieces that are just sheer mechanical perfection from tip to tail; objects which are clearly not destined to primarily earn their keep in daily use, but to be cherished in a private collection or museum as examples of the finest work that man can achieve. I am not criticising any craftsman or workshop that sees this as their major role, for it is all part of this individual choice of action that we have. I, too, attempt pieces from time to time with this same view in mind and will continue to do so; and I bear my share of responsibility for the present situation, but the point I wish to make is that this is not what *most* craft furniture makers are about for *most* of the time. We are out there to serve a discerning public that requires quality and individuality, but not at a price that limits it to two per cent of the population, and, equally important, to provide them with furniture that they are not terrified of actually using; furniture that, as James Krenov aptly remarked, still retains the thumb-print of the maker.

DESIGN

This area more than any other distinguishes the good from the mediocre, the professional from the amateur. It is pointless to devote endless man-hours and expensive materials to a piece of work which fundamentally does not work as an item of furniture and does not succeed visually. One might manage to seduce a few people by the beauty of the timber or the exquisite workmanship, but at the end of the day it is the design which will determine whether that item is successful and whether it will stand the test of time. Unfortunately it is also the most difficult area both to define and to carry out; it is the area where I and others like me devote most nervous energy and suffer most anguish.

It is often argued that because attitudes to aesthetics and design are so personal, it is a subject that cannot be taught successfully and is therefore best ignored, since no two people agree on what is good. The layman could probably be excused for holding this opinion, for furniture today does present a confusing and often contradictory picture to the world. This is largely because, despite forty years now of Design Council education, the greater part of the furniture industry does not employ designers but is content to reproduce the designs of past centuries or to leave it to the factory floor and production managers to come up with all the answers.

The few design conscious firms that employ good designers and produce good work are a regrettably small minority, and only a little of their trail-blazing work reaches the High Street stores, as most goes into the more specialised contract furniture field. There is, however, a welcome sense of design and simplicity at the lower end of the price range, which has been brought about by the production and distribution advantages of simple designs that fold flat into boxes, but the quality leaves much to be desired, with components whittled down to an unsatisfactory meanness for the sake of cost.

The craft furniture scene is also confusing for the student of design who could understandably come to the conclusion that anything goes. The recent emphasis on innovation and individual expression both here and in the States has thrown up a great variety of approaches, some of which should not be taken too seriously, being more closely akin to fine art and sculpture. In the main, this does no harm, and in fact the injection of fresh thinking, new techniques and humour can often rub-off on to the serious designer to his advantage.

Fig. 48 Ebony chair by John Makepeace. Without doubt a work of art, but it is also a practical and comfortable chair.

What always pleasantly surprises me is that, through the maze of different styles, personal approaches and changing fashions, the stamp of the good design is invariably apparent. There is a welcome unanimity in the opinions expressed by so many people when a piece of work is truly successful. The piece then, in a sense transcends personalities, style and fashion and becomes a product of its age and yet timeless in the lasting appreciation that it generates, and it becomes a work of art without that being the aim of the creator.

So what constitutes a satisfactory design? Opinions will inevitably vary on style but first and foremost it has to fulfil its function, whatever that may be, as a specific item of furniture. A dining chair, for example, that is uncomfortable to sit and dine in is bad design, however beautiful, clever or exquisitely made. But if a chair's function is different, as for example a ceremonial chair, or even a hall chair, the priority for the designer can quite rightly be visual, with comfort being of secondary importance.

It will also possess a visual and structural unity, for it is this quality of wholeness and harmony, this complete statement of intent with nothing added and nothing missing which is so vital for the success of any design.

For me personally, it must also have that element of visual simplicity and humility and talk to us as a product of our generation. And although the piece may have taken a long time and care to make, in the final analysis it must appear as a logical, honest, straightforward use of materials, construction and techniques.

Good design is not about style or personal taste or even current fashion, although no designer can ignore the latter. For too long judgements on what constituted good design in furniture in Britain appeared to be the sole prerogative of the Design Council whose role and purpose was, and is today, to promote good industrial design. But what is considered good design for a large furniture manufacturer, employing all the latest technology and relying almost entirely on man-made materials and expanding markets, is not necessarily good design for small craft-based workshops, using low technology, hand skills, and natural materials like solid timber, and producing only one or six items at a time.

Fortunately, our more recently established Crafts Council has recognised this fact to the point that much work on their selected index at Lower Regent Street, London, would not, in fact, be acceptable for the Design Council index only ¼ mile away in The Haymarket.

Although this situation must lead to confusion for the amateur and student, I welcome it as recognition that there need be no dictatorship of good design, and that it can take many forms. A good design for one interior situation and one method of production is not necessarily the best solution for another.

How, then, can the amateur or professional cabinetmaker, who has not been fortunate enough to have had the benefit of a three to seven year design training and yet seriously wishes to be better informed on design, set about sifting through this complex and often contradictory subject?

Whilst it is comparatively easy to find short courses on cabinetmaking, it is almost impossible to find similar courses on furniture design, and, although it would obviously be beneficial if all makers were to have a better understanding of design, because the subject is so complex, I believe most amateurs and many professionals would do far better and achieve greater success and satisfaction if they left design to the experts, both past and present, and concentrated on making good work. For myself, I would rather see a good, well-made reproduction piece of a noted period or designer than a bastardised attempt to produce an original inspired by Chippendale, Mackintosh, Krenov, Makepeace or Wendell Castle, or, in the worst cases, a mixture of all five.

Of course, every designer is, consciously or unconsciously, influenced by his peers and by what has gone before, but it is the experience and ability to interpret those influences and to translate them into a successful design that does not come naturally or quickly. Almost without exception, the successful designer-craftsmen of this century underwent a long design or architectural training, or trained in workshops where design and aesthetics were all-important. In contrast, many now planning to set up workshops have had only a

*Fig. 49   Chairs and table in brown oak, shown at the Devon Guild of Craftsmen exhibition 1984;
superbly made by Trevor Pate of Plymouth to a timeless early 1950's design of Edward Barnsley.*

smattering of design training, and a yet larger number have not even been so fortunate and
are merely self-taught. To these I say, don't feel you have to be the great creative artist
overnight; learn your craft thoroughly, and take simple designs and work to them until your
expertise matures.

There are many books now where good designs are featured for others to work to, and
many of the most contented men I have known have spent their lives working to other
people's designs and gained tremendous personal satisfaction from just making.

However, for those who wish to work to their own designs, it should be remembered that
furniture design has two important elements. There is, on the one hand, the bare skeleton of
the design, the brief, the restrictions that every serious designer must work within; and on
the other, the features or the designer's flair which gives the piece its individuality.

As soon as you consider the design of a basic item of furniture, such as a dining table, the
skeletal construction immediately becomes apparent. It must have a flat level surface to eat
off, at a height convenient to the diners. It must accommodate a certain number of chairs,
or be made easily adjustable to admit a variation on this. It ought to provide maximum
freedom of leg movement for the diners whilst still retaining rigidity in the top surface. It
will have to be made to a budget, either as a one-off or as a batch production design; either
way, it is most unlikely that cost will not enter into it. Naturally, it will have to be made
within the limitations of the materials chosen; and finally it needs to be an attractive item
within these limitations.

Now, given these restrictions, which have remained constant for a long time, it is obvious
that you are not going to shatter the world with startling innovation, but there is still the
second design element, the designer's flair, which could be a mixture of imagination,
artistic ability, or just an inner feeling for the rightness of things; but it is that vital element
which puts the flesh on the bones and distinguishes the good from the mediocre.

Add to these two design elements the skill of a master craftsman working in choice materials, and the result may be quite astounding, but I repeat, it will not shatter the world by its innovation. To do that, you have to remove some of those restrictions, and increasingly this is being done, particularly in the States, by a number of artist-craftsmen.

If the prime purpose of that table, that is, to eat off it in the conventional western way, is removed, then a whole new world opens up. It no longer needs to be flat, level, or a fixed height, and chairs no longer have to be accommodated. Remove, also, that other restriction on freedom, the budget, and the world is at your feet, for you can achieve a lot more innovation at £15000 a throw than at a £1500.

Whether the result is furniture, sculpture, art, or a subtle combination of all three is unimportant, but the whole question of the budget is of fundamental consideration in design, for, just as I believe that the best work does not come out of poverty, and that craftsmen should be well rewarded, I also do not believe that the finest work comes from absolute freedom from economic restraint. Work produced under these conditions can be self-indulgent and over-worked, for here lies the pitfall for the successful professional and the skilled amateur alike; with his consummate skills, given the time and unlimited budget, he could conceivably produce anything. Knowing when to stop is the important lesson for us all to learn.

Success takes many forms: for me, personally, to have to charge £15,000 for a dining table would not be success, but failure, and failure both as a designer and as a craftsman. I would hope that many students reading this will appreciate that it can be just as rewarding a challenge in life to design and make good quality work that half the population could with some sacrifice afford, as it is to make expensive works of art.

THE DESIGNER'S CRAFT

Although short courses on design are virtually unobtainable, there is nevertheless a great deal that the individual can do to acquire the skills of the designer's craft and to develop the visual awareness so necessary in order to make those crucial judgements.

Sketching

The importance and the advantages of being able to sketch easily and freely cannot be over-emphasised, for the ability to express on paper numerous ideas, and variations on those ideas quickly and confidently, is a major asset. Unfortunately, gazing at a piece of timber and waiting for the inspiration to come, as though the piece of wood is going to talk to us, is not how most furniture gets designed.

Sketching can be fun, as well as a means to an end, and I would advise all students of

Fig. 50   An ink and watercolour impression.

design to live with a pencil, and sketch anything and everything at the slightest opportunity; for in the process of drawing, whether from nature, urban environments or interiors, the very fact of looking closely at an object or scene in order to record it, develops an appreciation of shape and form.

It is not necessary to spend seven years at art school to acquire the ability to draw – any local art class could get you started and from then on it is up to you. Your aim is not to become a superb artist, but to acquire the ability to get ideas and thoughts on to paper quickly and well both for yourself and for prospective clients, and therefore it is more

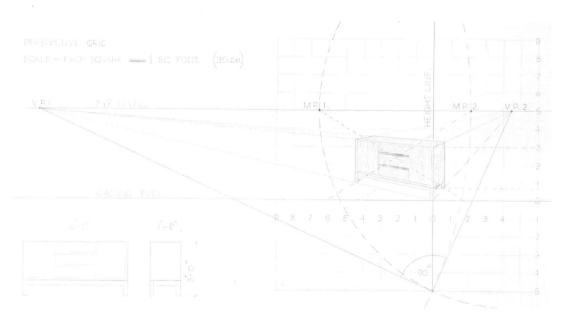

Fig. 51   Perspective grid.

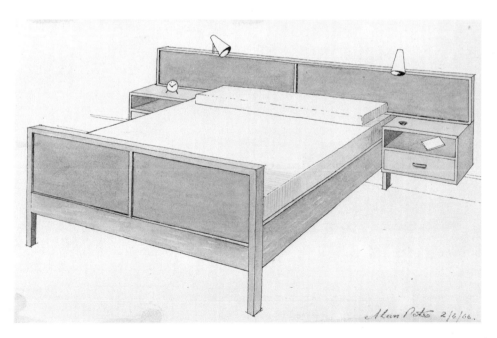

Fig. 52   An ink outline perspective drawing with washes of flat watercolour, 1966. (Produced on the type of grid shown in   Fig. 51.)

important to develop speed and freedom in sketching than laborious pictorial accuracy. However, as most cabinet and interior work is based on straight lines, angles and mechanical shapes as opposed to Nature's free curves, a knowledge of perspective is essential. Here again, just as sketching sharpens one's sense of form, learning the techniques of measured mechanical perspective, whether on a simple grid system or the more formal plan projection, will improve your ability to sketch furniture and interiors freely, for your eye will become accustomed to seeing drawings in true perspective, and you will become quite adept at pinpointing vanishing points and tracing the diverging lines of vision quite naturally in your freehand sketches.

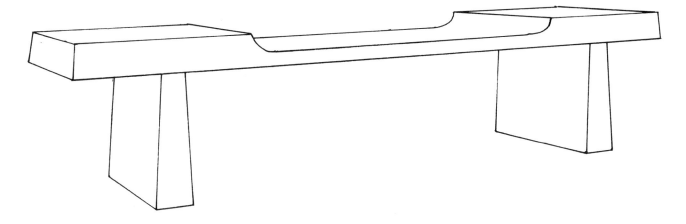

Fig. 53   Simple ink outline drawing built up on a perspective grid.

Fig. 54   An unlaboured pencil and crayon perspective (1976), typical of hundreds sent out to prospective clients.

Draughtsmanship

Draughtsmanship is a second major tool of the designer which in essence requires a little know-how, practice, and the steady hand which every cabinetmaker naturally has. At one time, basic draughtsmanship and the ability to prepare working and scale drawings was taught by the woodwork teachers in our schools an was related directly to the objects the pupils were making in the school workshops. Unfortunately, this very rarely happens any more, and drawing board time is now devoted to a syllabus of work for an examination which has elevated technical drawing to a dull intellectual exercise with a strong engineering and mathematical bias, with the result that many gaining good results in this subject would be hard-pressed in later life to draw up plans for a new garage or garden shed, let alone a kitchen cabinet. However, it should not prove impossible for most people to learn the basics of the subject from evening classes, examination courses, or books on the subject.

In practice, I find I am relying more and more on the practical workshop aspect of designing, but I must emphasise that the use of card and wood models, full-size layouts and full-size mock-ups, usually comes after the exploratory sketch drawings and preliminary scale drawings. But there are no hard-and-fast rules on the correct order of procedure, and indeed I sometimes produce accurate working drawings only after the job is completed, so that the piece can be repeated more economically in the future in the light of the experience gained from the one-off.

Fig. 55   This table, designed for Broughton Castle, near Banbury in 1978, has been drawn by single central point perspective. This very simple method lends itself particularly well to designs of this nature where the end elevation is such an important feature. This is a presentation drawing.

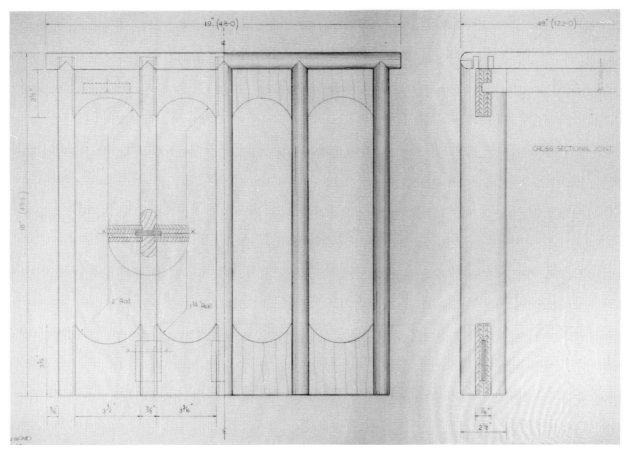

Fig. 56   Chinese Gothic table, working drawing.

Furniture Sizes and Planning

As a student of furniture design, along with your pencil and sketch pad, you should go armed with a pocket rule which comes out at every opportunity in order to measure the sizes of those pieces of furniture, and the dimensions of the component parts used in their construction, which you consider to be particularly successful, whether antique or modern. Make notes of this information beside your sketches and in this way the height of a dining chair, a low stool or a desk top will soon become second nature to you. There are books to assist you in planning both furniture and interiors, and these are widely used by architects and interior designers. They cover such areas as the sizes of everyday items which have to be accommodated in storage furniture, the optimum height for writing, eating or sitting, and designing for particular purposes, such as restaurant seating, where it is important to make the best use of the available space; but, generally speaking, this aspect of the designer's task which relates to planning and ergonomics is probably the easiest to master.

DESIGNING IN 3-DIMENSION

The strength of the designer-maker lies in the fact that he exercises complete control from start to finish over the making of his design. This allows the design process to be very much an on-going situation that continues throughout the making of the piece.

Having said that, it must also be said that we furniture makers do not have the advantage of the potter or glass-blower, who, because of the fluidity of the material they are working with, can achieve spontaneous and unexpected results. We do have to plan our work far more thoroughly and undertake considerable preparation before we commit endless time and expensive materials to any idea. Once having embarked on a particular design or course of action, I nevertheless try to leave as many options open as possible, although they are often quite limited.

Because of this, I have tended increasingly to rely less on drawings and more on full-size mock-ups of new designs. In normal carcase work, for example, storage units, bookcases and libraries, I can achieve most of what I require on the drawing board from ⅛th scale elevations, leaving constructional details to full-size setting-out boards and rods later. However, on more 3-dimensional objects such as chairs, library steps and many table designs, I find the time spent in actually making the complete object in full-size form is never wasted.

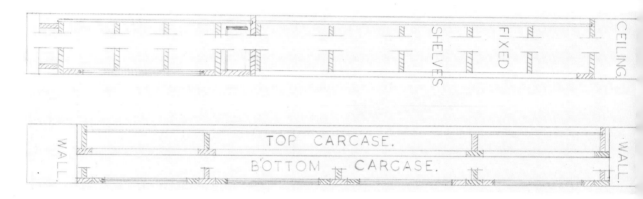

Fig. 57   Full size white painted setting out board of bookcase fitment. Height details on one side, plan details on reverse side.

I use any softwood that is available for this, and it is a good idea to have a plentiful stock of different dimensions easily to hand for this purpose. (It is also useful to have these sections available whilst designing on paper, just to get the feel of what certain sizes actually look and feel like). All the components of the mock-up are screwed together, never nailed or glued, because I often need to dismantle it to change various details. I also often paint it with emulsion paint in the colour closest to that of the proposed timber, for colour can quite transform some designs – a mock-up in soft, white pine can alter dramatically when executed in dense black ebony.

Craftsmen in the Gimson and Barnsley workshops rarely used mock-ups, working instead from ⅛th scale drawings and then full-size setting out boards which they prepared themselves. Maybe I lack their confidence, for I was never trained as an architect, but I find the sheer relief and satisfaction of knowing that I have solved most of the aesthetic and technical problems before I have committed myself *too deeply* to be well worth the time spent, for at the most I will have taken one or perhaps even two days, and if the design is not to my liking I can cheerfully scrap the whole idea and start again.

The production of a mock-up has another advantage in that the client, who may not be able to visualise your design simply from a drawing, can be involved at quite an early stage; and I will often load the mock-up into the van and take it to the site so that he can see it in situ, or invite the client to see it in the workshop and discuss any further developments that may be necessary.

I must add that, despite all these preparations, some decisions just have to be left, and are best left, until working in the actual material itself. In one-off work perhaps the final object is itself only a prototype or mock-up, in the sense that, until it is oiled or polished,

The three stages in a one-off chair: The chair in Indian padauk was designed for a client with an 18th century bureau/desk for which all normal desk chairs were too small. A mock-up was made to measure and tested for comfort before any padauk was touched.

Fig. 58   Original drawing.

Fig. 59   Full Mock-up.

Fig. 60   Finished chair.

constant decisions are being made, individually often quite minor, but collectively very important ones, which shape the finished piece.

Many of my design ideas I find come from constantly working with the material and the equipment I have. Whilst working on any one item, ideas will often present themselves which are no longer possible on that particular piece, but they can be remembered, recorded and used on future occasions. These opportunities would not arise if I only designed for others to make.

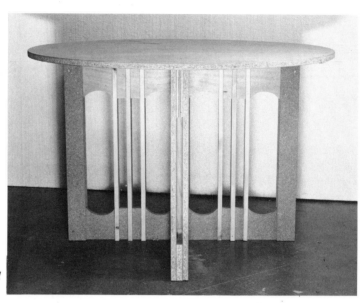

Fig. 61   Oak table's chipboard mock-up, designed to complement 4 existing chairs by Peter Waals, and entailed taking the mock-up on site for approval.

INSPIRATION, INDIVIDUALITY AND INFLUENCE

This last ingredient is not one that anyone can give you or positively teach you. All you can do is to work at it over a period of years, never ceasing to be critical of your achievements and always excited at what the present and future holds.

In the meantime, you study furniture, its history, its development, its construction. You visit museums and collections, not stopping at the furniture sections, but digging deep into whatever man has produced in his quest for beauty and utility. You visit every exhibition of quality work, see what your contemporaries are about, read every magazine on art, architecture, and design as well as the woodworking press. Gradually you will acquire your likes and dislikes, based not on your original biased ignorance, but formed through a wider knowledge and appreciation of man's achievements.

In trying to find your own voice, always be ready to listen to advice and opinion, but resist the temptation to produce work which you do not wholly believe in simply because others do. Gradually you will grope your way towards work and a style that others will recognise as being distinctively yours, and that you yourself feel pleased and comfortable with. However, you should avoid becoming obsessed with the desire to be different from your competitors at all costs, for with the field expanding at its present rate, it is going to be extremely difficult, if not impossible, for all to be so highly individualistic.

There must always be a place in society for the innovators in all fields, even the crazy ones, and they deserve support; but the problem is that this desire to be different can throw up work which attracts more attention and credit than it often deserves, simply because it *is* different, even though it may not be in any way superior to what it is replacing.

1

2

3

4

5

6

7

8

9

10

11

12

13

14

15

16

17

18

19

Stimulation from the East

Nos. 2, 4, 5, 6, 11, 13–16: The timber buildings of Korea.

Nos. 1 & 3: The formal and imposing wooden buildings of Japan.

No. 17: The sweep of Japanese thatch on a temple roof.

Nos. 7, 10 & 19: Korean furniture of the 17th, 18th and early 19th centuries.

No. 18: Eastern basket work.

No. 8: One of the many uses of bamboo.

No. 12: 12th century Chinese celadon vase.

No. 9: 15th century Chinese porcelain.

Four-panelled double-sided screen and lamp in Burmese teak; (hand-made paper by Gillian Spires).

$\frac{1}{4}$-*Fan table in rosewood inlaid in sycamore.*

Fan table in paldao and leather.

Walnut chest 1984. Designed to stand alongside an existing desk, it fulfils a very tight brief for specific storage requirements within a restricted space. It houses various sized papers and desk accessories and is the happy result of co-operation between the client and the maker.

Ash chest, commissioned as part of a complete room scheme. It is one of a pair that stand together thus accentuating further the pattern of the drawers.

(Detail) Chest of 13 drawers in English Walnut with brass and ebony handles. (See also figs. 135 & 136).

A reading table in quartered oak for the Craft Study Centre, Bath, 1981.

Chinese/gothic table first made in 1976 and so called because it was inspired by the carved arches on mediaeval pew ends of a Devon church and by the mitred joinery so typical of traditional Chinese work. Now in the 20th-century collection at the V & A museum, London.

1

2

3 ▲

6

4

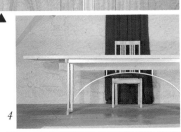

7

8 ▶

5

9

▲ 10

11 ▼

12 ▶

13 ▶

▼ 14

▼ 15

Alan Peters Furniture

No. 1: Chess table with monkey puzzle insets. 1976.
No. 2: (Detail) low table. 1981.
No. 3: Laminated handle and details on satinwood cabinet 1982.
No. 4: 12-seater dining table in aluminium and sycamore 1978.
No. 5: Walnut games box (chess pieces by Richard Kell) 1984.
No. 6: Carved mulberry bowl 18″ dia. 1982.
No. 7: 19″ bowl with carved interior from walnut root.
No. 8: Corner detail of cherry linen chest with ebony details 1983.
No. 9: Joint detail on oak sidetable. 1984.
No. 10: End detail of stack laminated dining table. 1982.
No. 11: Wine table (top detail) in kingwood, monkey puzzle
and boxwood. 1981.
No. 12: Ash nest of tables. 1984. (See also Projects section).
No. 13: Low elm table/bench. 1982–83.
No. 14: Part of room scheme in teak. 1981–82.
No. 15: Mock-up of a panelled paper screen. 1981–82.

Commissioned furniture for the Swiss Catholic Mission Chapel, Westminster 1977

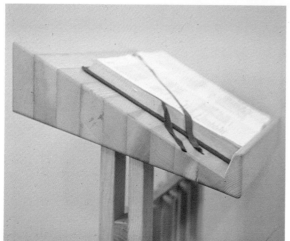

It is not so difficult to be different. What is difficult is coming up with something new that is worthwhile and of value to others besides the creator. Most of the major breakthroughs in design this century have come about as a result of new technology and new materials being exploited with foresight by a mere handful of designers; for the rest, most industrial furniture designers are planners and stylists – round legs this year, oval the next, like car manufacturers updating their new models. In fact, much of my own work of the early 70's, at the height of my period with aluminium, owes much to current industrial design, and most of us in the field of furniture design have to be content with only a degree of originality in what we do. And yet as craftsmen, as creative peiople, we cannot sit back and leave it all to Habitat. We still need to search for that uniqueness which craftsmen can provide, and this in turn often demands more fundamental thinking and subtlety than the mere inclusion of an attractive grain or a spattering of well-made joints. Indeed, if your aim is to be creative and not solely a designer or a maker or a combination of both, it is not enough just to produce well-designed and well-made work. Somewhere along the line there has to be a desire to push the craft forward in a personal way, for the creative craftsman has something definite and personal to say and says it in his work.

Design influence and inspiration are engendered by study and appreciation of work by others and by constant comparison with one's own results. My work, I am sure would have

Fig. 62   Library steps, 1972. Brushed aluminium tubes, rosewood and wool carpet.

Fig. 63   Sideboard in rosewood with aluminium, 1971.

Fig. 64   Curved desk in English walnut solids and veneers and brushed aluminium, 1972.

CPA–F

82

Fig. 65 & 66 Ebony cabinet made in 1975 just prior to my visit to Japan and at the height of my interest in inlaying metals; in this case, stainless steel. It was resold at Sotheby's in 1982 and is now in the loan collection of the Crafts Study Centre at Bath.

Fig. 67 Korean rice washing bowl, in which all decoration and shape derive from its function.

changed even if I had not visited Japan. Devon itself and that solid 16th century farmhouse home and large stocks of home-grown timbers, all, in a way, demanded a change of direction. In the mid-seventies I was interested in decoration and was experimenting with inlaying metal and wood sections, and using decorative veneer patterns on tables and cabinets, and it was at this point that I was awarded a bursary by the then Crafts Advisory Committee in 1975 with a view to researching this aspect in particular. In the hope of getting some new stimulus in the area of decoration, I chose Japan, a country not renowned for its furniture at all, but for its art. The result was quite different; I became intrigued by Japanese architecture as many before me had done. The wide use of timber, beautifully worked, and the sweep and curves of the roofs, both thatched and tiled, captivated me, as indeed did the magic of the joinery technique that went underneath them.

I was also impressed by some of the furniture I saw, but this, unknown to me at that time, was not in fact Japanese at all but Korean.

Fig. 68 The design of this oval dining table (1977) owes much to Edward Barnsley and to my visit to Japan. The latter caused me to redesign the feet in particular of a table made several years before.

Fig. 69   Fruit bowl in Burmese teak, 18" diameter,
1981.

Fig. 70   Fluted bowl table in ash and ebony, 1984.

Fig. 71   Table in Devon ash, 1983.

Fig. 72   Textured surface of shallow bowl table in elm,
1980.

In these tables I am keen to exploit a favourite theme of mine, the contrast between the surface produced from the
cutting edge of hand tools, in this case the gouges on the interior of the bowl, and the smoothness and nearest perfection
possible on the table surface.

I had, prior to this visit, been intrigued and influenced by the Chinese hardwood furniture of the Ming period, excellent examples of which I had seen in the V & A Museum in London. But my visit to Japan did more than increase my admiration for Eastern work; it was something deeper, a reinforcing of views and opinions that I had been forming for some time. Japan, and my later visit to Korea, strengthened my love of traditional crafts and craft objects. Most of what I admired in the East had not been the product of any one designer, but was the result of a gradual evolution over many centuries. It heightened my regard for those simple everyday objects made by craftsmen, *objects whose shape and beauty were derived chiefly from their function and the most logical and economic method of their making.*

The result of this is that since my return I have barely used decoration at all. I have instead become much more interested in form and variation in construction and more wedded to using solid timber, thus moving further away from the current industrial scene.

I am not suggesting that in 1984 we should not be moving on, but I think I, and others like me, who are still predominantly hand craftsmen and creative people, had become too influenced by the products of industry, and by the art and design college environment, which, in furniture at least, is basically the training ground for industrial designers.

Of course, many others have felt this disillusion with the blandness of so much industrial design, and this is the reason for the emphasis and importance now placed on innovation in both British and American craft furniture, with all the excitement and at times the sheer nonsense and gimmickry that this inevitably generates.

There was a complete absence of such gimmickry in the East, and whilst I was there the second time in 1980 my thoughts continually reverted to my apprenticeship, and to Gimson and the Cotswold School, and I developed a growing respect for their earlier work which, whilst breaking new ground and being quite revolutionary in its day, nevertheless had its roots in something much deeper and more stable.

Some craftsmen today have been quoted as saying that their work owes little or nothing to tradition. This is fine, for I think it matters little where one seeks inspiration as long as the individual develops and continues to say something in his work. For me, I need roots, the roots of old, well established cultures, be they East or West.

Six

Working to Commission

BACK in 1962 when I set up there was not much choice of action if one wanted to break through and make a living. There were no noticeable retail outlets for craftsmans' work beyond the British Craft Centre in London. There were no craft markets, fairs or shows, and exhibition opportunities were very rare. So the choice was only between providing either a personalised service (commissioned work) direct to the public or as a service to architects, interior designers and sections of industry on a sub-contract basis.

Now, one does have a wider choice. It is possible to produce furniture without a particular customer in mind and provided the product is good and the price right, sell it at one of the numerous craft shops, galleries, markets, or exhibitions up and down the country, as well as from one's own premises.

You might be tempted, in order to hedge your bets, to combine both one-off and batch work equally, but I don't advise it. For success, one area must take overall preference over the other and it is largely a question of individual temperament and ability as to which area one concentrates on.

In batch production and retail sales you will have to limit your sights to a few well thought-out designs and exhibition pieces. You will have to enjoy jig-making, machining and organisation. You may have to spend a lot of time away from the workshop promoting sales and in most cases you will not know who buys your work, but you will have the satisfaction that generally the design and creation is 100 per cent in your own hands.

In commissioned work you will be constantly, almost daily, tackling and solving design and technical problems. For if you employ other craftsmen and include unsuccessful enquiries you could easily be designing a hundred or more items a year. In return you will be giving personal pleasure and satisfaction to individuals who will become well-known to you and even good friends over the years.

You will never succeed in this area of commissioned work unless you readily accept that you are providing a service to the public in return for work and your livelihood, and that simple fact must never be forgotten however successful you may become. If, on the other hand, you secretly, or otherwise, consider yourself God's gift to the world of art and design and that it is an honour for anyone to possess your work you will not last long unless you really are brilliant.

In some people's eyes, working to commission, working within the requirements of others, is not considered truly creative and instead considered to be second best and a compromise of integrity and standards. Frankly, after 20 years of designing both for private clients and my own unfettered instincts I have yet to see how one can design and create anything successfully without the important element of compromise. I am convinced that working to commission can be as exciting, stimulating and creative as you choose to make it.

A large part of that much-maligned public out there is extremely receptive to new ideas and good work but quite rightly mistrusts gimmicks. Many will know very little about furniture, timber or construction and it is up to you to enlighten them – not in an aggressive way, but helpfully, and to suggest tactfully, alternatives to their original ideas should these conflict with your own interpretation of their requirements. But remember, you have only just started on the problem; your prospective client could have been living with it for months, so don't dismiss his ideas out of hand, simply build on them.

Naturally there will be times when it becomes all too obvious that they have approached the wrong workshop and then you simply politely suggest that they visit a colleague whose work is more sympathetic to their requirements. This, incidentally, is one of the bonuses of the great upsurge in workshops, that an alternative is never too far away.

Strangely enough, the more wealthy the prospective client is, the more likely he is to be prejudiced against modern work. For people brought up in an environment of good quality valuable antiques it is often genuinely difficult for them to see furniture in any other way. People who have not experienced this influence are usually more receptive to modern design and timbers beyond mahogany and rosewood. This is the chief reason why it is more difficult to break through and make any money pursuing creative work in this country than to reproduce or near reproduce the work of past centuries.

Fig. 73   Library steps in Zambesi redwood, 1978 (A full-size mock-up was made first).

Figs. 74 & 75   Detail of steps. The tall shaped upright is left straight from the spokeshave in contrast to the sanded flat surfaces.

My personal problem over the years and that of others like me is not any lack of appreciation for the work we do but the hard fact that, generally speaking, those that admire it most and would love to possess it, and I would love them to have it, are those very people least able to afford it, and for whom owning a commissioned piece means a genuine sacrifice.

Here I digress to touch on the dilemma of the creative cabinetmaker pursuing work in a way that is honest to himself when things are difficult. Do we pander to the whims and fantasies of the wealthy and fashionable pop world? The extravagant tastes of the Arab oil magnates? Or do we simply cash in on the stately home image of fine old English furniture as designed centuries ago, with its certain wide appeal?

I know the answer, but there, I have broken through and succeeded, but it is a much tougher dilemma and decision when the children are young and the bills roll in.

With only the odd lapse over the years, I have preferred when the chips are down to build honest oak doors, staircases or fit out a kitchen or two, for it worries me less, in fact I enjoy it and consider it a relaxation from cabinetwork.

ACQUIRING CLIENTS

I have one client for whom I have worked for nearly twenty years and made on average one piece a year, but this pattern is very much the exception. Most customers do not come on a regular basis, and it could well be two or even five years between orders. Many others never come back at all once their immediate problem and requirement has been met. This is not, I hasten to add, due to any dissatisfaction on their part, but simply that the British public in particular does not purchase furniture on a regular basis at all, and certainly not custom-built furniture.

So the result is that you, like me, will require throughout your working life a continual flow of fresh clients, and there are several ways of setting about finding them.

By far the best, and, moreover, the cheapest method is by personal recommendation of friends, relatives or business associates of well-satisfied clients. The big advantage here is that anyone who enquires as a result will have already seen your work at first hand in normal, regular use in the home or office. It is, after all, the work itself which is the finest advertisement for the craftsman, and how much better it is to see and examine it in use rather than on an impersonal exhibition stand. The problem is, though, that this on its own will not usually provide anywhere near enough potential clients, particularly in the early years when your collection of work and customers is not very large.

All other methods, with the exception of friends and relatives who might be helpful in hard times, and the very rare visitor who just walks in out of the blue and orders, will be the result of deliberately spending time, money, and effort, but this is a vitally important element and expense to be incurred in working to commission.

Exhibitions

Probably the easiest way for a craftsman to publicise himself and his work is at exhibitions, shows and fairs, where you can get your name and your work known to a wider public and promote quality craftwork in general at the same time. You should not, however; expect to make any direct money from an exhibition or show, since the sheer cost of moving furniture carefully around the country, the time involved, the commission on sales and other incidental expenses soon nullify any sales you might make. Exhibitions can and regularly do prove to be extremely depressing experiences, with your work being, at times, poorly displayed if you have no control over this, and possibly also being returned at the close damaged in some way, and the whole exercise apparently yielding no tangible results. And

Figs. 76 to 80   Two chests for Kirkham House, 1980, a lovely mediaeval house open to the public at Paignton, Devon. The first is in Devon oak with wrought iron hinges by James Horrobin, letter carving by Ronald Parsons. The second, with hollowed out top, is in ash with hinges of Zambesi redwood.

yet, who knows? Two years later, someone walks into your workshop and orders a desk. Why? Because he noticed your work at that exhibition and remembered you when the need arose.

Some furniture makers protest that they are far too busy to take part in a forthcoming exhibition. This is so often a mistake, for although you might be extremely busy at that period with some pressing order, you must organise your time to ensure as far as is possible a constant flow of work for the future. I would maintain that you must never be too busy to promote and to develop your work and business. If you want to physically make the furniture yourself you will never find enough time to do this adequately, but you must nevertheless still set aside enough time and energy in any one year for the furtherance of future work and the wider aims you may have.

If you are constantly rushed off your feet with orders and cannot find time to breathe, then frankly something is wrong. You are either extremely greedy and frightened of missing a trick, or you are simply giving consistently unrealistic delivery dates and possibly unrealistic prices as well.

There is no great merit in simply being busy with lots of orders – anyone can achieve this by offering something for next to nothing, promising the near impossible and lowering standards. What you should be aiming for is the ideal situation in which you receive far more enquiries than you can possibly manage as orders. This then gives you the freedom of choice and action that, as a creative person, you need. You are then able to offer realistic delivery dates and prices on the commissions you take up, and the rest fall by the wayside, possibly to be taken up by your competitors, or, if the clients are too impatient and less discriminating, by the High Street furniture retailers. You will, of course, have to be practical, and with the ever increasing number of opportunities there are to exhibit, you will have to be selective in deciding which and how many you can become involved in. But do continue to get involved, for the great merit in enquiries that come to you as a result of this kind of exposure is that the potential clients have seen your work, admired it, are familiar with your price range, and have come to you in preference to the three, four or maybe twenty other people exhibiting. These enquiries, believe me, are worth ten from a wider public just passing your door, the nett result of whose casual interest is all too often simply an interruption of your work.

Open Days

As you become better known, you will find that it is not difficult to get people into your workshop; the problem, particularly if you live in a holiday area, might rather be one of keeping them out, for the sad truth is that the majority of these visitors, whilst quite genuinely interested in your craft, will never actually purchase your work. Now, despite your desire to spread knowledge and goodwill, there is a limit to how much time you can afford to spend on being an unpaid educationalist, youth employment officer and entertainer whilst attempting to make a living as a small businessman.

You may be driven, as many workshops do, to limit visitors to certain days in the week, or see them by appointment only. What I have found extremely useful over the years in coping not only with this problem but also useful in promoting work and sales is to hold an open weekend once every two or three years. This provides an opportunity for local people, students and others to simply see what your work is about and to chat, and it also enables you to invite personally the local press and county magazines, plus a selected group of interested potential customers and past clients. Even if the latter do not actually come, you have gently reminded them of your existence.

I usually time an open weekend when I have a particularly interesting commission just completed, which adds interest to the event, and possibly results in press coverage, and I display all current work, both finished and under construction. People come because they feel under no obligation to buy and no guilt at wasting my time. It becomes a very pleasant couple of days as I renew friendships with clients I may not have seen for years and open up new ones with people who had simply been nodding acquaintances. To do it well requires a lot of preparation, but I have always found it worthwhile because people see my work in far greater depth than is ever possible at an exhibition, in a gallery or even in the normal workshop situation. It is also excellent for my trainees and assistants, for they see their own work and the workshop in a different light, and can share in the admiration of their skill which is all too often reserved for the master-craftsman. Also important, especially where young trainees are concerned, is that their friends and relatives have a chance to see and understand what their training is about.

Direct advertising

Advertising in newspapers and magazines has in my experience been the least successful method of gaining work, and I have ceased using it for many years. Again, much will depend on the nature of your work and the service you provide – if you are aiming at architects and interior designers, it is probably wise to advertise in their specialist magazines. Normally, I do not welcome working through a third party, so I am aiming at the general public, and I have found that direct advertising is far more appropriate to those engaged in batch production, who have a product to sell, rather than a specialised service to offer.

If such advertising is going to have any effect, it is going to be expensive. Quality work needs reflecting in quality advertising placed in quality papers or periodicals. But the chief drawback, beyond its expense, is that at best it only provides a more selected group of people who would be interested in receiving your brochure, for the advertisement cannot convey enough information to do any more than stimulate their curiosity. As a result, you may be rewarded by a flood of telephone enquiries which disrupt your day and raise your expectations, or receive endless superficial written enquiries which have to be dealt with. After a great deal of effort you might have gained two or three new customers.

Free advertising

Far more beneficial is free advertising in the form of articles and news items about you and your work. A half page spread in your local paper with photographs and a sympathetic article is worth a year's paid advertisements. Frequently, local papers and county magazines are hungry for well-written and interesting material, and if it can be used and presented in a way that does not involve them in much work or expense, they will often publish practically unedited news items for example, which in effect give you a free plug.

Writing and good photographs all take time and money, which really are the same thing when you are self-employed, and you may prefer to simply try and attract the reporters and freelance journalists to visit you. First, however, you have to have something to attract them, some important commission; an award you may have won; a story that can make news or create interest for their readers. The disadvantage of this, over presenting them with material, is that they can write what they like about you, and although in many cases they would let you see a proof, there is no guarantee of this and the finished printed article may contain material which you may wish was not there, but this is the risk.

Magazines have one very important advantage over newspapers, and even over radio and television, in that they are more timeless, finishing up weeks, months or even years later in doctors' waiting rooms, hairdressers and reception areas to be read by people with time on their hands. But again you need to be selective with these for best results. Woodworking and trade magazines might improve your image and position within your

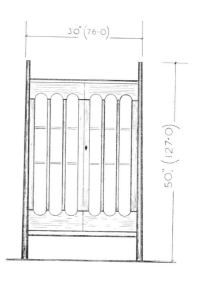

*Figs. 81 & 82   Cabinet in wych elm, 1984, and, front elevation
plan. Designed to relate to other pieces previously designed for the
same room. The tapering of the two ends was particularly
successful and was repeated on the oak side table exhibited at the
Crafts Council Open Exhibition 1984.*

Figs. 83 & 84   Display unit and detail, commissioned in 1983 to display the work of potter Lucie Rie. A heavy piece in solid tropical olive, it is designed to provide visual contrast and physical security to the delicate and precious items to be displayed.

own profession but rarely find you a client. The whole point of publicity is to get yourself known for the work you do and known to people who not only become interested in what you do but who can also be persuaded to purchase it.

When you first set up, in most cases no one knows you from Adam and whilst "Let the work speak for itself" might be a worthy maxim to follow, good work will not in itself guarantee you a living. A workshop or house full to the brim with beautifully executed furniture without a purchaser in sight will not pay the bills. Most people taking the plunge today into self-employment have to create a market for their work and services from the word go, and you won't do it by sitting back basking in modesty, and waiting for people to beat a path to your door.

Appearing on television and radio can be a daunting prospect for some and an exciting one for others, and there is no doubt that many craftsmen in all media have benefited from this kind of exposure, particularly on television, where their actual work is presented for thousands or even millions to see.

Cabinetmaking as a visual process is not in itself very exciting – it all takes so long and involves so many processes before anything worthwhile materialises, so we are at a great disadvantage compared with the potter, woodturner or glass blower who can make things really happen before our eyes. But, having said that, many furniture makers have been featured on television, the most notable being John Makepeace in 'Touch Wood', a full feature programme in 1982 which dealt exclusively with his work, workshops and students. If you have the stomach for it, it is a question again of plugging away at your local radio and television station, letting them know of any events or commissions, or anything topical which might interest them in you, a humble cabinetmaker. An additional bonus is that they will often pay quite well if they can feature you on a prominent magazine-type programme, or an educational feature film.

The whole future prospects of television, with its increased number of channels and specialist programmes, is an area, I am sure, that can and will be exploited by more and more craftsmen, particularly as this expansion of television coincides with the drive to prepare the population for its increased leisuretime – ironically a precious and diminishing commodity for the self-employed craftsman.

The Crafts Council have recently issued a free guide *Working to Commission* available on request to the Information Section, 12 Waterloo Place, London SW1.

DESIGN PROCEDURE FOR COMMISSIONED WORK

Arriving at the Brief

A brief is simply a designer's term for evaluating all the requirements and data needed before you can actually begin to design anything at all seriously.

Few prospective clients are capable of giving you a clear brief of their requirements, and it is up to you to prepare one from the information they give you and that you seek out in your meeting. Preferably you will meet in person, either in the client's home or office, or at your premises, but at times this has to be conducted over the telephone or by letter, or by a combination of both.

It is difficult to be precise about what one should be achieving during this initial contact; for example, you obviously will not be able to take site measurements or photographs unless you are meeting on site, and these, if they were required, would have to wait until a subsequent meeting.

However, certain fundamentals should be established:-

The function and nature of the work and service you are being asked to supply:

Establish the priorities. Is it basically a storage problem, and if so, what is to be stored? If it is a dining area, will they require chairs? If so, how many? If not, whose chairs will be used? Could the over-riding priority of the piece or pieces be aesthetic, to enhance a room or entrance hall? Will the project involve site work and fitting? How quickly is it required? – and so on.

The room or site:

Study the general environment of the room or office, the decor, the way they live and work, whether the floor is carpeted, etc.

Take careful note, even if they seem irrelevant, of the position of heating vents, pipes, radiators, electrical plugs and wiring etc. Note the height of the ceiling, skirting board, picture rails, architraves. Notice and record which way the doors open and where the windows are positioned.

If site work is anticipated, take particular note of the evenness of walls, floors, and any potential obstacles.

Always take note of the ease of access into a room. How embarrassed you will be 12 months later if the table you have made will not go up the stairs, through the door, or round that awkward corner.

Take all necessary measurements and photographs if you have to do extensive planning.

If your briefing cannot be on site, then try and establish as much of the above information as you need from your meeting and telephone conversations.

The clients:

Note their particular preferences and prejudices. They may, for example, hate metal or light coloured timbers, detest handles on drawers, or be highly prejudiced against veneer and adore inlay.

The competition:

Find out tactfully whether you are alone in the field or merely one of several hopefuls who have been approached. If the latter is the case, will the clients pay for the initial design work, for if not you may decide that it is not worth the candle. Six independent craftsmen battling away with designs for a £500 order may not be your idea of fun, but if it is a boardroom worth £20 000 you might perhaps think differently.

The decisions:

Do all the major decisions lie with the person or persons you are talking to, or is there a committee, a partner, an architect to consider; or, in the case of a private house, a wife, husband or mother-in-law in the background, who could be footing the bill?

The terms:

Mention the terms on which you work – maybe so much for the initial sketch design, or money on account as the work progresses. In fact, soften the impact of your more formal letter to follow, and thus avoid having to give any unpleasant shocks and surprises later.

The budget:

In order to avoid unnecessary waste of time on both sides, it is important to establish right at the outset, not a firm commitment to cost, but a general understanding of the budget within which you will be expected to design and work.

Naturally, people are often reluctant to talk about money, preferring to discuss every other detail under the sun, but unless you do break the ice right at the start you could be designing in a vacuum, not knowing whether that desk has to be made for £1000 or £6000. It could well be that your client's requirements simply cannot be met within the budget

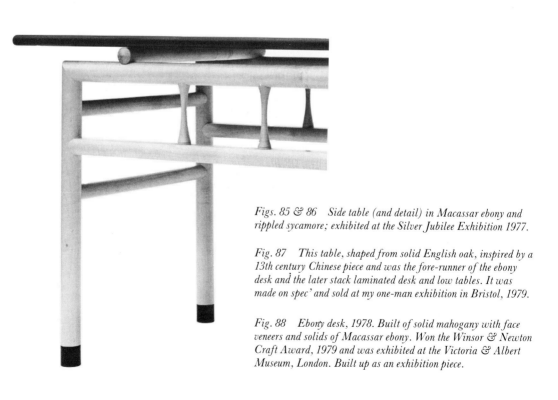

Figs. 85 & 86   Side table (and detail) in Macassar ebony and rippled sycamore; exhibited at the Silver Jubilee Exhibition 1977.

Fig. 87   This table, shaped from solid English oak, inspired by a 13th century Chinese piece and was the fore-runner of the ebony desk and the later stack laminated desk and low tables. It was made on spec' and sold at my one-man exhibition in Bristol, 1979.

Fig. 88   Ebony desk, 1978. Built of solid mahogany with face veneers and solids of Macassar ebony. Won the Winsor & Newton Craft Award, 1979 and was exhibited at the Victoria & Albert Museum, London. Built up as an exhibition piece.

proposed, in which case the sooner you point this out, the better; not after you have spent a tiring week on design work. You are then in a position to offer, on the spot, less expensive alternatives and at the same time to indicate the advantages to be gained by increasing the budget. We are not talking about quality here, for I assume you would not be offering anything else; it is design decisions and choices of construction and materials that we are discussing – not bad construction or unsuitable materials, but different, less expensive ones. In some cases your client may have absolutely no idea of what costs are involved in having an individual piece of furniture designed and made to order, and you will have to enlighten him and give him some idea of the range of costs his enquiry might incur. You would be ill-advised to leave him completely in the dark whilst you take a fortnight to prepare an estimate he cannot afford.

You may well have to allow him time to consider your meeting and the project before he will be prepared to give you any guidance on the budget available. So you will just sit tight and wait, and if you do not even hear any more, this is still preferable to designing in the dark, and possibly wasting a great deal of time and effort on a non-starter.

In general, then, when attending a meeting away from your premises, always ensure that you have all your information and facts at your fingertips. Always carry a measuring tape, a sketchbook, photographs of past work, particularly, but not only, those pieces which appear relevant to the enquiry, and have timber samples and your camera tucked away in your car.

It may be that, as a result of your photographs, you will not be required to design anything new, only to repeat or modify slightly an existing piece, and there are obvious advantages in this, as you can price pretty accurately on the spot and get an immediate reaction and there are no real design costs. It can, however, also be a lost opportunity to move on in your work. Photographs of past work are extremely useful but they can also be traps for the designer wanting to continually develop but restricted by having to reproduce his past successes. Fortunately, the converse is also true – perhaps you have been itching to have another crack at a particular desk or chest of drawers, and improve on it, and this could be the opportunity. As the years go by, you will become more expert at turning situations to your own advantage, and with a growing collection of photographs you will also become much more adept in selecting the ones you want to present.

The Immediate Follow-up

Following the briefing, write immediately clarifying all the points discussed, and do this before undertaking any serious design work. He will have had time to sleep on it, so suggest that he lets you know any further thoughts or suggestions he may have. Outline your terms and conditions, and do not commit yourself to very much at this stage.

Generally, I must stress the need for flexibility in handling clients. One walks a tightrope between business efficiency and simply frightening clients away. In theory, as a designer, you should charge for site visits and preliminary sketch proposals as well as more formal design work. In practice, as a craftsman, this is not always feasible; one must expect at times, particularly if the brief is an exciting one, to gamble a certain amount of time and effort in the hope of obtaining an eventual commission.

This procedure I have described is aimed particularly at new clients. With old established ones one obviously becomes less formal but not less business-like, or less efficient in dealing with their enquiries.

Below is a specimen letter written on the day following a meeting at a prospective client's house:

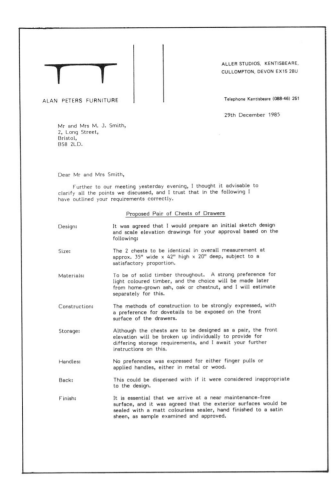

Preliminary Sketches and Proposals

This is the most important and difficult part of the design process when working to commission and clients often imagine that you can produce a handful of sketches and ideas in a few minutes. This can be so far from the truth. The whole concept of the design, which may eventually lead to weeks or even months of bench work, is reflected in that initial work. Clients will often ask for ideas and suggestions. Don't give them ideas in the plural but one idea developed with confidence and clarity and with variations on a theme if you feel that this is necessary and desirable in order perhaps to give some flexibility in the cost. A blanket chest, for example, of the same basic design can be hand-dovetailed in prime oak for x amount or machine jointed in prime chestnut for y amount.

Always remember that the sketch proposal will have to be made to the budget you agree. Give it careful thought and make sure that it can in fact be made and within the price. You may have to do a considerable amount of homework within the workshop to ensure it is all possible before committing those proposals to the post.

I can't over-emphasise how important this area of work is, at times to be unpaid, in the development of a designer/maker. Of course, it is easier to produce a near copy of something you have done before and there are at times excellent reasons for doing just that, but also remember that each new enquiry is an opportunity and a challenge to make and develop something fresh.

I always recall a conversation with a depressed furniture maker, now forced out of business, who said that he had not been able to design any new work for several years simply because his clients were not able or willing to pay for the design time and the development, and barely even paid for the making time. The mistake in this thinking is that it automatically assumes that good designs or new designs are going to be expensive. But, if you have done your homework correctly and obtained a full brief of your client's requirements and the budget allowed, there is no reason why a good, new, fresh design should not involve much less work in the making than your client's first intentions, or indeed yours, and thus could even save money both for you and for him. You do however stand to lose the time spent on the initial design work should your client decide not to proceed further and should you not have previously negotiated any fees – or more frequently an insufficient one – for this work.

I consider it a gamble worth taking frequently, and only experience will tell you how much of this unpaid design work you should do in a year. But do record the time spent on it, for, if the project were interesting enough in the first place, it is never wasted and is there for future reference, maybe for the next exhibition piece, or perhaps another client may be persuaded of its merits. And sometimes time will tell you that the whole idea was not up to much anyway; in this case you can conveniently forget it, tear it up, and be thankful that you never got the job.

Final Specification and Client's Drawings

At some time, and in extreme cases it might be after several meetings, letters and even modifications to those initial sketch proposals, you will need to send your prospective client a specification and drawing of what you are finally proposing to do for them.

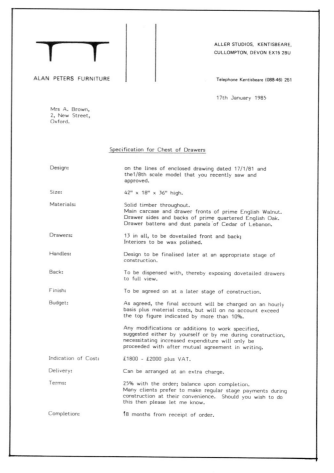

Fig. 90   Specimen letter

This specimen letter to Mrs Brown of Oxford is typical of those sent out at this stage, when everything has been verbally agreed but the need still remains to confirm it in writing both for your records and for your client's.

The specification is an instant record for you of the requirements for that particular job which will be much easier to refer to in two months' time than wading through many letters, especially if they are hand written ones, to find just those details you need.

Hopefully the order will soon follow with the cheque for the deposit, so that you can then proceed if you wish. Never proceed without it, for it is surprising how people and their circumstances can change almost overnight; but once having sent out the deposit and made a financial commitment it is extremely rare for people then to have second thoughts.

Upon receiving the cheque you must receipt it and thank them for the order, not just bank it and then quietly forget all about the client for the next three months while you concentrate on more pressing matters.

Do keep people informed of progress. They have made a commitment in terms of money and effort, so don't ignore them but involve them in the process; invite them down to see the piece under construction, or ring them up from time to time.

Procedure for Working to Commission

1. Obtaining the clients
2. Arriving at the Design Brief
3. Design Procedure
    a) Following up the brief
    b) Preliminary sketches and proposals
    c) Terms, fees, estimates; copyright
    d) Design development – models, mock-ups & working drawings
4. Workshop Procedure
    a) Ordering and checking on materials
    b) Organising sub-contract work well in advance
    c) Preparing templates,
        setting out boards and rods,
        cutting lists.
    d) Cutting out the materials
    e) Keeping clients informed of progress; possible meetings and consultations during construction.
    f) Monitoring and confirming any major alterations to design and price that might arise due either to your client's or your decisions.
5. Delivery; Site fixing; Liability

Seven

Batch Production

THE dilemma that has faced every craft furniture maker is how to make furniture of quality and distinction without either living in near poverty, limiting one's work to a handful of wealthy people, or subsidising the workshop by some other means. Many have lived out their lives in near poverty, and few can undertake the middle course without some pangs of conscience, even if they do possess the rare ability necessary to attract this very limited clientele. So naturally, over the years, many furniture makers have explored ways of reducing the cost of their work to make it more widely available.

The increasing availability and use of light machinery and power tools has assisted in this quest, but it has not completely solved the problem. The one-off commissioned piece, despite all the equipment now at our disposal, must by its very nature be a relatively expensive luxury for many people, and therefore subject to a restricted market.

So the answer must lie in some form of batch production, where the cost of the design and development, and the setting up time for the various processes in construction, are spread over many pieces. This thinking is not new, and it has its parallel throughout the history of the functional crafts from pots to sheep hurdles. In cabinetmaking shops, however, as opposed to factory production, it has never been so common or successful, for the sheer complexity of the operations and the components used in traditional cabinetwork has not lent itself to efficient batch production in situations where both working capital and space are so often at a premium.

This is still largely true today, in that batch production of complicated cabinetwork rarely gets beyond three or four-off; it is with the smaller items of furniture and woodware, such as low tables, wall mirrors and chairs where it becomes more practical to plan in large numbers. This type of item can make greater use of standard sized components, or use very few; they can be stacked both before and after assembly thus taking up little space, and where space is important, as it so often is, it makes sense to tie up say, £50 worth of time and materials in an object such as a wall mirror, that can pack flat into a small box, than in an awkward piece of furniture that requires fifty times that space.

The success of batch production, and the reason so few practising it are really successful, lies in making the ideal product that appeals and sells readily in quantity and at a price that can absorb the heavy retail mark-up, and the promotional and distribution costs. For the problem with batch production is that normal workshop orders, however vigorously they are encouraged, rarely keep pace with output, so that one is forced to consider mail order, an endless round of craft fairs and markets or, more commonly, selling the work wholesale to retailers and galleries. In order to achieve this economically the whole operation must be highly and efficiently organised, for, in sharp contrast to commissioned work, you are not producing a personalised service that people expect to have to pay for, but goods which will have to take their chance in the market place in direct competition with everything else that is there. Your name, and the fact that you are an excellent craftsman, will mean little, unless you are very well established; everything, absolutely everthing, stands on that product and its design, its visual appeal, its quality, its uniqueness, and its price in relation to these qualities. Thus, design considerations are even more vital than in commissioned work, for a weak design in a one-off is a great pity and best quickly forgotten, but a weak design repeated a hundred times could prove an expensive disaster and a long-standing embarrassment.

Figs. 91 — 93 Occasional tables in brushed aluminium and a variety of dense hardwoods. Batch produced in the early 1970's through to 1980.

So, the product must be designed in relation to the consumer as well as to its manufacture, for the pitfall with simply considering the efficiency and streamlining of the making is that the end product can so easily become nothing more than a mere echo of industrial production. If there is nothing left in your product to let the world know that a caring sensitive individual has been concerned with its making, then why bother? – for all you are doing is running an inefficient factory – a pointless exercise and a wasted opportunity. Potters do not suddenly start producing Stoke standard industrial ware simply because they are making in quantity. Yet how often, in this desire to emulate the convenience and style of industrial production, do we see solid wood table tops with razor

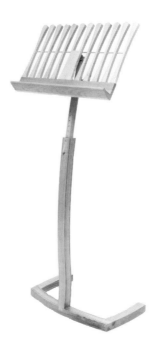

Fig. 94   Chair in steam bent ash by David Colwell.

Fig. 95   Gimson-style chair by Neville Neal.

Fig. 96   Adjustable music stand in yew with ebony stringing by Peter Kuh.

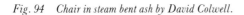

Fig. 97 Occasional table designed to be made in small batches of 4 to 6 at a time. A simplification of my Chinese/Gothic design. Around 50 have now been made in a variety of timbers and dimensions to meet individual requirements.

sharp edges and corners, as though the product were of chipboard with an edge veneer that restricted any other treatment? Or so-called easy chairs and settees with uncomfortable arms of flat, squared up boards of timber just crying out for a craftsman's touch to soften and humanise them?

No, batch production from craft workshops does not imply that we should throw all hand skills and our spokeshaves overboard in order to compete with the lowest end of the retail trade – what is wrong with the middle or the upper brackets? Neither should it be regarded as a necessary, but rather tedious way of paying the bills, whilst our creative energies are reserved for those few one-off masterpieces that keep us sane. It can in fact be a very rewarding and satisfying way of working and running a craft workshop, and the challenge of competing more directly with industry and involving a wider public is an exciting one. For instance, the chairs of Neville Neal and David Colwell, both specialists in batch production, come over as craftsman-made pieces even though they are made in considerable quantities. This is not because they are fussy or elaborately decorated, but because they have that sensitivity to the qualities of the ash they are made from, and possess an overall feeling of elegance and sheer quality that puts much industrial work in wood to shame. Peter Kuh's music stand, aimed at a smaller, more specialised market, proves too, that a fine cabinetmaker, helped along by such equipment as the spindle moulder, can get that caring, sensitive craftsmanship into a relatively inexpensive article that is produced not in hundreds but in small batches alongside his one-off commissioned work.

When designing for quantity production it is not necessary to search deliberately for originality; if a product is right and well thought-out, this so often follows anyway. Rather, you should choose what it is you wish to produce, research the market thoroughly, examine the weaknesses of the available alternatives and their prices, and perhaps, if you are particularly inventive, you might succeed in coming up with an entirely new approach and a wholly original product, in which case comparisons simply won't be there. Either way, test the water gently at first to gauge the response, perhaps at a few selected exhibitions, before committing yourself to a large number. And once launched, still be prepared to let the design develop in the light of the experience of both making and selling, ensuring that your modifications improve the product or its making, and are not simply a whittling down and weakening of the design in pursuit of a larger profit.

Batch production does not refer exclusively to products from craft workshops designed for resale through some retail outlet, even if that outlet is the craftsman's own small

Figs. 98, 99 & 100   Chair in sycamore. Originally a one-off commission in the Crafts Council's collection, it was later developed into a dining chair and is now one of my standard designs.

showroom. It can also include larger scale commissioned work such as the college refectory or office boardroom; and the chapel with 40 to 100 chairs will require the same careful planning and organisation in making as did the fifty small but intricate ship's chronometer cases that I made a few years ago. Once, I even did a project involving 300 drawers, all hand dovetailed, front and back, as a commission. Also, many craftsmen, myself included, have some set designs and whenever possible it is advantageous both to the craftsman and the client if several orders can be combined. In this way, for instance, four sets of six dining chairs could be made up together, although maybe in different timbers and upholstery, and produced as one batch of twenty-four chairs. What one has to do here is to explain the financial advantages to be gained by waiting to those who were first on the list!

Limited Editions

Some distinction needs to be made at this point between the true batch–designed product, which can be produced in endless quantities as long as demand exists, and which utilises simplicity of construction and techniques in order to make it viable, and other repeatable pieces, which are better classified as limited editions.

The latter are pieces with a more specialised appeal; pieces that can demand more of the cabinetmaker's skill, and involve many hours in their making. They may well have been conceived as one-off pieces, but because the designs have proved so successful you wish to make them more widely available and also recoup some of the design and development costs. They will, nevertheless, still be expensive and appeal to a limited clientele who will quite rightly expect to receive something very special whilst benefiting also from the economic advantages of small batch working. For this reason the maker must be strictly honest and limit production to ten, or maybe fifty, depending on the piece, and it is a good idea to actually number each one. They need not all necessarily be produced at the same time, but the limit must be set, stated openly, and adhered to. It would of course be better financially to make the whole set together, but it is often a matter of how long people will wait whilst you first collect the orders and then complete the batch, so you may have to take the gamble of going ahead with only three or four actually spoken for and use your own judgement to determine how many to make. The all too frequent nightmare then, is that one is left with one or two which would readily have been sold had they been made in a different, usually a richer, and darker timber than the one you chose; so it is less worrying if you can pick up the orders first.

Workshop Organization

It is impossible to be too specific here as much depends on the temperament of each individual craftsman, the workshop facilities, the product, and the style of marketing adopted. However, given perfect conditions, it would be more sensible and sounder economically, to make a run of say a hundred nests of tables and work each process in turn on the entire hundred right through to eventual completion. But there are snags with this approach, the biggest of which being that only when the full hundred are completed can any of the considerable capital outlay involved be recouped. Also, there will suddenly be a hundred nests to be distributed and sold, or alternatively stored. Lastly, retailers frequently require a steady flow of say two sets a month and are unwilling to wait indefinitely for that first consignment.

The compromise most craftsmen make is to machine up and prepare all the materials for the hundred sets, agonise over just how many joint and machine operations to complete before shelving the whole lot away very carefully and then taking down maybe four or six sets at a time to work on till completion.

I never cease to be surprised by the differences in the number of hours required to make a chair as one of a batch of fifty, as opposed to one of six, or, worst of all, a one-off. This is why I am convinced that for success in this field it is wise to specialize and produce the largest batch possible, compatible with avoiding boredom and bankruptcy.

In larger workshops, such as my own which specialize in working to commission, there is also a place for batch-designed products, even though these will not prove to be particularly viable economically, for the reasons already given. It is essential that those involved in these workshops, whether they are employed or still in training, should be constantly busy, since there are few things more frustrating than enforced idleness. But, the larger the workshop, the more difficult it is to ensure that someone does not run out of work at three o'clock of an afternoon due to some unforeseen hold-up – maybe the glass that was ordered did not arrive, or the client one needs to contact with a query is away on holiday. For these and many other reasons, it is useful to have a few batch products neatly stacked on the shelf which can be brought down and worked on at such times. Furthermore, there is no better training for apprentices than work which involves some repetition, which is not usually present in one-off pieces; because the exercise of repeating a process many times, perfecting it, and executing it faster each time, is so essential in developing the skills and attitudes needed for economic survival.

Fig. 101   *Apprentice Stephen Hopper working his way through a small batch of stool seats and mastering the drawknife at the same time.*

Fig. 102   *Three-legged stool in sycamore. First made in 1962 and used constantly since as a training exercise.*

Marketing of Batch Products

The finest aid to selling will always be the product that people just cannot resist buying, but the public must be aware of its existence and its qualities. It needs to be presented or displayed in a manner that does it full justice, not tucked away half forgotten in a corner of a shop where no-one notices it. Nor, if it is a table, should it be displayed with such an assortment of beautiful objects placed upon it that no-one notices the table underneath, for while it may be very comradely to provide a good surface for fellow craftsmen such as potters, sculptors and glass artists, it is not exactly in your own interest.

Sadly, once out of your premises, you may have no further control over the display of your products, so the commercial success of your work is not entirely in your hands but in the hands of the retailers and others who deal directly with your public. You may well argue that this does not matter provided that the retailers purchase the work in the first place, but this is not so, for they are hardly likely to re-order while they still have unsold stock, and the public can hardly be expected to wax ecstatic over a piece that has been collecting dust and bruises for the past six months.

For these reasons direct selling could prove to be a better proposition. It is naturally attractive to the maker, if only because it avoids the retail mark-up which can be as high as 100 per cent or more; but, whether it is done direct from his premises, by mail order, or through a continual run of craft fairs, exhibitions and shows, it is very time consuming, and it should always be remembered that if you are actively selling you cannot be actively making. Now to some, this aspect of selling can be as exciting, exhilarating and as important as the actual making of the product – or it can be a bore and a frustration which gets in the way of the real work, the actual working at the bench. Those in this latter category should perhaps question whether batch production is in fact right for them, and if it is, they should leave the selling to others and look to retail outlets.

These can be the traditional furniture stores which are found in every town and can often be persuaded of the merits of craftsman-made work provided that the price is right. Alternatively, there are the more specialised craft shops and galleries that have mushroomed throughout the country these past ten years. Contrary to what many makers think, the retailer or gallery director does not make a killing out of selling craftwork; and usually the better the shop or gallery the more difficult it is for them to survive themselves, for, unfortunately, inexpensive trash is less difficult to sell than quality work which must command a high price. A good gallery will usually respect your work, and you as an individual craftsman, and will make strenuous efforts on your behalf once you have gained their confidence.

A good starting point for selecting suitable galleries and craft shops, as opposed to the more normal retail furniture outlets, is the Craft Council's leaflet on Craft Shops and Galleries, but this is by no means an exhaustive list and others should also be sought.

When approaching retailers of any description, always bear in mind that they are very busy people who are inundated with travellers offering them their wares; never just call in on the off-chance, always write or telephone first for an appointment, stating clearly the purpose of your visit and what it is you wish to interest them in. They will soon tell you if they are not interested at all, and thereby save you a fruitless journey. Always arrive on time, and take along first class finished work, or if this is not possible, good quality photographs of what you wish to sell, rather than attempt to interest a buyer in some vague idea that you wish to pursue. (This is something you might consider later, once you are accepted and known.) Be selective in what you show; it is always better to present a few perfect objects than a dozen mediocre ones.

You may be a creative artist, but in dealing with retailers do not give the impression that you are woolly-headed as well. Do your homework well in advance so that you know the prices you need to get, and be positive about it; you will soon be told if your figures are ridiculous, and they often are, for beginners are as likely to overvalue their time as undervalue it. You should also be prepared to listen to advice and criticism of your products and prices, since these people are much nearer to your public than you are; and confidence must be built up between you the supplier, and them the eventual sellers of your work. They want to rest assured that you will always deliver the goods at a consistent quality and at the times agreed, and you need to be assured that your work is being adequately presented to the public at what is a fair price to you, to the retailer, and to the customer.

Many galleries and craft shops are not in a position to purchase outright items of furniture and they may suggest retaining them on a sale or return basis. In this case, the retailer will not actually buy your work but he will display it for you and take a commission, usually an agreed percentage, for selling it. When a retailer purchases work, all the risk is

Figs. 103 — 108   Stools and Benches.

Figs. 103, 104 and 105   A simple, basic stool, 12" high, my first piece after returning from Japan. It has since been produced in some quantity, primarily as a training exercise, but the joint, as detailed, is really too time consuming for batch production.

Figs. 106 and 108   Small table/bench in olive ash. The joint has been simplified to a straight–forward mitre. These are still made in a variety of sizes and timbers.

Fig. 107   Stool in ash with curved seat first designed in 1976, since when a couple of hundred or so have left my workshop.

his, and he may never sell it, or have to sell it off eventually quite cheaply. When dealing on a sale or return basis, all the risk is yours; you are stocking that store or gallery at your expense and therefore the mark-up or commission on eventual sales should reflect this and be considerably less than if the gallery has purchased your work outright. You should also be paid promptly after a successful sale, not three months later in order that your money can work for them.

Given these obstacles, and the fact that you are responsible for the delivery of the goods, collection at some later date, and even in some extreme cases for insurance whilst your work is on display, one wonders why craftsmen ever get involved in such a one-sided transaction. The answer is that the craftsman, and the furniture maker in particular, needs exposure in order to generate sales, and he would rather have his work on display in prominent towns than sitting idly in his workshop. In addition, this system does have an advantage for the maker in that it encourages galleries and the better craft shops to take and display more adventurous and expensive items than they would be prepared to risk if they had to purchase.

Although I dislike this arrangement intensely, unless the retailers are in some way subsidised, most simply cannot take the risk of purchasing major items of furniture, and we as makers can only sympathise with their situation. Much help has come the craftsman's way these past ten years, but the major problem of marketing their products in a way that gives a fair return to all concerned, not least the galleries and shops, still remains to be tackled.

The Future Development of Batch Production

One of the other major obstacles which hinders the development of good, inexpensive, craft-inspired furniture in Britain is that, whilst there is no shortage of talented designers in this field, there are very few who either want to, or are in a position to, actually make and produce their designs in any quantity once past the prototype and development stage. Coupled with this, all too few other craft workshops are interested in doing this for them either, preoccupied as they are in doing their own thing in their own search for something new and individual.

There is, therefore, a great need for more, larger production workshops that will work to the designs of other designers. This could be done in one of two ways: either by simply providing a making service and acting as a sub-contractor to a designer or architect, or by engaging a designer who is sympathetic to craft production, to design for them and thus launch their own company products in a professional way, much as the Danish cabinetmakers did so successfully in the 1950's and 1960's. Either way, it goes without saying that the integrity of the makers and the quality of the work they produce are of the utmost importance.

However, this development is hampered by attitudes that imply that there is little dignity, satisfaction or recognition to be gained by simply being a maker of things. In fact, quality workmanship is often ridiculed or ignored by those in a position to influence, who place artistic ability on such a far higher pedestal than skill in making. This is a nonsense, and more people, particularly young people entering the field, need to be reassured that there is nothing demeaning or inferior in living out their lives, as Bert Upton has done, in simply making to the best of their ability. Many do not possess either the wish or the aptitude to be the great exciting artist or designer as well as the maker, but this is no reason for them to feel inadequte or unfulfilled, for cabinetmaking, even without the glamour reserved for the successful designer, is a most exciting and rewarding profession in its own right, and a lifetime is never long enough to master all its many facets.

Those cabinetmakers who are interested in collaborating with a trained craft designer should consult the Craft Council's slide index to find the individuals whose work is most sympathetic to their requirements.

Eight

Training

I T is encouraging, despite an educational system that, eighty years on from William Morris, still by and large looks on manual labour as being beneath anyone with a modicum of intelligence, that so many gifted young people reject this and the lure of the white collar in favour of getting dirty with polish or clay under their finger nails.

Within many of our schools, designing, or rather the problem-solving aspect of it, is now a respectable academic subject, and as a result it is daily getting further divorced from using materials, working with tools and experiencing the sheer joy of making. The sad consequence of this is that in general the standard of woodwork achieved in schools now is lower than it used to be twenty years ago. It could of course be said that the horizons of the pupils are now much wider, but it does seem strange that, at a time when we are supposedly educating for increased leisure time, and when there is a strong possibility of no normal formal employment for much of our school population, less and less time should be devoted to actually making things and workshop experience. I have long since ceased to take much notice of the work which an aspiring apprentice brings along at the interview, for all too frequently it is merely a sad reflection on his or her school's indifference to craftwork. It is because of this ingrained prejudice against manual work in British education that I and others like me are inundated with requests for training from young people who have been steered by the system into an advanced academic education which did not provide them with fulfilment, only frustration. If I had the stamina, I could fill my workshop many times over with disenchanted university graduates who see nothing demeaning in working with their hands as well as their heads.

Sadly, the problems of training do not end with the schools, for the sheer demand now for workshop and design training for the would-be designer-maker in furniture far outstrips the facilities available, and this is the reason why so many take the plunge and set up their workshops virtually with one hand holding a how-to-make-it book. For, despite the incentives of grants that are available, all too few practising craftsmen are prepared to take trainees into their workshops, and of those who do, this rarely means more than one apprentice or student every two or three years.

Another problem is that, despite having more art and design schools than probably any other country in the world, there are nevertheless so few which run courses directed at the aspiring craftsman in wood. If your chosen craft is ceramics, glassblowing, textiles or silversmithing, an art school will give you a sound, craft-based design training. If on the other hand it is wood, the nearest you are likely to encounter is an industrial design course, sometimes with furniture design as a separate discipline, but more often part of a general 3-dimensional industrial design study. The problem here, however, for the would-be maker is that, having acquired the quite high academic qualifications necessary for entry to these degree courses, and after having spent four or even seven years of study if post graduate training is involved, he or she may still know very little about how to make a piece of furniture. For this reason so many design students upon completion of their courses still have to search for workshop training to gain the skills and business know-how that establishments such as Parnham House and Rycotewood give their students in a very concentrated two years.

It is quite easy, and often fashionable, to criticise the art schools, but the fact remains that the majority of successful craftsmen in Britain at this present time are products of that system. The design discipline learnt and the visual awareness that comes from such a long leisurely training is I suspect the modern equivalent to the equally lengthy architectural study that practically all the 19th century furniture pioneers undertook.

But it is not ideal if your aim is to be a designer-maker and you cannot afford the luxury of four to seven years design training. Since I often suspect that the most valuable period of that long training is in fact the first year, the foundation art studies, which the majority of our students encounter before entering the more specialist 3-year degree course, I would recommend taking just this year at a good school of art as a prelude to specialised training either in a workshop or in one of those establishments listed which specialise in teaching the skills that are needed to become a successful maker.

TRADE TRAINING

The Guild of Master Craftsmen have issued an excellent booklet called *Practical Guide to Woodworking Careers' and Educational Facilities* in which there are listed over 250 training establishments throughout the United Kingdom offering City and Guilds courses in timber trades, so why, you might ask, is there any shortage of training facilities? Simply because of that 250 plus, just 36 offer furniture crafts, and these courses are basically intended for trade apprentices. In other words, you have to be employed in the furniture industry or within a workshop before most of these courses are open to you.

And what of the courses themselves? First one has to look at the state of the British furniture industry and to realise that its chief successes are in the fields of metal and plastic; that much current practice in cabinetmaking is downright shoddy and bad; and that close on a hundred years of cheapening of a noble craft has taken its toll to the extent that most cabinetmakers within the mainstream of industry could not match the skills and accuracy of a second year apprentice from a good craft workshop. One cannot blame the individuals concerned, since their sights and expectations have been destroyed by a lifetime of having two minutes allowed to fit a drawer on an assembly line, and sadly this has rubbed off on to many of the training establishments that cater for the industry. The exceptions, however, are good, and the fortunate apprentice often gains his only opportunity in a lifetime to pursue good work and give of his best whilst attending day release or block courses.

The purpose of these courses is to give the trainee a wide and thorough understanding of the whole of the furniture industry and to expand what may well be a very narrow training indeed that he or she may be receiving in their regular employment.

The course most relevant to the trainee cabinetmaker, and the one most commonly available throughout the country is the City and Guilds 555 Furniture Crafts Part I and II which are usually obtained after three years' part-time study. This can be followed by Part III which can be either Advanced Studies in Furniture Crafts (ACF) or Advanced Industrial Studies in Furniture (AISF), although unfortunately there are only 18 centres in the United Kingdom for these courses.

The City and Guilds 586-1 Machine Woodworking Crafts course is a three year equivalent to Furniture Crafts I and II for trainee wood machinists, and it too can be followed by a one year advanced course, 586-2.

The City and Guilds 579, Furniture Design and Construction, is a part-time course designed to extend the experience of the qualified craftsman in the drawing and design of furniture and intended for those who already possess the 555 craft certificate. It can be followed at only 5 colleges: London College of Furniture; Manchester College of Building; Jacob Kramer College, Leeds; Liverpool Central College of Further Education; and Basford Hall College of Further Education, Nottingham. It should be a useful course for practising craftsmen, who might even gain entry by virtue of experience, even without a 555.

And finally there is City and Guilds 564, 1, 2, and 3, Cabinetmaking for Mature Students. This is a 3 year open evening course which is held only at the London College of Furniture.

The aspiring craftsman should perhaps ask himself whether a bad training is better or worse than no training at all, and whether it is harder to drop bad habits than to acquire good ones. On a personal note, one of the best craftsmen to work in my workshop trained in a small but good joinery shop where speed and accuracy went hand in hand, and I would strongly recommend such a good basic training in joinery in preference to poor cabinetmaking training. There is much to be said for joinery – it instils speed and a directness of approach; up and down the country there are far more opportunities to get enrolled on good courses from which one could acquire a good basic training in wood machining and machine maintenance as well as joinery construction, instead of getting bogged down in wood stains and fake antiques.

Training in Craft Workshops

This type of training is difficult to obtain particularly in those workshops which specialise in high quality and individual work. It is slightly easier to come by in larger scale production shops, where the more repetitive nature of the work enables the master-craftsman to make greater economic use of apprentices or other trainees.

Training in established workshops takes the form of either a three or five year apprenticeship. It is usually begun between the ages of 16 to 18, and often, but not always, includes day or block release to attend City and Guilds courses in an appropriate local college.

Alternatively, the trainee pays the master-craftsman a premium in exchange for a concentrated one or two year period of training in his workshop. There appears to be no set formula or set premium for this, it is simply a question of the craftsman and the aspiring pupil coming to some amicable agreement. This method of training is as old as the Arts and Crafts Movement itself and was used by Gimson. It is particularly suitable for the mature person, too old for the normal apprenticeship, who requires concentrated workshop experience and is prepared to pay the true cost of gaining it. Unfortunately however, there are still all too few practising craftsmen who can be persuaded of the economic advantages to them of taking a mature but nevertheless raw recruit into their shops and lives.

Similarly, not many can be persuaded of the advantages of taking an apprentice either. Many prefer to soldier on for a lifetime, working on their own, or within the family or a partnership, and do not welcome the restrictions put upon them once they become employers, even if that employee is only one 16 year old school-leaver. Over recent years, increased legislation introduced, with every good intention of increasing safety, improving working conditions within the furniture industry, and reducing the exploitation of apprentices, has simply made the situation that much worse as more craftsmen choose not to employ or to train at all.

Because of this, both the Crafts Council and CoSIRA run what on the surface appear to be very attractive schemes to help to finance the initial year's, or in the case of CoSIRA two years' training for apprentices, in workshops which they consider to be of high enough calibre to attract this financial help. In both cases, it is the craftsman and the workshop that makes the application and receives the grant, and in return he guarantees a minimum wage to the apprentice and certain safeguards for his training. CoSIRA, for example, insist that some part of the apprenticeship is spent in their own training workshops at Salisbury.

The fact that so few craftsmen take advantage of this is proof that, welcome as it is as an incentive, it goes nowhere near far enough. The advantages of both these schemes, but especially the Crafts Council one, go mainly to the apprentice who receives a minimum wage which absorbs all the grant and more besides. The craftsmen, however, particularly those of national repute, find no shortage of applicants prepared to pay for their training, or simply work for nothing in return for the experience, and so they lack the incentive to commit themselves to a three- or five-year apprenticeship scheme and prefer to retain their independence of action.

Training an apprentice thoroughly in a small craft workshop can be time consuming and frustrating, but, like all teaching, it can also be extremely rewarding. Sadly, many more craftsmen need to be convinced of the latter. Worthwhile apprenticeships will continue to die out in Britain until someone recognises that if the state can support an art and design student for up to seven years at art school it should also support an apprentice of limited means through a recognised craft training, not for a year, but for as long as it takes. It would be an interesting exercise to evaluate the true cost to the public of art school training per student, and to compare that with the pittance that is available nationally for workshop training.

The apprenticeship system as practised in Britain, Germany, Japan and other European countries is the envy of the newer countries of the world, and it is significant that it is strongest in Germany and Japan, the two industrial giants. Here in Britain we are destroying it fast in the mistaken belief that it is outdated and that the new need is for flexibility. Having been through an apprenticeship myself, I am convinced that it provides a training for life that cannot be equalled; once trained in one craft, the discipline can be so easily transferred to any other medium or indeed any other walk of life, for a craftsman is a craftsman, not merely a potter or a joiner. What he learns in his training is not just to manipulate wood or metal or clay, but something far more important – the ability to size up a situation and problems and to overcome them with a discipline, directness and economy of working which usually puts the apprentice-trained tradesman at an advantage in so many walks of life.

Both the Crafts Council, with its Index of Craftsmen, and CoSIRA, with its handbook of country workshops, are good starting points in tracking down this elusive workshop training, but neither of these are fully comprehensive in their coverage and many craftsmen and workshops, including some very good ones, are not featured in any publication or index. Apprenticeships are rarely advertised in job centres or anywhere else. All one can do is write, enclosing a stamped addressed envelope, enquiring about any future vacancies and giving a brief description of your own experience, situation and aspirations. Do not be too downhearted or surprised if you receive no reply – there is obviously no vacancy, and with more people searching than there are possible openings, it is bound to be a depressing experience, and many craftsmen are hard pressed to follow up all enquiries. Start looking early, pick up possible names and addresses from craft fairs, guilds, markets and local craft exhibitions; many craftsmen advertise their services locally but are unknown nationally, so look through local papers and county magazines for their names and addresses and keep plugging away. Furniture making as a career is demanding so perhaps this initial search for suitable training is in itself valuable in developing the determination, perseverance and resourcefulness necessary for eventual success! But finally, although you may be convinced that you would prefer practical workshop training to that of a college course, do keep all other options open, so that if all else fails you have at least enrolled on some form of training course, even if it has to be for a year ahead.

Formal Training

The following list is of those schools and colleges specialising in craft furniture making:

The London College of Furniture

The college is situated in the East End of London where it was established in 1899 to cater for the large furniture and cabinetmaking industry centred on Shoreditch and Hackney. Most of that industry which grew up over several hundred years has now moved out of London, but the college remains as the main training establishment for the furniture industry in Britain.

The college is vast, and now occupies six floors of a modern factory/office block building which it moved into in 1971 in order to accommodate the 550 full-time students and the 1500 or so who attend its part-time courses. The courses, too numerous to list, cover the whole field of the furniture industry and include interior design, textiles, soft furnishing, as well as a very thriving department for making musical instruments.

The facilities here are excellent for the student of furniture design, production and management but less so for the acquisition of hand skills. But, having said that, no time spent in this college could ever be wasted; for so diverse are the courses and so wide is the range of equipment and facilities here, that the accumulated knowledge of the staff that is assembled under one roof is quite staggering.

It is natural that, given its history and its vast capital involvement, its main role remains that of meeting the training requirements and research needs of a more streamlined industrial furniture industry. However, it does possess the facilities to extend its training courses to include those relevant to the potential self-employed maker, although at the moment most of the hand skills and workshop practice of real note take place in the excellent department for musical instrument making. Encouragingly, its interest in, and involvement with the needs and aspirations of the individual designer-maker is already growing, and for two successive years now, the college has prepared more than a dozen students for the Licentiateship of the Society of Designer-Craftsmen.

When weighing up the merits of individual colleges, it is worth noting that the realism of an industrial design and production training can be a useful counter-balance to the extravagances of the artist-craftsman, and this London college is particularly suitable for those who see their future as makers of sound, functional furniture in small batches, tailoring production techniques to the needs of a small workshop.

For a prospectus, write to: London College of Furniture, 41 Commercial Road, London E1 1LA or telephone: 01 247 1953, where the full range of courses is listed. The following five courses are of particular interest and relevance being open to all:

A. City and Guilds, 555 -1-2, Furniture Crafts.
    This is a one year, full time furniture making and craft skills course designed for 16/17 year olds who wish to reach a high level of craft ability. It covers timber preparation, hand-made furniture construction, metals and plastics construction, and both traditional and modern upholstery and finishing. No fees are payable for students under the age of 18 on the 1st September and applications for grants should be made to local Education Authorities. Applicants should be 16+ and must be keen and motivated. Evidence of ability in hand skills would be advantageous.

B. T.E.C. Diploma in Furniture Studies.

A two year full-time course leading to the Technician Education Council Diploma Award in Furniture Studies, this course prepares students for entry into the furniture industry, or craft/restoration workshops, in supervised positions. Upon successful completion of the course, students may continue their studies for a further two years on the T.E.C. Higher Diploma Course in Furniture.

Applicants should be 16+ and have achieved passes in 3 subjects at GCE O-level, or equivalent similar qualifications. However, students not possessing these qualifications who are able to produce suitable evidence of ability to succeed in the course, may be admitted at the discretion of the Principal.

C. T.E.C. Higher Diploma in Furniture.

In this 2-year full time advanced course leading to the Technician Education Council Higher Diploma Award in Furniture, students are able to select from one of the four major areas of study contained within the T.E.C. Course. These have been evolved to meet the many faceted requirements of an industry ranging from large production enterprises to the single workshop. The subjects are: furniture design; furniture designer/craftsmanship; furniture production technology and management; and furniture restoration and conservation. Submissions for Diploma membership of the Society of Industrial Artists and Designers, and Licentiateship of the Society of Designer Craftsmen are also strongly encouraged.

Applicants should be 18+ and have completed the T.E.C. Diploma in Furniture Studies or its equivalent. Alternatively, appropriate GCE A-levels or industrial/craft experience will be considered by the course admissions panel. Again, unqualified students who are able to produce evidence of ability to succeed in the course may be admitted at the Principal's discretion.

D. City and Guilds, 555-1, Furniture Crafts.

This is a one year, 21 hours per week course in craft skills related to furniture. It is aimed at 16/19 year olds who wish to study to reach a basic level of craft ability and it introduces the study of timber preparation, hand-made furniture construction, metals and plastics construction and traditional and modern techniques of upholstery and finishing.

As with A above, no fees are payable for those under 18, and all applicants must be 16+, keen and well motivated. Again, evidence of interest in hand skills and modest academic attainment would be advantageous.

E. Cabinet making for Mature Students 564-1-2-3

This is a 3-year evening course which studies cabinetmaking to an advanced level.

The John Makepeace School for Craftsmen in Wood

This school was established as recently as 1977 in a lovely Elizabethan manor house set in the depths of the Dorset countryside. It offers a very intensive 2-year residential course in craft skills, design, and business management. It is the only course on offer in Britain where the sole aim is to train students for self-employment as artist-craftsmen or designer-makers, and it does not compromise that aim by offering any study in furniture restoration, making of period styles or large scale industrial production.

Its intake is restricted to ten students a year, and the course is certainly not for the faint-hearted. The working day is organised very much on disciplined workshop lines, beginning promptly at 8 am, with none of the leisurely art school approach. At the head of the training programme is Robert Ingham, an excellent craftsman and a perfectionist, who combines the post of Principal with that of being the leading tutor in cabinetmaking skills.

This course has the advantage of having some two dozen visiting professional lecturers each year, ranging from leading industrial designers to photographers, accountants, and a wide range of practising craftsmen of international repute. This gives the course the edge over any other in that the training provided is thoroughly professional at all levels and the students being exposed to numerous design approaches.

Excellence in all fields is very much the goal at Parnham House, with John Makepeace's own furniture making workshops alongside setting the pace. Students here further benefit from the fact that Parnham has become an international centre for creative work in wood, and they can participate in and gain stimulation from the numerous seminars, lectures, exhibitions and general traffic of top designers, artists and craftsmen visiting the house each year.

The school is run as a non-profit making charity with fees of £7000 per annum. A few scholarships are available. Enquiries to: The Secretary, The Parnham Trust, Parnham House, Beaminster, Dorset, DT8 3NA. Tel. 0308 862204.

Rycotewood College

This was the first and is now by far the major source of training for the self-employed cabinetmaker. Although it is not set in such idyllic surroundings as Parnham House, it has the advantage of being situated on the edge of an attractive and busy market town and, far more important, is within easy reach of London, Oxford and other cultural centres.

At present it runs a 2-year full-time course (Datec Diploma) with 50 entrants per annum, although during their first year many students work at nearby Banbury Technical College. After two years the students can opt for a third year's study leading to a Datec Higher Certificate in Design Crafts, in which business studies and management play a larger role, making this third year particularly advisable for younger students planning to set up their own workshops.

In addition, the college runs a one year full-time course for mature students with some previous experience. This course has an entry of 25 a year and is particularly valuable for those practising craftsmen who have not previously enjoyed any formal training but who could with sacrifice manage 36 weeks away from their business as a sound investment in their future. It is also ideal for carpenters and joiners seeking a change of direction into fine cabinetwork.

Rycotewood has a staff of highly skilled and qualified craftsmen, backed up by visiting lecturers, who are usually practising designer-craftsmen, and as its emphasis is towards self-employment, the teaching of hand skills is very much to the fore. The standard of work achieved here by the majority of students in two years is remarkably high, and puts most of our other training establishments to shame.

It covers the whole repertoire of cabinetmaking, covering furniture restoration and the reproduction of the work of past centuries as well as a progressive programme of designing and making, all in a two-year course. It argues that by doing so its students are better prepared for the real world outside and thus have a higher chance of survival and success. There is much emphasis here on the realities of earning a living as a craftsman, and on the economic problems that the students will inevitably face; and much of the effort here is directed not only towards acquiring skills but also the necessary speed in the execution of these skills that is essential for economic survival.

The facilities at Rycotewood are good, but space is at a premium as the course continues to grow and outstrip its resources. Due to this pressure on its facilities, perhaps the time will come when it will have to be more selective in its entry and concentrate its efforts on catering for the aspiring creative craftsman, the designer-maker, and leave its reproduction work and antique restoration to other establishments which could fill this role equally well. What they could not do is fulfil Rycotewood's main function of providing that vital middle road between the very limited and elitist opportunities available at Parnham House and the pure design oriented courses available at our leading colleges of art and design with their high academic entrance requirements and their sheer inability to understand and teach hand skills.

Rycotewood is administered by Oxford County Education Authority, and local authority grants and other financial help for mature students are freely available for all its courses. Due to this, it is always very much over-subscribed and early application is essential.

Enquiries to: The Secretary, Dept. of Fine Woodworking, Rycotewood College, Priest End, Thame, Oxon. Tel: 084 421 2501

Shrewsbury College of Arts and Technology

The prospectus speaks of vocational courses in furniture design, which is misleading, for the true merit of the two courses run here is that they are all about hand skills, craftsmanship and small craft workshops. I quote from the prospectus: "These two full-time courses are designed to satisfy the need for basic training in Furniture Making skills for mature students wanting to re-train as craftsmen and school leavers unable to obtain craft apprenticeships."

This 2-year programme is growing in stature yearly under the direction of its Tutor, John Price, and is a useful alternative to Rycotewood. It is more modest in its claims as to what it can achieve in two years than either Rycotewood or Parnham, preferring to stress that its students will be ready for gainful employment in small workshops, rather than necessarily being equipped for self-employment, although some do achieve this.

The actual syllabus of the courses is based on City and Guilds 555 part II and Part III advanced, and students are prepared for this final examination. But this course differs from the general run of 555 courses in that it is of two years duration, full-time; the academic requirements are more stringent; and the students are not already in regular employment in the industry.

Students should be aged 17+ and show evidence of skills in woodwork, design and/or technical drawing. The basic entry requirements are 5 GCE O-levels at Grade C or above and an interview. A limited number of mature students are accepted on a one-year course which is recognised by the Training Services Department for grant purposes. Shropshire students aged 18+ on the Part III course are eligible for County Further Education Awards, and some other Education Authorities are also prepared to support both courses in this way.

Application should be made to: The Principal, Shrewsbury College of Arts and Technology, London Road, Shrewsbury, SY2 6PR. Telephone Shrewsbury 51544.

Short Courses

CoSIRA at present run nine short courses at their Salisbury workshops for practising cabinetmakers and upholsterers who wish to extend their skills. These range from a four-day course in furniture restoration to a two-day course on veneering techniques. They also run many other short courses in furniture making and wood machining which are aimed primarily at trainees, and as these are remarkably flexible, if you reside in a small town or rural area, they can be a great source of help and knowledge.

Contact: CoSIRA, 141 Castle Street, Salisbury, Wilts., SP1 3TP.

West Dean College, a private college in a beautiful setting near West Dean in Sussex, runs many short courses as well as its one-year full-time course on Antique Restoration. The facilities here are excellent, and besides the various aspects of furniture restoration, in which the college has considerable expertise, the courses most relevant to the cabinetmaker cover wood carving, upholstery, cottage or stick furniture making based on traditional craft methods, and musical instrument making.

Contact: West Dean College, West Dean, Chichester, Sussex PO18 0QZ. Tel: 0243 63301

Many individual craftsmen run courses from their own workshops. The Guild of Master Craftsmen's book, *Practical Guide to Woodworking Careers* lists quite a lot, and others are advertised regularly in such magazines as *Crafts*, *Woodworker*, and *Practical Woodworking*, and in America, *Fine Woodworking*.

Evening classes run by local education authorities have frequently been the starting point for many craftsmen. They are never ideal, however, as two-hourly sessions are all too short, although if one is lucky one might obtain some excellent tuition and inspiration. More often, though, you will simply gain the opportunity to use a school workshop with its benches and tools, whilst the hard-pressed tutor, usually the school craft teacher, works hard to keep everyone sweet and busy. Other evening classes in Technical Colleges can prove more worthwhile, but at best these evening sessions should be regarded as an introduction, not a training.

DESIGN COURSES

The Design Council publishes a booklet listing all the design courses available in Britain, and of these the following are those most appropriate to the furniture student. Where details and first hand experience of the individual courses are known these are commented on, but this does not imply that some of the other courses on offer are not equally as relevant or useful.

Degree Course

These are 3-year full-time courses, preceded by a one-year general Foundation course in Art and Design, and lead to a BA Hons degree in 3-Dimensional Design. These CNAA degrees are awarded in Interior Design, Silversmithing, Metalwork, Jewellery, Ceramics and Glass, as well as Furniture Design, but some establishments have better facilities for the furniture student than others, and generally speaking it is preferable to choose a college where furniture is stressed as a separate subject.

Entry requirements are generally standard: applicants must be 18+ on entry, have successfully completed a one-year foundation course, and have attained the following GCE standards: 5 O-levels, or 3 O-levels and 1 A-level, or 2 O-levels and 2 A-levels, or 3 A-levels and evidence that other subjects have been studied. At least three subjects must be academic and at least one must be a subject which provides evidence of the candidate's ability to use English. O-level passes must be grade A, B, or C and a grade 1 pass in CSE will be accepted as an equivalent. However, occasionally, where an applicant shows outstanding artistic promise or possesses some specialised experience or ability, he may be considered for these courses without having undertaken the foundation course or fully satisfying the entrance requirements. All students without exception are interviewed by the college concerned and they should be prepared to show a portfolio of drawings, sketch books, evidence of 3-dimensional work in photographs or slides or small objects as evidence of both design and care in execution.

The following colleges offer furniture as a chief study:

Birmingham Polytechnic, Perry Barr, Birmingham B42 2SU
Kingston Polytechnic, Penrhyn Road, Kingston upon Thames, KT1 2EE.
Leeds Polytechnic, Calverley Street, Leeds, LS1 3HE.
Leicester Polytechnic, PO Box 143, Leicester, LE1 9BH.

Loughborough College of Art & Design, Loughborough, Leicestershire, LE11 3BT.
Trent Polytechnic, Burton Street, Nottingham, NG1 4BU.
Ulster Polytechnic, York Street, Belfast, BT15 1ED.
Buckinghamshire College of Higher Education, Queen Alexandra Rd., High Wycombe, Bucks., HP11 2JZ.
Gwent College of Higher Education, Clarence Place, Newport, Gwent NP5 0UW.

Of these, Buckinghamshire College of Higher Education in fact consists of seven schools, and its School of Art, Design, Furniture and Timber, set as it is in High Wycombe, the traditional home of so much of the furniture and chairmaking industry, has its roots still very much in that industry, and it runs the familiar City and Guilds craft courses as well as those design-based ones. Because of its history and position, it has similarities to its bigger sister, the London College of Furniture, but because it is also a school of art and design, its activities cover a broader spectrum of design work than is available at L.C.F., having departments of ceramics, glass, silversmithing and jewellery as well as interior design and timber technology. It also offers a one- or two-year foundation arts course, an additional advantage, as this course constitutes a very good grounding for furniture studies.

When *Furniture* is chosen as the *Chief Study* on the BA Design Course, the college encourages a creative and experimental approach to design, allowing the students to develop fully their individual styles and interests, whether it be in craft or quantity production. However, due no doubt to the college's close links with industry and its deep rooted craft traditions, the design work achieved here is by and large more realistic and geared to man's needs rather than some students' excesses seen in the more experimental design courses. It has for many years entered students for the Licentiateship of the Society of Designer Craftsmen, and its interest in the needs and aspirations of the designer-maker is stronger than is generally found in many colleges of art and design that offer furniture studies.

Othe colleges which offer a more liberal 3-dimensional design course within which individual students may choose to specialise in furniture, are as follows:

Brighton Polytechnic, Moulsecoomb, Brighton, E. Sussex, BN2 4AT.

Bristol Polytechnic, Clanage Road, Bower Ashton, Bristol, BS3 2JU.

Newcastle upon Tyne Polytechnic, Squires Building, Sandyford Road, Newcastle upon Tyne, NE1 8ST.
3-year BA Hons course in Design/craftsmanship.

Wolverhampton Polytechnic, Castle View, Dudley, Wolverhampton.
BA Hons 3-Dimensional Design in wood, metal and plastics. This course, whilst not specialising in furniture, is sympathetic to the needs of the designer-maker and allows much individual direction by the students. The results are exciting and yet, because of the great emphasis laid on fundamentals like drawing, they retain a strong sense of realism. It is a very good place for the student who may love wood, but who does not necessarily wish to be restricted to cabinetmaking or furniture, but wishes to explore any other creative opportunities for this material.

Middlesex Polytechnic, 114 Chase Side, London, N14 5PN.
BA Hons 3-Dimensional Design in wood, metal, ceramics with glass. The emphasis here is on a quite wide design training with furniture students being expected to study the question of environmental design as well as individual pieces.

Manchester Polytechnic, Grosvenor Building, Cavendish Street, Manchester.
BA Hons 3-Dimensional Design in wood, metal, ceramics with glass. This course is very closely allied to the needs and development of industrial design in a wider context than furniture.

Ravensbourne College of Art & Design, Walden Road, Chislehurst, Kent, BR7 5SN.
BA Hons in Furniture and Related Product Design. For many years the college has entered students for the Licentiateship of the Society of Designer Craftsmen and is sympathetic to aspiring designer-makers.

Post-Graduate Design Training

Royal College of Art, Kensington Gore, London W8
3-year post-graduate course in Furniture Design. Entrants usually possess a BA degree, but exceptions are made for exceptional ability and equivalent experience.

Buckinghamshire College of Higher Education, Queen Alexandra Road, High Wycombe.
a 4-term full-time course in Furniture Design leading to an MA degree.

London College of Furniture, 41 Commercial Road, London E1.
a 1-year post-graduate Diploma in Design of Furniture and equipment for the disabled.

Non-Degree Courses

Chesterfield College of Art and Design, Sheffield Road, Chesterfield, S41 7LL.
a full-time course leading to the Diploma of the Society of Industrial Artists and Designers (SIAD)

London College of Furniture, 41 Commercial Road, London E1.
Furniture Production and Design courses directed at the Diploma of SIAD and the Licentiateship of the Society of Designer Craftsmen.

In 1981 the first ever BA Hons in Crafts was initiated at Crewe and Alsager College of Higher Education, Hassall Road, Alsager, Cheshire, ST7 2HL. It is a combined study that considers the role of the artist/craftsman and examines the creative and integrated uses of wood, metal, ceramics and textiles. Its aim, beyond training versatile artist-craftsmen, is to provide a unique training for future craft and art administrators and gallery directors.

ORGANISATIONS OF ASSISTANCE TO THE CRAFTSMAN/DESIGNER

National Bodies supported by the Government

The Design Council

The Design Council's main aim is to promote good design in everyday industrial products from motor cars to toast racks, and also to encourage a wider appreciation of the importance of design amongst the general public.

Its main vehicle for doing this is the Design Centre in London's Haymarket, which is visited by many thousands weekly, and its famous kite symbol, which manufacturers can display on their work when it has been accepted by the Council as an example of good product design.

Over the years many craftsmen have had their work displayed in the Centre and thus exposed their work to this large public. Anyone is free to submit work for inclusion in their photographic index, but it is generally more relevant to those engaged in batch production.

The Centre, generally, is a must for anyone visiting London. It has a shop selling smaller objects to the public and some craftsmen sell work this way. Its library of design, architectural and craft books and periodicals, all of which are for sale, is excellent, so too is the coffee and snack bar facilities.

The Design Council, 28, The Haymarket, London, SW17 4SU.

The Crafts Council

The role of the Crafts Council is to promote the work and interests of the artist/craftsman in England and Wales and it takes as its criteria for granting support the quality and aesthetic standard of the work the craftsman produces rather than his potential business ability. It is highly selective, and most of its grant aid, which includes help in setting up a workshop, providing training facilities in established workshops, and workshop loan schemes for established craftsmen, is gained through quite stiff competition. This is the one body which is likely to help the person who has neither money nor security provided he has considerable talent. It has two slide indexes of craftsmen's work, one selective, one non-selective, in its very smart and cheerful premises in the centre of London. It is always worth a visit, as there is a continual programme of exhibitions on a whole range of crafts in the adjoining gallery. The coffee bar upstairs is conveniently situated next to the slide index and stand of current magazines and booklets on craft topics, which includes their excellent paperback *Setting up a Workshop*, as well as much other invaluable information.

The Crafts Council, 12, Waterloo Place, Lower Regent Street, London, SW1Y 4AU.

Arts Council and its Regional Arts Associations

The Arts Council of Great Britain does not embrace the crafts, least of all furniture making. However, its affiliated Regional Arts Associations do now have a responsibility for the crafts in their areas and receive money from the Crafts Council for this purpose. They are also funded by the Arts Council and by the Local Authorities, but even so, this is never sufficient to cover all the aspects of art support required, and their budget varies tremendously from region to region in accordance with the amount of sympathy local authorities have for the arts. The crafts come under the Visual Arts section, which also includes painting, sculpture and photography, and the percentage of the annual budget which each Association allots to this area again varies across the country.

It is really a matter of luck whether you reside in an area where the crafts are taken really seriously or in an area where they are regarded as something that has been foisted on them, but it is worth finding out what your local association can provide. The person to contact is either the Crafts Officer or The Visual Arts Officer.

Directory of Regional Arts Associations

GREATER LONDON ARTS ASSOCIATION
Covers: London Boroughs and the City of London
Contact: Lesley Greene, GLAA, 23/25 Tavistock Place, London WC1 telephone 01 388 2211

NORTHERN ARTS
Covers: Cleveland, Co. Durham, Tyne & Wear, Northumberland and Cumbria.
Contact: Barbara Taylor, Crafts Officer, NA. 10 Osborne Terrace, Newcastle onTyne NE2 1NZ.

SOUTH EAST ARTS
Covers: East Sussex, Kent & Surrey (excluding areas within the boundary of Greater London).
Contact: Richard Moore, SEA, 9–10 Crescent Road, Tunbridge Wells, Kent TN1 2LU telephone 0892 41666.

NORTH WEST ARTS

Covers: Lancashire (except W. Lancs), Cheshire, Greater Manchester and the High Peak District of Derbyshire.

Contact: Sally Medlyn, Viual Arts/ Crafts Officer, NWA, 12 Harter Street, Manchester M1 6HY telephone 061 228 3062.

WEST MIDLANDS ARTS

Covers: West Midlands Metropolitan County, Hereford, Worcester, Salop and Warwickshire.

Contact: Lisa Henderson, Fine Art/Craft Officer, WMA, Lloyd's Bank Chambers, Market Street, Stafford ST16 2AP telephone 0785 59231.

EAST MIDLANDS ARTS

Covers: Derbyshire (except High Peak District), Leicestershire, Northamptonshire, Nottinghamshire and Milton Keynes.

Contact: David Manley, Visual Arts Officer, EMA, Mountfields House, Forest Road, Loughborough, Leicestershire telephone 0509 218292.

MERSEYSIDE ARTS

Covers: Merseyside Metropolitan County and West Lancashire.

Contact: Roman Piechocinski, MA, Bluecoat Chambers, School Lane, Liverpool L1 3BX telephone 051 709 0671.

YORKSHIRE ARTS

Covers: North, South, West Yorkshire.

Contact: Simon Roodhouse, Visual Arts Officer, Yorkshire Arts, Glyde House, Glydegate, Bradford, Yorks telephone 0274 723051.

LINCOLNSHIRE & HUMBERSIDE ARTS

Cover: Lincolnshire and Humberside.

Contact: Diana Pain, LHA, St. Hugh's, Newport, Lincoln LN1 3DN telephone 0522 33555.

EASTERN ARTS

Contact: Jane Heath, EA, 8–9 Bridge Street, Cambridge telephone 0223 6707.

SOUTH WEST ARTS

Covers: Avon, Cornwall, Devon, Gloucestershire, Somerset.

South West Arts, Bradninch Place, Gandy Street, Exeter EX4 3LS telephone Exeter (0392) 218188

SOUTHERN ARTS

Covers: Berkshire, Hampshire, Oxfordshire, West Sussex, Wiltshire.

Contact: Marilyn Carr, Visual Arts Officer, SA, 19 Southgate Street, Winchester, Hampshire telephone 0962 550099.

Regional Arts Associations within England (except Greater London Arts) run their own grant schemes and you should contact the association for the area in which you live and work for details. In London the Crafts Council operates grant schemes for individuals and details of these are included in their Grants & Loans leaflet.

Most Regional Arts Associations also run regional indexes of craftspeople/artists within their area and will give help and advice where required.

Council for Small Industries in Rural Areas (CoSIRA)

This body provides the greatest assistance to the greatest number of craft workshops because its schemes are open to all who live in rural areas. It exists to promote small industries in the countryside, which includes small towns with a population of up to 10000. It is far more likely to be impressed by your potential ability to run a successful business than by your abilities as a craftsman, designer or artist. It is also very keen to create employment, so if your plans include employing, training and future expansion you will be welcomed with open arms, particularly as furniture making has always been considered one of the more suitable industries for rural areas.

They are therefore most helpful in obtaining suitable premises or planning approval; in fact in every aspect of starting up and running your business, from finance down to machinery and workshop layout. However, although it is non-selective as far as the aesthetic qualities of your products are concerned, its officers have a keen business sense and they will not be taken in by woolly, half-thought-out proposals; they should be approached in the same business-like way one would adopt in asking a bank manager for a loan.

Like all organisations, it is as good as the people who run it. CoSIRA has many regional offices run by local organisers, some of whom are more energetic and helpful than others, and some more sympathetic to the one-man band and his limited ambitions.

CoSIRA also publishes an excellent booklet *Craft Workshops in the English Countryside* where craftsmen and their services are listed county by county. This can be a useful source of inexpensive advertising.

CoSIRA: Regional Offices

**Head Office: Information Section, CoSIRA, 141 Castle Street, Salisbury.
Tel: (0722) 336255**

NORTH

Barnsley, Council Offices, York Street, Barnsley, South Yorkshire S70 1BD.
Tel: (Barnsley) 0226-86141.

Darlington, Morton Road, Darlington, Co. Durham. DL1 4PT
Tel: (Darlington) 0325-487123.
For Durham, Tyne & Wear, Cleveland.

Howden, 14 Market Place, Howden, Goole, N. Humberside DN14 7BT
Tel: (Howden) 0403-31138.

Morpeth, Northumberland Business Centre, Southgate, Morpeth, NE61 2EH.
Tel: (Morpeth) 0670-58807 or 514343 (via Business Centre).

Penrith, Ullswater Road, Penrith, Cumbria CA11 7EH
Tel: (Penrith) 0768-65752/3.

Preston, 15 Victoria Road, Fulwood, Preston PR2 4PS
Tel: (Preston) 0772-713038.

York, The Lodge, 21 Front Street, Acomb, York YO2 3BW
Tel: (York) 0904-793228.

SOUTH EAST

Bedford, Agriculture House, 55 Goldington Road, Bedford MK40 3LU
Tel: (Bedford) 0234-61381. *For Beds & Herts.*

Braintree, Bees Small Business Centre, Hay Lane, Braintree, Essex CM7 6ST
Tel: (Braintree) 0376-47623.

Guildford, 2 Jenner Road, Guildford, Surrey GU1 3PN
Tel: (Guildford) 0483-38385.

Lewes, Sussex House, 212 High Street, Lewes, Sussex BN7 2NH
Tel: (Lewes) 07916-71399.

Maidstone, 8 Romney Place, Maidstone, Kent ME15 6LE
Tel: (Maidstone) 0622-65222.

Newport, 6–7 Town Lane, Newport, Isle of Wight
Tel: (Newport) 0983-528019.

Wallingford, Wallingford, The Maltings, St. John's Road, Wallingford, Oxon
Tel: (Wallingford) 0491-35523.
For Oxford, Bucks & Berks.

Winchester, Northgate Place, Staple Gardens, Winchester, Hants SO23 8SR
Tel: (Winchester) 0962-54747.

EAST

Bingham, Chancel House, East Street, Bingham, Notts NG13 8DR
Tel: (Bingham) 0949-3922/3.
For Nottingham and Leicester.

Cambridge, 24 Brooklands Avenue, Cambridge CB2 2BU
Tel: (Cambridge) 0223-35405.

Ipswich, 28a High Street, Hadleigh, Ipswich, Suffolk IP7 5AP
Tel: (Ipswich) 0473-827893.

Northampton, Hunsbury Hill Farm, Hunsbury Hill Farm Road, Northampton NN4 9QX.
Tel: (Northampton) 0604-65874.

Norwich, Augustine Steward House, 14 Tombland, Norwich, Norfolk NR3 1HF
Tel: (Norwich) 0603-24498.

Sleaford, Council Offices, Eastgate, Sleaford, Lincs.
Tel: (Sleaford) 0529-303241.

SOUTH WEST

Bristol, 209 Redland Road, Bristol, Avon BS6 6YU
Tel: (Bristol) 0272-733433.

Dorchester, Room 12/13, Wing D, Government Buildings, Prince of Wales Road, Dorchester, Dorset
Tel: (Dorchester) 0305-68558.

Exeter, Matford Lane, Exeter, Devon EX2 4PS
Tel: (Exeter) 0392-52616.

Salisbury, 141 Castle Street, Salisbury, Wilts SP1 3TP
Tel: (Salisbury) 0722-336255.

Taunton, 1 The Crescent, Taunton, Somerset TA1 4EA
Tel: (Taunton) 0823-76905.

Truro, 2nd Floor, Highshore House, New Bridge Street, Truro, Cornwall TR1 1AA
Tel: (Truro) 0872-73531.

WEST

Malvern, 24 Belle Vue Terrace, Malvern, Worcs. WR14 4PZ
Tel: (Malvern) 06845-64506.
For Gloucester, Hereford & Worcester.

Telford, Stickland House, The Lawns, Park Street, Wellington, Telford, Shropshire TF1 3BX
Tel: (Telford) 0952-47161/2/3.
For Cheshire, Staffs & Shropshire.

Warwick, The Abbotsford, 10 Market Place, Warwick CV34 4SL
Tel: (Warwick) 0926-499593.

Wirksworth, Agricola House, Church Street, Wirksworth, Derby DE4 4EY
Tel: (Wirksworth) 062982-4848.

British Craft Centre

First established as The Crafts Centre of Great Britain in 1948 at Hay Hill, off Piccadilly, it is at the present time benefiting from a move to Covent Garden in the mid-sixties. Now, after being in a position of near isolation for so many years, it is at the centre of an exciting development which has transformed this part of London into a very lively pedestrian shopping and browsing area.

Its original aim, way back in the forties, was to provide a shop window in London for the best of British craftwork, and after many years of constant change and uncertainty it now appears to be fulfilling those same aims, by providing a permanent retail outlet and a changing exhibition programme on its two quite spacious floors. It is partly a self-help organisation, a legacy from its origins in the amalgamation of several craft guilds, as its members are all professional craftsmen who pay an annual subscription, keep its shelves stocked with goods on sale or return, and provide its elected Council of Management. The everyday running of the Centre is left to a paid Director and staff, and it attempts to be more than a mere shopwindow by inviting the membership and involvement of regional craft organisations and Friends of the Centre who pay a nominal subscription.

Its policy and thinking on the crafts are quite closely akin to those of the Crafts Council which gives the Centre a tidy subsidy each year and without which it would probably fold. However, its area of support in terms of providing exhibition opportunities and London exposure for craftsmen's work, is much wider than that offered by the Council's own more specialised gallery at Waterloo Place. Recently, in the wake of the regrettable closure of the Prescote Gallery at Banbury, the Crafts Centre has taken an increased interest in furniture and now has the largest permanent display area available to furniture makers.

For further information on membership apply to:
The Secretary, The British Crafts Centre, 43 Earlham Street, Covent Garden, London WC2H 9LD.

British Council

The British Council exists to promote wider knowledge of the UK and the English language abroad and to develop closer cultural relations between the UK and other countries. It organises British exhibitions touring abroad and can help craftspeople make contact overseas.

They are able to offer grants towards travel and other expenses to craftspeople who have been invited to attend overseas conferences as British delegates or who have been invited to exhibit by a foreign gallery.
British Council, 10 Spring Gardens, London SW1A 2BN. Tel: 01 930 8466

Professional Bodies

Society of Industrial Artists and Designers (SIAD)

This is the professional body for designers in Britain and although within its ranks it does have a few designer/craftsmen its main membership is confined to industrial and graphic designers and those working in art and design education for whom it is an additional professional qualification. The majority of its members join as students direct from design training, but membership is open to all who are able to satisfy a selection procedure based on the applicant's design work.

The fact that so few professional designer-makers are members probably has more to do with choice than lack of merit, and perhaps this choice is influenced somewhat by the annual membership fees required. There also appears to be a general reluctance among furniture makers to belong to any organisation, from the SIAD down to the Regional Craft Guilds, and certainly if one belongs to them all the annual outgoings can be quite considerable. Much will depend on the nature of your business and the type of work you propose to do, but membership of SIAD would be most appropriate to those wishing to work in close collaboration with industry, architects and the Design Council.

Society of Designer-Craftsmen

First established in 1888 by William Morris as *The Arts and Crafts Exhibition Society*, it is now a professional body for designer-craftsmen in all media. It attempts to play a similar role for them to that performed by SIAD for the industrial designers, but it is very much the poor relation as its limited financial resources tend to restrict both its activities and its facilities. However, what it lacks in finance and smart headquarters it makes up for in the optimistic enthusiasm of its elected officers.

It holds regular exhibitions for its members; has annual lectures and weekend conferences; issues informative newsletters; in fact it provides all the advantages and comradeship which derive from belonging to a professional body of like-minded people. It needs and deserves wider support from practising furniture makers, for one of its chief values, over and above the personal benefits to be gained from membership, is that it is an independent democratic voice for practising craftsmen in a way that government aided or sponsored organisations can never be.

Like the SIAD, it has three categories of membership: licentiateship, open to students, LSD-C; full membership, MSD-C; and fellowship, FSD-C.

For further particulars apply The Secretary, Society of Designer-Craftsmen, 24 Rivington Street, London EC2A 3DU.

The Guild of Master Craftsmen

This is a national organisation which receives no government support and is more in the nature of an organisation of professional craftsmen bonded together in self-interest. It interprets the word craftsman more literally than other bodies to mean a master of a trade, whether it be a potter or a plasterer, a boat builder or a master baker. It chooses not to make any aesthetic judgements and is interested in supporting fine craftsmanship and the small business enterprises connected with it.

The benefits of membership are similar to those of most professional bodies: it provides advantageous insurance rates, regular newsletters, and it publishes the magazine *Woodworking Crafts*. Its directory of members is widely distributed to architects and interior designers, and its promotion of work and mutual assistance are two of the most helpful features of membership of such an extensive and wide ranging organisation.

Full details of guild membership can be obtained from: The Secretary, The Guild of Master Craftsmen, 170, High Street, Lewes, East Sussex, BN7 1YE.

Regional Craft Guilds and Associations

Unlike most other crafts, there is no professional guild exclusively for furniture makers, but they are readily welcomed by the many regional and county craft guilds. Sadly, many of our leading makers do not see the need to belong to these, perhaps because some, but by no means all, run as they are by volunteers, do present an unprofessional face to the world. This is unfortunate because the more that practising craftsmen do get involved, and not only join but assist in running these organisations, the more useful and relevant they become. Running any society calls for people to give unselfishly of their time for the benefit of others, and sometimes this does not come too easily for the ambitious, self-motivated craftsman, but it can also bring its own rewards. Being a self-employed cabinetmaker in a rural situation can be a lonely existence, and the friendship of other craftsmen and the opportunity to learn and understand about other crafts besides the one we practise can be most stimulating.

CPA-I

Most regional guilds run at least one annual exhibition and some have their own retail outlets. Almost all would welcome an increase in membership, particularly amongst young people at the start of their careers, and would hope that they would continue to belong even when successful in later years, as their experience and work would enrich the guild as a whole.

Current information on addresses and selection procedures can be obtained from local CoSIRA offices and Regional Arts Associations.

Other Organisations

Winston Churchill Memorial Trust

In 1965 thousands of people throughout Britain contributed £3 million as a tribute to Sir Winston Churchill. This has since been used to provide travelling fellowships for around a hundred men and women every year from all walks of life, including a dozen or so who have been connected with furniture making, either within the mainstream of industry or as self-employed craftsmen.

The fellowships are awarded to people displaying some degree of initiative in wishing to pursue some form of study or experience not normally covered by ordinary training and study facilities. Awards are available in around ten different categories each year, which vary annually to cover different interests and professions, and they are open to anyone within those categories regardless of age or qualifications. Applicants simply prepare a study project related to their trade or profession and if selected they are expected to make their own individual arrangements and programme to achieve their objectives within the scope of the grant. Further details can be obtained from:
The Winston Churchill Memorial Trust, 15, Queen's Gate Terrace, London SW7 5PR. Application forms are available from August onwards for completion by the end of October each year.

The Worshipful Company of Furniture Makers

This title is a little misleading in that it conjures up visions of craftsmen beavering away in little craft workshops, whereas it is actually an association of large furniture manufacturers and retailers. It does however offer a number of travel and study scholarships annually to people employed within the furniture industry and to students both in manufacturing and design training.

For further information and application forms apply to: The Clerk, The Worshipful Company of Furniture Makers, Grove Mills, Cranbrook Road, Hawkhurst, Kent, TN18 4AS.

Nine

Techniques

TIMBER

I still do not trust kiln dried timber although I use it from time to time. I also know that with many species and dried under perfect control the results can be fine. Perhaps it is the perfectly controlled conditions that are so often lacking which leads to my mistrust and bad experiences.

I am fortunate in that I live in the country with plenty of space to season and to store timber, and most of my home-grown stock is felled within 10 or 15 miles of where I work, by people known personally to me, and it is sawn under my guidance at a small mill five miles away and delivered by tractor and trailer. This way I have absolute control over what comes out of each log: maybe four boards at 2″ (50mm) thick, three at 1½″ (38mm) then six at 1″ (25mm) and so on, depending on how I see that log developing as it is being sawn, and how I see its future use. Sometimes the log may be turned 90 degrees or so to explore a better grain pattern or to avoid a fault. Some woods, particularly walnut, can vary so much in colour and grain from log to log that it is often desirable if not essential, to get a complete piece of furniture, or maybe even a room scheme, from one log, so we need a variety of thicknesses.

This juggling around at the sawmill end to get the best and most economical use out of each tree is quite time consuming but rewarding and often quite exciting, and, years later, when actually using the timber, I can vividly recall those on-the-spot decisions.

We take time in stacking and spend money on good, accurate pine battens or stickers, not using just any odd bit of wood. Much of it then sits there for four or five years, and often much longer, depending on the thickness, the species, and our particular needs at the time. Thin chestnut or cedar may only take 18 months or so. Also, we can often speed up the process by up-ending thicker timber for a while prior to stacking it, and we always do this with timbers like sycamore which are very prone to batten staining. Or quite often we will bring some boards indoors, particularly in winter time, into the warmth of the shop, and where possible cut them into smaller dimensions to reduce the drying time.

Some woodworkers feel that if they purchase kiln dried timber with a moisture content down to say 10 per cent, then all their problems are over. Unfortunately they are not. Wood

132

Fig. 109

(a) An unlikely log which yielded some spectacular, richly figured walnut.

(b) & (c) A small walnut log being cut up.

(d) This slab of ash, rejected by the sawmills, revealed some interesting grain.

(e) Various logs drying in an open shed but not exposed to midday or afternoon sun.

(f) Yew logs drying slowly, well away from direct sun.

(g) Timber stacked carefully with accurate clean pine battens.

(h) Assistant craftsman Keith Newton roughing out elm boards.

(i) Future jobs conditioning during the winter in the warmth of the roof space.

is like a sponge, and what is far more important in quality cabinetmaking is the humidity conditions under which the work is made. Put that 10 per cent kiln dried timber into a damp workshop in December in Britain and it will soon be up to 20 per cent or more, particularly if one lives on the western coast. Take a piece of furniture made in these conditions and put it into a centrally heated house or office and a few weeks later in January things will start to happen, kiln dried or not. Keeping the damp or humidity out of a workshop in Devon's winters is one of my headaches. Doors and windows should never be left open in damp conditions however mild the day; cold, frosty weather is fine, but damp fogs, mist and rain are quite the reverse.

So, my workshops are well sealed off in winter; insulated and heated night and day seven days a week, with a de-humidifier working whenever the humidity is high. It is expensive, but makes for pleasant working, and I do not get pieces coming back; I can think of nothing more soul destroying than having work returned because something has gone wrong. It is really no use just blaming central heating, for central heating is what we and our furniture have to live with today. We have to design and construct our work accordingly, and to take all sensible precautions before delivery. It is largely because so much of industry cannot cope with this problem that most of our High Street furniture is no longer made of wood.

I also take the precaution of cutting out the timber and planning my work well ahead. During September and October in a dry spell when my timber in stick is at its driest, I cut out all the jobs to keep the shop going until April or May. It is cut out full of the cutting list dimensions, rough machined, and then stored carefully between battens and under weights on the upper floor of my shop, the driest and warmest area, and there it sits doing all the things that timber likes to do, before being brought down, re-machined, and made up three or four months later. I always cut out more than I need – for example, 28 chair legs rather than 24, so that I can reject any that have proved unstable or unsuitable in that time. It is far better, and cheaper in the long run, to waste some timber and to have the problems now, rather than to have them six months later in the client's home 200 miles away.

Also during this winter period, I make sure I have a quantity of boards of various thicknesses and species just sitting inside the warmth of the shop in case of an emergency or a sudden rush job.

All this, I know, is a far cry from the country chairmaker working with some green timber in a corrugated iron shed; but that is a completely different world from fine cabinetmaking in the late twentieth century.

Timber Selection

This area I consider vital for the success of any item of furniture and it is simply a continuation of the all important design process. One can change the whole mood of a piece simply by the choice of grain pattern, let alone anything so drastic as changing the species used. For such is the rich repertoire that timber offers that we are to an extent like the artist with a large palette to hand. A dab of strong, vibrant grain here, framed by straight mild timber, with heavy grain and colour coming into the base rails for balance, or maybe even contrasting timbers or inlays – just a couple of the aesthetic decisions one may make daily when choosing timber for any particular job. Often the care and attention that I give this is not always glaringly apparent to many people. It is a little like the rules of proportion and harmony – when you add all these facets together, the piece should possess a wholeness and a quality that instinctively looks right, without people being fully aware of why, or of the efforts you have put in to achieve it.

But, important as these aesthetic decisions are, they must be matched by equally important structural requirements, concerning movement, structural weaknesses such as knots or sharp grain, the elasticity of some timbers and the brittleness of others. Certain

Fig. 110   End view of ash chest for Kirkham House. Note the careful grain selection both on the end itself and on the end-grain projections.

Fig. 111   Low chunky table/bench made from an exceptional log of dark brown, sometimes almost black, ash. Top and ends constructed of 13 pieces carefully chosen to provide a random yet balanced pattern of grain and colour.

Figs. 112–114   Two wych elm dining tables, the tops of each from single slabs of timber. One has the advantage of a removable top, the other the satisfying corner joint first developed on the low stool. Both are designed to withstand central heating with top and underframing moving in one plane. Note heartside on top surface and straight mild grain for the end sections.

designs may be perfectly feasible in one species but highly dangerous if executed in another. Weight, hardness and softness are three other considerations when deciding which species to use and what dimensions the members will have to be. Nowhere near enough attention in training establishments is paid to the properties of timber, or one would not see the endless mistakes in construction in the work of so many students.

One of the problems here in Britain is that most of our colleges of art and design, where furniture design is taught, are firmly wedded to industrial design and production which rarely uses solid timber except in small dimensions; but many students wish to work in solid wood and do, although all too often their designs are better suited to veneered construction. Solid timber is a marvellous material but it needs to be treated with respect, and you cannot ignore centuries of tradition in working it without carefully considering appropriate alternatives; to do that one needs to understand pretty fully what is going to happen to that expanse of solid timber in six months' time in centrally heated conditions.

ADHESIVES AND SOLID WOOD CONSTRUCTION

I remember in the sixties, whilst undertaking some art school teaching, that I was criticised for still concentrating on joints in construction to my students. I was told that modern super glues and bolts rendered such time-consuming activities as cutting dovetails and tenons to the scrap heap of history. 20 years later I do recognise that bolts and engineering practices are a positive move in furniture construction, particularly in industrialised production. But despite all the advances in adhesives nothing will stop a piece of timber moving if it so wishes and the conditions allow it. With the obvious exceptions of veneering and laminating, which must depend on the strength of the adhesive (but which also have large surface areas and thin materials and no end grain to complicate matters), I try in my construction never to rely solely on glue. Indeed much of my furniture would in fact stand up and survive without any glue at all.

How often in modern industrial furniture does one find edge lipping falling off; plastic laminates lifting, or coming away at the edge? How often, also, in old furniture do we find butt joints in table tops and carcase work coming adrift? As part of my development as a cabinetmaker I have made a very careful study of craftsman-made furniture of the past, in particular of the handsome pieces of the Cotswold School, to discover how they have fared over the past 80 years, particularly in conditions of modern heating. Most have stood up remarkably well, but things do happen; as a consequence I try to avoid them happening in my own work, or I take into account in the design and detailing that I do that some movement will be inevitable over the years. The art is, I believe, in designing for what solid timber might do, and allow for it, rather than trying to fight it.

It is this allowing timber to move rather than restricting it which leads me to favour the PVA type adhesive for the greater part of my work, including veneering. The very thing that it is criticised for, its slight elasticity, is to me an advantage, in addition to its more obvious ones of ease and convenience in use.

There are many excellent workshops and craftsmen who will not touch the stuff – to each his own opinion; but I have used it successfully for the past 18 years for 90 per cent of my work, and it is a proud boast of mine that in all that time only two pieces of furniture have ever come back with any structural defect, and one of these, a set of chairs, was glued up with a urea formaldehyde resin at the request of the client because he had under-floor heating. The back leg joints had cracked at the shoulders and the whole joint was working loose. The joints were cleaned and reglued ten years ago with a PVA glue and no further trouble has emerged.

It is my belief that many resin glues are far too brittle to allow for the natural movement that must occur in such a joint as a mortice and tenon where the grain on the tenon is at 90 degrees to that of the mortice.

Much of my success in terms of avoiding trouble and returned work, is due partly to very careful timber selection and conditioning and partly because I do not take unnecessary risks in construction, using fairly conventional time tested methods. When I do deviate from these it is only after very careful consideration.

Equally important, is that I never take chances with unseen construction, all my mortice and tenon joints fit, not just those that protrude through the surface for the world to see. All my lippings, butt joints and stack laminated tables contain hidden well-fitting cross-ply tongues.

It is this time-consuming hidden construction that no one will ever see, rather than unnecessary fuss on hidden surfaces that someone may just possibly see one day, which is important to me. It is so easy and tempting to leave hidden joints out and rely on glue; for after all the finished piece will look exactly the same, at least for a while, and maybe with luck for ever. But I prefer not to take the risk and it is this interest for the *future life of the furniture or product which is what I believe craftsmanship and integrity is really about.*

Also, on a more practical note, once I have completed and delivered a piece of furniture I never want to see it back in my shop again, the humiliation is too great, to say nothing of the expense.

If one wants to prove that glues like epoxy resins are not God's gift to the woodworker, try laminating a sheet of aluminium or any other rigid material between two layers of any thin, dense hardwood, say ebony or yew. Give it a fair chance by keeping the width down to 4 or 5 ins (100–125mm), then let it live in the extremes of humidity and temperature that your furniture will be expected to stand in most parts of Britain, and you will see what I mean when I say that nothing will stop timber moving and the sooner this lesson is learnt the better. However, this simple fact is at times ignored by not only students, who can be excused, but even by professionals who allow their search for visual appeal to override this fundamental question of movement that, for centuries, even the most uneducated village carpenter understood and took into account. We see solid coopered doors mounted within a fixed carcase which swell and won't close or open when we have a few foggy days; we see solid panels that crack because they were glued at the edges. No village carpenter in his right mind would ever have done that traditionally in Britain where the frame and loose panel construction has been used successfully for centuries.

An extremely interesting and useful book on solid timber construction for the 1980's is Karg's *Modern Cabinetmaking In Solid Wood*. Here we see nothing but solid wood exploited intelligently and progressively, and what a welcome relief much of it is to those acres of flush veneered panels that have filled the world's company boardrooms for so long, and equally, to the mock rusticity of moulded plastic dressed up to look like Jacobean oak that looks set to engulf us.

Fig. 115   *Assistant Allen Malpass gluing up an oak bench.*

Fig. 116   *A section through a bowl table showing hidden construction.*

138

Figs. 117 Three stages of gluing the ebony desk. A PVA based adhesive was used throughout the construction including veneering.

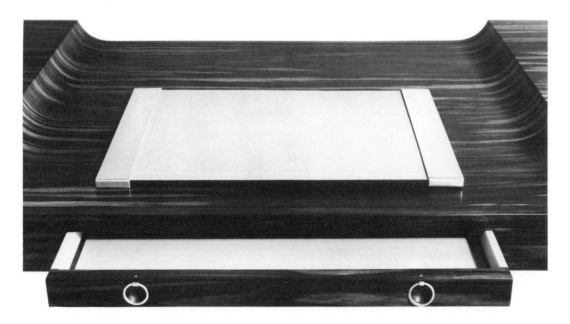

Fig. 118 The veneered surface of the ebony desk. Here a precious and difficult timber is used sparingly in veneered form, but protected by generous solid edge facings.

Figs. 119 & 120   Cherry table showing the decorative possibilities of veneer and laminated construction. This table could not be made using only solid timber.

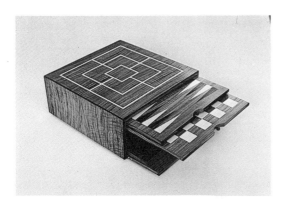

Fig. 121   Veneered games box in walnut, ebony and boxwood, 1984.

VENEERING

One can understand the public's distrust of veneer. The very word conjures up superficiality, no real substance, and visions of covering up inferior materials, and this distrust has been justified by much of the furniture industry's reluctance to protect the vulnerable edges of veneered panels. They have preferred simply to glue on a strip of veneer, which all too readily in use peels off or chips to reveal the chipboard underneath.

What is less excusable, is when professional cabinetmakers join in this condemnation of veneering, using the public's ignorance and mistrust to promote their own solid wood products.

Veneering, as many will be well aware, is an ancient skilled craft practised as far back as the Egyptians although not introduced into Britain until as late as the 17th century. If it is to be done well, it requires more skill and much more time than working in solid timber.

I can fully understand an individual deciding to make furniture only of solid timber, or a client purchasing only solid timber designs. It is his right and choice, but for most of us veneering is just another string to our bow, and one that opens up so many more design opportunities which would not be possible working solely in solid timber.

It is important that veneering should be recognised and appreciated for what it is, an ancient skilled craft, and that when using it we should be exploiting its advantages, telling the world openly what we have done, and not deliberately giving the impression that the object is of solid timber. For used intelligently and honestly, veneering allows us to use timbers and grain in a way that is not practical in the solid form. It can, for example, enable us to build up surface designs and patterns which are impossible by any other means. It can mean stability and lightness in structures; it can provide the designer with unlimited scope for combating the problems of central heating and designing for modern living.

Equally important, using veneer can mean the economical use of rare materials, the supply of which is rapidly becoming exhausted. To build, for example, rows of bookshelves in solid English walnut or Brazilian rosewood, whatever the budget allowed by the client, is something I could never contemplate because it would be such a criminal waste of a rare material. If the client were adamant in his desire for solid timber I would find one that was readily available or offer it veneered with generous solid edge lippings that became a feature of the design.

LAMINATING

This technique is used extensively in mass produced furniture and the building industry to achieve either stability in flat planes or to construct shapes and curves which would not be practical in solid timber. The three main methods employed are cross-ply laminating, single direction laminating and stack laminating.

Cross-ply laminating

This consists of gluing thin layers or veneers of timber at 90 degrees to each other, making the plywood, in fact, of commerce. This can either be pressed flat into boards or into moulds to form curved and shaped chair seats, panels, etc. For the craftsman, this technique can be exploited to build up box lids or small falls and flaps, where the edges become a dominant decorative feature by using layers of different coloured timbers in the construction. I use this method often, using at times just one species of timber, whenever I require maximum stability and restricted movement in all directions, and yet do not want to resort to standard ply and face veneers. However, for any large quantity of laminated shapes, for example, chair seats and backs, it is usually more practical and more economic to get this done to your template by a specialist firm.

Fig. 122   Jewel box in ebony and sycamore, shown here unfinished to illustrate the decorative qualities of cross-ply laminating.

Single direction laminating

Here the grain of the layers (laminations) is all running in the same direction to give maximum strength within the length of any component. This method is used extensively for curved beams and bridge structure in building, and in furniture for chair production and building up complicated curved and shaped rails and underframes of tables.

Again this method can be exploited and used by the craftsman, not only to solve structural problems, but also decoratively, with different coloured timbers being used, as well as solid wood inserts, to give variation on the width and shape of components. (See wine table illustrated on p. 142.) I also use this method primarily to provide a decorative answer to a particular problem; as for example in the wide swirling rim of the cherry-wood circular table, or the half-moon insert on the fan table. Here I only use one species, but with plenty of colour variation within the layers. Edward Barnsley's workshops in particular have made very wide use of this laminating technique over the years to produce serpentine shaped drawer fronts and rails, and many of his beautiful dining table underframes have been built up in this way.

I cut all my laminations on a fine toothed circular saw and aim not to touch them again, partly because my ancient planing and thicknessing machine cannot be trusted with stock much thinner than $^3/_{16}$ths (4.5mm), and partly because I like the gluing qualities of the sawn surface. Barnsley's shop would however achieve great accuracy from the planer, and they successfully produce planed laminations as thin as $^1/_{16}$th inch (1.5mm).

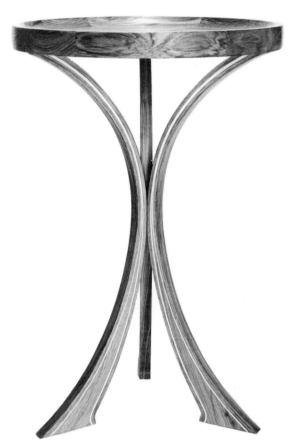

Fig. 123   Walnut wine table with contrasting laminations in sycamore, 1983. Note the solid wood insert giving increased width at the base of the legs.

Fig. 124   Detail of decorative laminating on rosewood fan table.

Fig. 125 & 126   Low-backed chair and stool in ash. The individual pieces were accurately cut on the tilting arbor saw before assembly.

Stack laminating

In both of the other methods we are relying on thin flexible layers of timber or veneers. In this third method we are simply building up a width or sometimes a mass of solid timber, but using smaller dimensions glued and bonded together with the grain running in the same direction.

Normally there are three main aims in using this technique rather than simply using larger sections of timber in the first place:

a) Stability – the smaller the sections, the greater the stability.
b) To build up widths and thicknesses of solid timber which are just not practical or even possible in many species of timber, such as holly or mulberry for example.
c) To use small section timber of any species, often including off-cuts or forest thinnings; an important and praiseworthy consideration in a world becoming ever more denuded of prime mature trees.

This method has been very successfully exploited by Ercol Furniture of High Wycombe, one of the few large firms left in Europe producing solid wood furniture exclusively. In this way they were able to overcome the inherent instability of a cheap natural timber like elm and eliminate the necessity of matching grain and colour; a tiresome problem for industrial production. So, by simply reducing all their timber to a basic small dimension and gluing it

Figs. 127 & 128   Fan tables in solid rosewood. Detail of decorative laminated section. (See previous Fig. 124.)

Fig. 129   Font cover in a combination of light and brown oak, made for
Williton Church, Somerset in 1978. Letter carving by Ronald Parsons.

together again into the various widths required, they were able to produce quality solid wood furniture from a native raw material that no-one except coffin makers really valued until recently. Many other firms and countries now do this, particularly Scandinavian countries, with their abundance of small dimension birch and pine logs that readily convert to more stable, wider material; and Spain, with its abundance of beautiful but unstable olive wood.

What has fascinated me these past few years however, has not been the three aims mentioned, but the possibilities that this technique opens up for design and decoration which are not feasible when working on a large expanse of solid timber or veneer. So much of my work recently has been founded on the simple fact that by working on these individual components before they are glued and assembled I can achieve results easily that would either not be possible at all, or at least not be logical or economical done any other way.

My first attempts were solely to obtain shapes that would be difficult for me to achieve by any other means, such as my curved topped stool in 1976 and my first low backed chapel chair in 1977. In both cases, the individual components are accurately cut on a tilting arbor saw to the angles required, grooved for accurate stopped tongues, and glued together, with the final shape being achieved quite easily on a flexible pad sander. The added bonus I was getting, in such timbers as ash and acacia in particular, was the fascinating pattern of end grain that was displayed, and which I have since gone on to exploit quite extensively in my work; also, I found that the random but carefully balanced strip construction, as on my later bowl tables, had a striking visual effect that had much to commend it over a single slab of timber.

The next stage came when I realised that I could so simply and easily inlay each component by quick passes on a fine circular saw, and that when glued together I could build up endless patterns quite effortlessly. Many of the results were quite garish, and I restricted this technique to a few quite simple weave patterns as on the first rectangular tables and the later fan tables. I could shape as well as inlay the individual pieces, and, with the aid of a jig on the spindle moulder (shaper), the first fluted fan tables emerged, followed by the obvious combination of both fluting and inlaying.

People quite naturally have questioned the usefulness of these fan tables, but, produced in dense hardwoods such as rosewood, satinwood or ebony, they are surprisingly tough, and one can slide a wine glass over the fluted surface without it tilting. But, having said that, their main function is to enhance an entrance hall, a recess, or a corner of a room rather than to do any appreciable hard work. The function of an item of furniture can take many forms, and that of fulfilling an aesthetic need has long been a legitimate one, dating long before Sheraton came along with his extremely delicate but quite useless inlaid tables which were ruined the moment anything was placed on their beautifully patterned top surfaces.

This process of shaping as well as inlaying led to many more related designs; some one-off commissions, like the font cover for Williton Church; desks of solid timber, where the drawer apertures and hollowed top section were removed and accurately shaped before assembly; and bowl tables and laminated bowls, where the bulk of the waste is removed on the bandsaw before assembly, a method which not only saves timber but much carving as well. My two most recent designs which exploit this strip construction are the music and magazine storage unit in cherry, and the nest of tables designed for *Practical Woodworking*, both in the projects section.

It will be obvious to most that laminated construction is not so economically viable for the one-off commission. Laminating invariably involves quite extensive use of machinery, jig and mould making, setting-up time and planing, and whilst many of the designs illustrated here may not be ideal for quantity batch production, they do lend themselves very readily to repeat orders, and to making in small batches of four to six at a time.

DRAWER CONSTRUCTION

I have purposely not dealt with cabinetmaking techniques, holding the view that many books already do this quite adequately, but I have made an exception in the case of drawer construction and fitting, an area that I find is so often a weakness amongst those not fortunate enough to have had professional training. It also relates to the drawer construction required for the dresser project.

The Carcase

However well the drawer itself might be made, if the aperture to receive it is not equally true and well made the drawer will not fit well. So check the drawer apertures and true up if necessary with a shoulder plane, ensuring that the sides are flat and straight, and that the measurements at the rear of the carcase are never smaller than at the front. After checking it should be carefully sanded and wax polished.

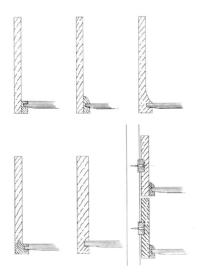

Fig. 130   Alternative methods of fitting drawer bottoms. (Bottom left example is used on the ebony desk shown over page).

Materials

Drawer sides should only ever be made of top quality, mild grained, and preferably quarter sawn timber. What you are looking for is timber that planes easily and cleanly for fitting and can be relied upon to remain straight and be subject to the minimum of movement. At the top of the list I put mild Honduras mahogany, and most of my drawer sides come from old mahogany furniture, much of which is probably 80 or more years old and therefore as stable as it is ever going to be. Running it very close is quartered English oak, and my choice is determined by the timber on the drawer fronts for I always aim for a contrast in colour, so mahogany would normally be used with very light coloured drawer fronts, such as ash or sycamore, whilst oak would be used with walnut and rosewood for example. From time to time I also use other timbers, such as teak, because of its very good wearing properties, cedar, and occasionally mild rippled sycamore for a few special cabinets or desks where the visual quality of the sides is very important, although the interlocking grain can cause problems in drawer fitting.

For drawer bottoms I almost always use solid cedar of Lebanon. I love the smell, and so do my clients, and it keeps the moths and worms away. The exceptions are when I require extremely thin bottoms in order to get the maximum depth inside the drawer, and then I use thin, cedar veneered plywood.

It goes almost without saying that for drawer making the timber must be thoroughly dry, so leave it stacked for weeks if possible in the warmest part of the shop, always allowing the warm air to circulate round each member. Do not simply leave it in a pile unless you are absolutely convinced they are thoroughly dry when you first cut them out. If your shop is not heated or as dry as it might be, bring them into the house as long as you can before construction, stacking them flat between accurate battens and weighting them down.

Construction

If you have the choice, and most cabinetmakers do, never make or fit drawers on damp or humid days, but wait for a dry spell and give yourself a better chance.

Ensure that all your wood is true and flat with one accurate shot edge and of even thickness. I usually like to check mine over with a hand plane before starting, and whilst doing this I carefully mark the grain direction on the sides so that on the completed drawer I can plane easily with the grain from front to back when fitting.

Whether there are 2 or 50, I cut the drawer sides accurately to length on a fine circular saw. I then pair them up into Right and Left for each individual drawer, and mark and number them to coincide with the drawer fronts, backs and apertures. Then, taking each pair individually, I edge shoot them accurately to fit for their entire length.

Step-by-Step Procedure for Normal Dovetailed Drawers

1. Check and true up carcase interior; sand and wax polish.
2. Accurately prepare drawer materials from timber previouly machined and left to dry out thoroughly.
3. Fit tightly drawer back. (Keep at full width)
4. Use the back as a template to mark off size. Then fit drawer front on all 4 edges but with very slight taper so it enters only approximately ¼″ (6mm).
5. Select drawer sides for grain direction. Number to correspond with back and front of each drawer. Plane and then edge shoot to fit snugly for entire length.
6. Groove front and sides for drawer bottoms unless using drawer slips.
7. Bring back of drawer to width and finish top back edge.
8. Gauge off all shoulder lines, remembering to allow the drawer sides to protrude slightly from the front and back.
9. Mark out and cut dovetails on drawer sides, working on the pair together. Complete this process on each drawer to be made.
10. Clean out the waste and accurately scribe to front and back in turn, cutting each row immediately after scribing and marking.
11. Clean out waste on front and back. Test fit to enter only by approximately ⅛″ (3mm).
12. Sand up and wax all interior surfaces.
13. Glue up, using glue sparingly. Do not fit bottom at this stage. Cramps should never be used when gluing dovetailed drawers; simply drive the dovetails down with hammer and hardwood block.
14. Test for winding and square. Then set aside carefully until glue is set.
15. Fit and glue drawer slips if these are to be used. Carefully flush them off on the bottom edge once glue is set.
16. When glue is set, drawer bottoms can be accurately fitted, taking care not to bulge the drawer sides. Do not fix at this stage as they may need to be removed.

Fig. 131   Through dovetails on ebony cabinet.

Fig. 132   Lapped dovetails on ebony desk.

17. Using an accurate, sturdy drawer board well secured to the bench; carefully plane drawer sides to fit. Plane from front to back in the direction of the grain previously selected.

18. If your initial fitting was right, you should only need to carefully plane true and flush to the front and back endgrain, and remove all sharp edges, and the drawer should enter.

    The wax on the carcase will mark the drawer enough to show you the high spots to remove to eventually get that perfect fit. This is not a time to hurry or panic, but for care, patience and intelligence, so that shavings only come off where required.

19. Finally sand the drawer sides and all running edges, then wax.

This procedure would require modifying when using oversail or overhanging drawer fronts. Much skill is required here to get a perfect fit in the conventional cabinetmaking tradition. For this reason, industrially made drawers of this kind are made small and hung on runners fixed to the carcase, and any fitting required is done on the removable runners themselves which fit into recesses in the drawer sides.

Fig. 133   A simple, inexpensive chest of drawers in macrocarpa with drawer sides and handles of dark mahogany, 1974. First example of my use of through dovetailing on drawer fronts as a strong visual element.

Fig. 134   Chest in a combination of white and olive ash. A Korean-inspired design, the chest has a deep blue interior and the laminated handles run through the drawer fronts.

Fig. 135 & 136   Solid walnut chest of 13 drawers. The bold use of the ebony and brass handles which accentuate the pattern of the drawers was a major decision. The rear, with the back of the drawers exposed, as a formal back was dispensed with in this instance.

WOOD FINISHING

This is the final act of worship on a piece of work which might have taken 400 hours or more. The layman, rightly or wrongly, will often not notice the imperfections in construction that bother you, the craftsman – the dovetails that did not quite make it, or the carcase that glued up two degrees out of square; but that same layman will stroke and caress that top surface and will be quick to notice any imperfections in the finish however small.

So, whether we like the situation or not, the quality of the finished surface of a new piece of furniture has become the hallmark of its quality and standard of craftsmanship in the eyes of much of the public. At times this disturbs me, for the surface that some admire and some craftsmen strive to satisfy has little to distinguish it from a piece of plastic laminate; for that is precisely what the surface has become, after the grain has been filled and endless coats of plastic film have been applied and painstakingly rubbed down.

On the other hand, one must admit that many busy people do not want furniture that demands constant attention, that will mark too readily, or generally become a source of worry and concern to them in use.

So what is the answer? Natural wood finishes, such as oil and wax, are very susceptible to marking in their early stages and do require care and attention. Frankly, this dilemma of finding wood finishes that leave the material looking like wood, resist marking, and improve rather than deteriorate with age, has dogged me and often defeated me these past 20 years. The honest truth is that there is no complete answer; no finish which fulfils all the requirements I want of it, that is suitable for all timbers, all forms of construction, and all situations, and this is just one of the reasons why I prefer to work to commission, because I can then explain this dilemma to my prospective client, and together we arrive at a timber and surface treatment that best suits the needs of the situation and their life style. For example, a scrubbed finish to an oak dining table, so favoured by the Cotswold School, is a beautiful surface, immensely practical in use, improving with age and developing a wonderful surface texture which would look fine in many situations, especially in the older farmhouse or cottage-style dwelling, and for most of the time it requires no more than a wipe over with a damp cloth after a meal.

However, it is also virtually colourless, just a bland uniform silvery grey. It has none of the colour variation of say a rosewood veneer or an oiled elm surface, and it is this richness of colour and grain that many of us find attractive about wood, so one has to move in this instance to a finish which heightens and preserves these characteristics.

The actual construction of the piece of furniture should also be considered when choosing the type of finish. Oiled and scrubbed finishes act by a deep penetration of the surface, for one is building up a resistance to marking within the wood itself, and this is clearly incompatible with a veneered surface which may be only a millimetre thick. Here one has no alternative but to protect the vulnerable surface by applying quite heavy coats of a tough resistant lacquer.

Another consideration where solid timber is concerned is that movement is always present. The more natural the surface finish, the more susceptible it is to movement; the more the surface is sealed, the more that movement is restricted. But, when it does occur, it could well crack a very heavily lacquered surface.

Finally, a finish should be chosen that is appropriate to the design and style of the piece of furniture. For instance, recently I saw some pleasant ladderback chairs, something between a Gimson and a Shaker design in English oak and as unpretentious in design as the originals, but completely ruined in my eyes by heavy coats of shiny polyurethane-type lacquer. The technique was faultless, a beautifully smooth and even finish, but the immaculate finish was so inappropriate for such a basic country-style design.

Visitors to my shop, on the whole comment very favourably on the finish we achieve, and

I am beginning to think that after 20 years of experimentation and development we are beginning to get things right, but it still remains one of the most difficult areas of our craft, and one that continually provides headaches and problems.

There are excellent books which go into great depth on the techniques of wood finishing, and these are valuable; but all too few explain why or when a particular finish is preferable to another, and even fewer consider the aesthetic considerations that should be taken into account. These, in the main, are the finishes I now use:-

Waxed Finishes

With the exception of very small items, small stools, boxes and occasionally blanket chests, I do not use wax as a finish for important surfaces for although I visually like the result I can get, it is far too susceptible to marking to be taken seriously as a wood finish in its own right. However, I do use it extensively for most interior surfaces of cabinets, linen chests, all drawers, back panels, etc.

Wax is easy to apply and does not interfere with the natural smell of the timber, which is very important to me with timbers such as cedar, oak and chestnut. In fact, I positively dislike the smell of sprayed plastic finishes one gets when opening a sideboard door produced in a factory. Compare that with the smell of wax and chestnut which I often use on the inside.

When making furniture, I am appealing to all the senses and this whole question of smell is quite important.

Wax also has the great advantage that it can be applied quite accurately (unlike oil or spraying) to just these areas required. So, for example all the interior surfaces of a drawer or cabinet can be waxed and completely polished off before assembly without fouling the dovetails which are simply masked off with a strip of tape. Any spilt glue after assembly will then simply peel off the wax when dry and no awkward corners have to be dealt with later.

Many books recommend using wax after sealing with other finishes. I never do this, for all it ever seems to do is to produce a lot of hard work and a shiny, easily finger-marked surface – two things I try to avoid.

Scrubbed and Washed Finishes

Ten years ago on moving to Devon I needed to make a pine kitchen/dining table quickly for our own use. Today, it is a beautiful golden colour similar to old stripped pine with not a bruise and hardly a scratch to be seen. We do not use a table cloth, only place mats, and we have never treated it at all gently. Yet all that it has received in treatment or finish is a regular wipe over with a damp cloth after use and, once a month perhaps, it is thoroughly washed and scrubbed with hot water and household detergent. The hot water raises any bruises and scratches and the table looks like new, or rather, even better than new, for it has acquired a lovely patina now. There is no comparison with the treacly, bruised and scratched polyurethaned surfaces so often encountered with modern manufactured pine tables.

A scrubbed finish is not restricted to pine, and I have used it for dining and kitchen tables and sideboards in oak, chestnut, pine, cedar and also sycamore. In the case of the latter, if an occasional wash with household bleach is substituted for the detergent, a beautifully white spotless surface will result.

My only regret is that I cannot persuade more of my customers to have this finish. Sometimes they look on it as hard work, which in fact it is not, and sometimes they feel it is only applicable to the kitchen. It seems to me that we must be honest and tell our prospective clients that any lacquered, french polished or sealed surface finish, however well we do it, must by its very nature deteriorate if subject to heavy and continuous use.

Liming Paste

This is again a traditional finish for oak and really consists of rubbing white lime paste into the open grain of oak. It had a great renaissance in the 1930's with Heals and Liberty's selling acres of limed oak bedroom furniture.

It works well with other timbers besides oak and is quite effective when combined with fuming as the contrast of colour is so much greater. Acacia, mulberry and ebonised ash all take it quite well.

It is possible to buy lime paste already mixed in tins ready for use from specialist wood finish suppliers such as Fiddes in Cardiff or Jenkins in Tottenham, London.

Fuming

I have an innate objection to one timber being coloured up to resemble another, so generally speaking I do not use wood stains. I have less objection to coloured dyes, and I use black dye quite frequently, not to imitate ebony, but because I want black; black ash in particular, with its bold open grain, can be most attractive. But what I use most to alter the natural colour of a timber is fuming, which is not in fact a stain or a dye, but a process of exposing the finished object to the fumes of 0.880 ammonia.

Traditionally, this was often done with oak, particularly for church work, where centuries of maturity of colour could be achieved overnight. The result is quite remarkable, especially as it penetrates deeply with none of the disadvantages and patchiness of surface stains and dyes.

I do not confine its use to oak, finding it equally effective on chestnut, acacia and mahogany, and in fact many other woods are affected to a greater or lesser extent, and this can be exploited.

First you have to ensure that the surface is absolutely free from grease and glue. Then erect a polythene covered frame over the piece; this will allow you to monitor the degree of fuming. It must be completely airtight as the fumes are most unpleasant, and shallow dishes of ammonia are put inside. The longer the work is exposed to the fumes, the darker are the tones achieved.

Oil Finishes

Since these work by deep penetration of the timber, they are obviously only suitable for solid timber surfaces.

On domestic woodware, such as salad bowls and cheeseboards, I use a good quality vegetable cooking oil. It is colourless, odourless, harmless and inexpensive, and the user merely continues the same treatment in use.

Where furniture is concerned, almost any solid timber can be oiled, but this type of finish is most successful on hardwoods such as teak, afrormosia, elm, brown oak, walnut and rosewood; all timbers where I want to deepen and enhance the richness of colour, and where the open grain allows deep penetration of the oil. It goes without saying that I never fill a surface to be oiled; surface preparation would be either direct from the cutting tools or glasspapered carefully in the direction of the grain.

All too often I sense an oiled finish is used as a simple way out, with just a quick coat of linseed oil being slapped on a couple of days before delivery and the rest left to the customer. But a true oiled finish is much more than that, and it requires much effort and time, with the surface being built up over many weeks or even months. Naturally I would expect the customer to treat the surface with respect initially and to continue to build it up over a much longer period of time, but the main task of producing a tough, resistant surface should have been done in the shop before delivery.

It is difficult for me to say just how many applications of oil I would make, as so much depends on how absorbent the piece of timber is and how it is going to be used. Dining table tops, for example, and low tables would receive far more time and attention than, say, the vertical surface of a chest of drawers or indeed the under surface of the same table.

Procedure

I mix up a solution of 50 per cent raw linseed oil and 50 per cent white spirit. In the past I used pure turpentine, but beyond the strong smell there appears to be no great merit in this and I find the less expensive, lighter bodied white spirit does a better job of driving the oil deep down into the timber without allowing it to become sticky on the surface. For the same reason I use raw instead of boiled oil; at this stage I do not want a drying oil but one that will stay fluid and penetrate. I apply this solution liberally over a period of several days – in fact, as long as the surface will absorb it I continue to apply it, the whole purpose being not to build up a surface coating but to drive the oil down as deep as possible in order to give non-oily timbers in particular, like elm and oak, the same natural oily resistance to water as teak. On the more absorbent timbers, like some species of elm, I would increase the percentage of oil, and even finish up applying pure oil, but not ever allowing it to build up or dry on the surface.

It is no good being in a hurry if you require the best result. If you need a quick finish, then spray a lacquer. It is not that oiled finishes take up so many hours of actual work, but the work must be carried out over a long period of time.

Having ensured that there is no build-up of surplus oil anywhere, no dribbles on the bottom edges of the table top for example, I would now prefer to leave well alone for a week at least, even several if I have the time and space.

By this time the colour will have matured somewhat and the surface will be quite dry to the touch, often with the grain raised, especially in elm. So I now lightly sand the surface, while it is dry, not whilst it is dripping with oil as some experts favour.

The surface is now ready for the second stage, in which I use neat, raw linseed oil more like a polish, putting it on and then polishing it off again. I might well do this last thing every night for a week, many light applications being preferable to one heavy one. One can cover a whole dining table top in about two minutes, and I must repeat that I would not go to these lengths on anything other than the vulnerable top surfaces and edges.

Finally, when I am convinced that the surface will not absorb any more oil without becoming sticky, I again leave it alone for a week at the very least, and usually for much longer, before moving on to the third stage. In this I use a proprietary Danish oil, which closely resembles Tung oil and dries quite quickly overnight. I use it solely to achieve a degree of top surface protection and sheen. Used to excess, it can build up like a treacly yacht varnish, so do not allow your clients to use it. I use it very sparingly, again, more like a polish, applying thin coats which are polished off before they have time to dry. Again, two minutes every night for four nights is a much better method than applying one heavy coat. I am not aiming to seal the surface, which is what it will eventually do if too much is applied, for the whole point of oiled finishes is that one does not seal the surface but allows the timber to continue to absorb oil or Vaseline over a continuous period of use.

This done, I would again leave it, maybe for a week, until the day before delivery. The top surface will now be quite hard, and if there is a too-heavy build-up of sheen it can be lightly cut back with fine steel wool. Finally, the whole piece can be polished with Vaseline, which I purchase in 7lb tins.

On some timbers, in some situations, for example on padauk and rosewood, I can sometimes omit all the previous processes and simply treat the raw timber with Vaseline, which gives a lovely matt finish but it is not so resistant to marking as the true oiled finish.

You might question the feasibility of following such a lengthy procedure as I have outlined with the kind of delivery dates you are confronted with. All I can say is that after 20 years I have reached the ideal situation in that I will not make anything in a hurry, explaining to prospective clients why I require time and why, if they are patient, they receive a better result. Most of my furniture, and hopefully yours too, is made to last well beyond the lifetime of the client: why put it at risk for the sake of an extra month?

Maintenance

With oiled finishes in particular, the client must know what to do; what to use and when. It is very helpful to give them the appropriate finish in a small bottle or can that will at least see them through the first year. In this respect, it is advisable to suggest finishing materials that are readily and widely available to the general public, for if they have problems in obtaining the one you have specified later, they may simply move over to some widely advertised aerosol finish and ruin your masterpiece. I give them two choices: one, polish with Vaseline, once a month. This is quite hard work even when the Vaseline is heated, but I prefer it because it leaves the surface matt and dull; or, secondly, apply a proprietary Teak Oil, not Danish Oil, very sparingly, like a liquid polish. This is by far the easiest option and is best done last thing at night after having wiped off any marks with a slightly damp cloth. Again, as in the workshop, it is better to do this once a week sparingly rather than saturate it once every three months.

It is worth noting that I very rarely use oil on any interior surfaces and certainly never on drawers or working parts; never where paper or linen is to be stored, as the future seepage of oil in warm surroundings could be a great problem. Likewise, bookcases and shelving are sealed rather than oiled.

Sealed Surfaces

Despite my growing preference for natural finishes that feed the timber such as oil and Vaseline, much of my furniture is either sprayed or hand finished with a tough resistant colourless lacquer and this has many advantages for both me, the maker, and also the client. I use it particularly in the following situations:

a)   On all veneered surfaces where I am aiming to protect a vulnerable surface;
b)   On light coloured timbers like sycamore, white ash, oak or satinwood when I wish to preserve that lightness of colour which oil would soon darken; and
c)   Bedroom and Storage furniture – furniture where the surfaces are not subject to continuous hard and heavy use, where what is required is a pleasant surface that only ever requires a wipe with a clean duster. Here I would also include all those acres of bookshelves I have done over the years.

Clear Lacquered Finishes

The chemists in recent years have given us a wide choice of finishes, far superior in their resistance to marking and fading than our traditional french polish or the pure cellulose used so extensively in industry in the past.

I have tried most of them over the years and have now settled for three as being most suitable for the limited facilities that I have:

a) **Pre-catalysed Matt Melamine** (suitable for spray application only)

This is very easy to spray. As it is a cellulose-based finish it dries rapidly and the fumes are not that unpleasant. I use it for 80 per cent of all spraying. An item of furniture sprayed one day can in an emergency be delivered the next, although for maximum curing of the surface the longer one can leave it the better – preferably more than seven days.

b) **2-Pack Matt Acid-catalyst Melamine** (suitable for both hand and spray application)

A very tough durable finish that tends to darken many timbers more than the pre-catalysed matt melamine. It is extremely unpleasant to use with fumes that cause distress to the user. Because of this, I use it rarely and only on table or sideboard surfaces which are subject to heavy use and drinks.

c) **One-Pack Matt Polyurethane** (suitable for hand application only)

This is very slow drying and with my facilities unsuitable for spray application. It is particularly good on open grained light-coloured timbers like ash, chestnut and oak where I wish to keep as close as possible to the original colour. With this material I am able to achieve a finish with quite a high degree of surface resistance, but with most of the visual characteristics of a natural oil or wax finish. However, it is not as resistant as the 2-pack matt acid-catalyst melamine and does require more care in use.

This has one big advantage over spray finishes in that table tops, and the like, can be resurfaced very easily on site at any time either by the client or yourself.

For maintenance I suggest the client polishes weekly with a light application of teak oil.

Surface Preparation

On examining normal sprayed furniture which is only ten years old or less I have found that the edges of tables, etc., have frequently chipped revealing bare wood which quickly discolours, or, commonly, surfaces of chairs such as arms or top rails have simply worn away, again revealing bare wood. It appeared to me that what was happening was that a very fast drying heavy bodied material was simply forming a film over the surface and not becoming part of the wood itself and that grain fillers and sanding sealers were simply adding to this situation by sealing the surface before the spraying occurred. Therefore over the years I have developed a technique that owes much to that used on my oiled finishes and achieves, initially, a similar result. It is a technique which can be used with all three lacquers whether they are sprayed or not.

I never use grain fillers or sanding sealers except in some veneered work where I am attempting to build up a heavy protective layer on top of the veneer, rather than drawing the finish into the timber as I am with solid material.

All three finishes are first thinned with at least 50 per cent thinners in the case of the melamine lacquers and with white spirit for the polyurethane.

After careful mixing this is fed liberally into the wood as if it were oil. With polyurethane one has plenty of time to brush it well into the grain before wiping off any surplus from the surface with a soft, non-fluffy cloth, always carefully in the direction of the grain.

With the two-pack acid-catalyst melamine, one has less time before the surface will begin to dry, and with the pre-catalysed variety a lesser time still, and when large areas are to be covered it pays to increase the percentage of thinners used.

In the case of surfaces to be sprayed, one application is enough and spraying should commence as soon as the finish is touch dry, for when spraying I believe in building up one harmonious layer rather than spraying several layers at intervals on to bone-hard surfaces.

When hand finishing I leave the surface for 24 hours; very lightly sand if necessary and repeat as before. In most cases I would do this a third time and that is all. But where I require a heavier bodied finish the third coat would be neat polyurethane or acid-catalyst applied extremely carefully and evenly by a good quality brush, checking any runs on edges etc.

Once thoroughly dry it would be carefully cut back with a fine paper if needed and then lightly gone over with 000 grade steel wool, wiped off with a clean dry cloth and then left to mature and harden, preferably over several weeks before delivery.

Spraying

Here I have to accept that I cannot get the result I would like. I do not have the expertise or equipment that is available to large scale industry where a man will spend his lifetime perfecting the technique.

I simply cannot achieve the quality of finish direct from the gun that some of our manufacturers do so effortlessly and I am convinced that the best results with matt and satin finishes do come straight from the gun. However, I only ever achieve this on small objects and most of my pieces have to be rubbed down and worked on after spraying to get a satisfactory smooth surface which in turn destroys some of the visual qualities.

One of the big problems for the small cabinetmaker is whether to go to the expense of setting aside a large area for a polishing and spraying shop which may only get used once a month or so, particularly if one is engaged in one-off work where spraying constitutes a very small part of the overall time spent on any particular piece. It can also be an expensive item in terms of insurance, so I do all my spraying at the weekend when the workshop is empty and I can thoroughly vacuum out one end. It is not entirely satisfactory but at least I do get the continual heat and dryness of the workshop which is an important element in winter finishing, and I can also accommodate any size of table or cabinet with ease. I simply wheel in a portable compressor and a powerful dust collector which takes most of the fumes away but it is obviously primitive in comparison to large scale industrial finishing.

French Polishing

I confess I have never used this finish and cannot see its relevance to new work. If a protective surface is required, then modern lacquers are so much more resistant to damage and fading. It is of course essential, and perfectly justified in restoration work, and I suppose, even reproduction of period pieces if one is logical, but it is an area of which I have no experience, and the subject is a craft in itself and adequately covered in many other books.

Ten

Projects

1 MUSIC STOOL

THIS design uses one of my favourite themes, the hollowed out top surface, and is a simplification of a hinged one completed in yew a few years ago as a commission. The tapered ends give it an elegance and feeling of stability, but render the piece less suitable for batch production than if they were parallel. It can be made in a variety of timbers but preferably ones that are mild and easy to work because of the hollowing of the top surface. I suggest straight grained olive or white ash, chestnut, cherry, or brown oak if a dark timber is required. Visually, this piece works best with one centre joint both on the top and ends, care being taken to balance the grain from that centre line.

Construction

Tapering the ends: With extreme care, much of this can be achieved on the surface planer, but for final accuracy the No. 7 hand plane is used. This tapering, like the hollowing of the top surface, is done after the centre joints are shot, grooved and glued.

Hollowing the top surface: It is advisable to cut the mortises first and temporarily fill them with unglued softwood. The top should then be accurately cut to length and the exact curve marked out on each end from a prepared template. For the actual removal of the waste much will depend on the equipment available. I used a tilting arbor circular saw to come in from each side, and the centre core that was left was largely removed by several shallow passes over the table saws. Next came my latest piece of technology, the curved sole wooden jack plane, followed by a contoured scraper and cork glasspaper block. The final finishing is left until after assembly when the protruding wedged tenons are flushed off.

Finishing: This is an unpretentious piece and a natural oil finish seems most appropriate, but do allow plenty of time for the oil to dry from the surface before using the stool.

Fig. 137   Music stool perspective.

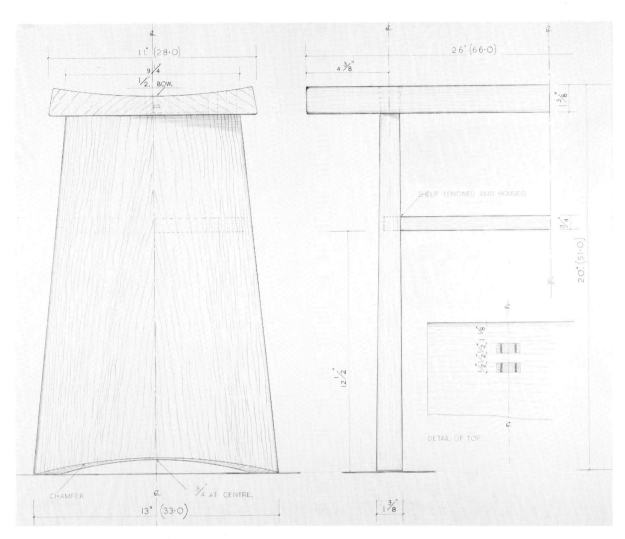

Fig. 138   Working drawing.

material and cutting list		music stool			
		FINISHED SIZES			
No.	**REQUIRED FOR**	**L.**	**W.**	**TH.**	**NOTES**
2	Top	26″	5½″	1⅜″	
		660mm	140mm	35mm	
4	Ends	20″	6½″	1⅜″	Top, ends & shelf to be jointed
		510mm	165mm	35mm	at centre
2	Shelf	17¾″	4¾″	¾″	
		450mm	120mm	18mm	

2 NEST OF TABLES

This design first appeared in *Practical Woodworking* magazine in February 1984 to a brief that required the use of two homegrown timbers and a mail order supply of the materials. My solution was to design with one basic component, strips of timber prepared to 50mm × 18mm.

I found that the design works equally well using one timber only, but if contrasting timbers are preferred it appears more successful to me when the contrast is not too extreme; for example, a combination of white and brown oak, white and olive ash, ash and brown oak, rather than sycamore with mahogany or rosewood.

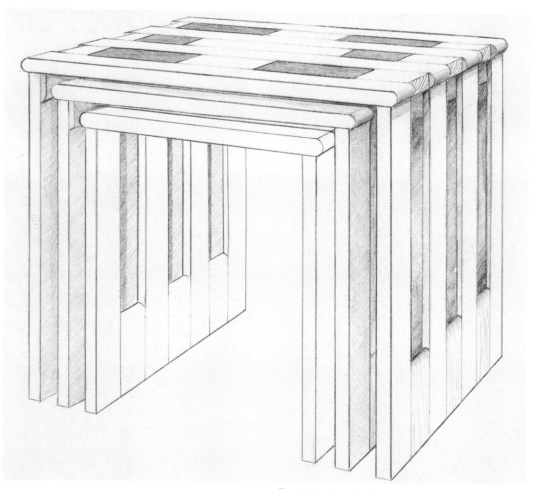

Fig. 139   Nest of tables perspective.

163

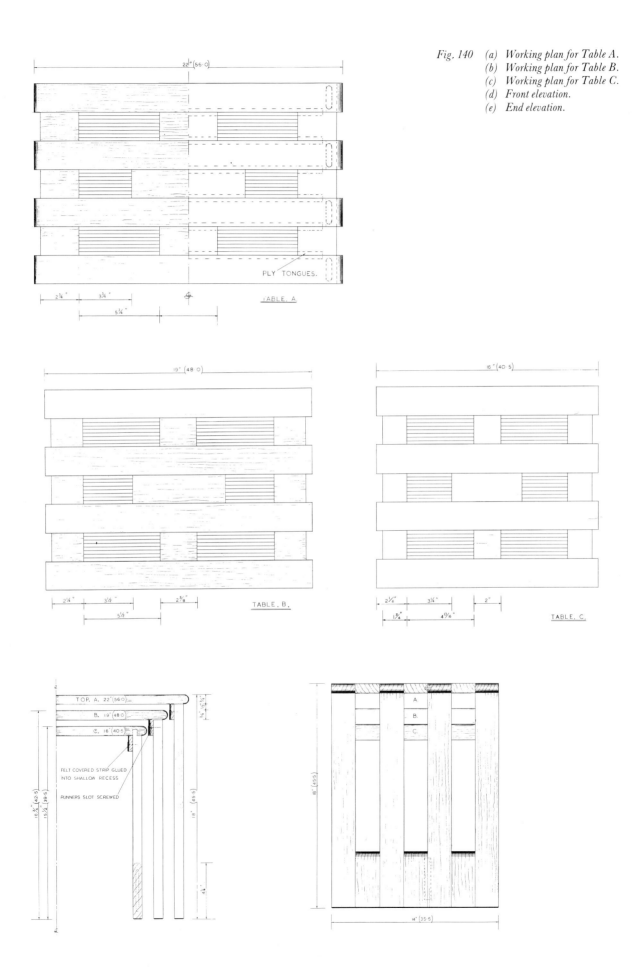

Fig. 140 (a) *Working plan for Table A.*
(b) *Working plan for Table B.*
(c) *Working plan for Table C.*
(d) *Front elevation.*
(e) *End elevation.*

22" (56·0)

PLY TONGUES.

2¼"   3¼"

5¼"

TABLE. A.

19" (48·0)

2¼"   3½"   2⅝"

5½"

TABLE. B.

16" (40·5)

2¼"   3¼"   2"

1¾"   4¹³⁄₁₆"

TABLE. C.

TOP. A. 22" (56·0)

B. 19" (48·0)

C. 16" (40·5)

FELT COVERED STRIP GLUED
INTO SHALLOW RECESS

RUNNERS SLOT SCREWED

16 ¾" (42·5)

15½" (39·5)

18" (45·5)

4"

A

B.

C.

18" (45·5)

14" (35·5)

material cutting list		nest of tables			
No.	**REQUIRED FOR**	**L.**	**FINISHED SIZES** **W.**	**TH.**	**NOTES**
	Tops				
4	Table A	22″ 560mm	2″ 50mm	¾″ 18mm	Straight grained mild timber
4	Table B	19″ 480mm	″ ″	″ ″	″
4	Table C	16″ 405mm	″ ″	″ ″	″
1	Table A	14″ 355mm	″ ″	″ ″	To be cut into 3 lengths as drawings
2	Table A	10″ 254mm	″ ″	″ ″	″
1	Table B	11½″ 292mm	″ ″	″ ″	″
2	Table B	7½″ 190mm	″ ″	″ ″	″
1	Table C	9″ 228″	″ ″	″ ″	″
2	Table C	6″ 152mm	″ ″	″ ″	″
4	Table A panels	5¾″ 146mm	″ ″	″ ″	Contrasting panels
2	Table A panels	3¾″ 95mm	″ ″	″ ″	″
4	Table B panels	5½″ 140mm	2″ 50mm	¾″ 18mm	Contrasting panels
2	Table B panels	3½″ 90mm	″ ″	″ ″	″
4	Table C panels	4¾″ 120mm	″ ″	″ ″	″
2	Table C panels	3¼″ 82mm	″ ″	″ ″	″
					Total length allowing for waste = 7½ft. or 2.3 metres approx.
	End frames				
8	Legs Table A	17¾″ 450″	″ ″	″ ″	Straight grained mild timber
8	Legs Table B	16½″ 420mm	″ ″	″ ″	″
8	Legs Table C	15¼″ 387mm	″ ″.	″ ″	″
18	End spacers	4¼″ 108mm	″ ″	″ ″	″
6	Guide rails	13¾″ 350mm	1¼″ 32mm	¼″ 6mm	Same timber as contrasting panels.
	Plywood tongues	6mm plywood cut into 12mm strips; approx. total amount required = 30ft or 9 metres.				

3 MAGAZINE STORAGE/TABLE UNIT

Like the nest of tables, this again exploits the use of just one strip component simply cut to different lengths. It can be either free standing on feet, or more readily moveable on mini castors. It is made with the minimum of equipment and the design lends itself to jigging up for large or small batch production.

Construction: The top and bottom are produced first, with hidden tongues for location as much as for strength; all the mortises, slots and tenons follow. The through jointing illustrated on the top, bottom and ends is not vital and adds considerable time, and consequently expense, to the end cost. It is, however, important not only for the extra strength it gives, but also as a visual confirmation of the interlocking nature of this strip component design.

Materials: With such small dimension stock, this design is ideal for using up the many off-cuts and narrow strips that tend to litter a workshop, and the variations in colour and grain from doing so can be a positive advantage, particularly on the top and bottom, in order to emphasise and exploit the strip construction. The timber needs to be mild and stable, and the design works best in rich dark hardwoods such as walnut, teak, padauk, mahogany or any of the exotics. Yew and cherry, if carefully chosen for stability, also look good but are time consuming to work; coarse, open grained timbers such as elm, or light coloured ones such as ash and the pines, are less suitable.

Fig. 141 Magazine storage/table unit perspective.

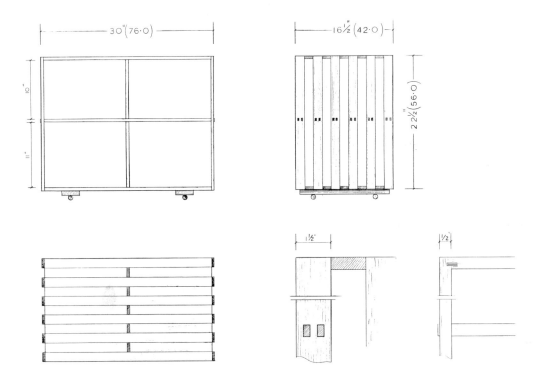

Fig. 142   Working drawing.

material cutting list		magazine storage/table unit			
		FINISHED SIZES			
No.	**REQUIRED FOR**	**L.**	**W.**	**TH.**	**NOTES**
28	Horizontal members	30″	1½″	½″	All straight grained
		762mm	38mm	12mm	
17	Vertical members	22½″	1½″	½″	
		570mm	38mm	12mm	
2	Feet	16″	1½″	¾″	
		46mm	38mm	18mm	

4 DRESSER/BOOKSHELF UNIT

This is a very functional piece of furniture which is equally at home in the living room with books and open display shelves, or in the kitchen with storage jars and china. It is simple and inexpensive to construct, and for those with the skill and the time to spare, the machine joints and dowelling can be replaced by dovetailing and wedged mortise and tenons. This is another example of how one basic design can be produced adequately and well but to different budgets and requirements. The piece also lends itself to being built in or otherwise adapted to fill recesses either side of a fireplace. In this case, care should be taken to match the height of the base rail with the skirting boards, and the proportions should be watched carefully, for alterations may well become necessary to the overall height and the cupboard top as a result.

Materials: It is designed for solid timber, with chestnut, ash, macrocarpa, Scots pine and larch being particularly suitable where economy is important. Brown oak might be considered for a living room situation where a darker timber is required, or carefully selected Dutch or wych elm.

Finishing: Both oiled and spray finishes are suitable for this design, but if the piece is to be used for book storage a sprayed finish is preferable.

Fig. 143   Dresser/bookshelf unit perspective.

168

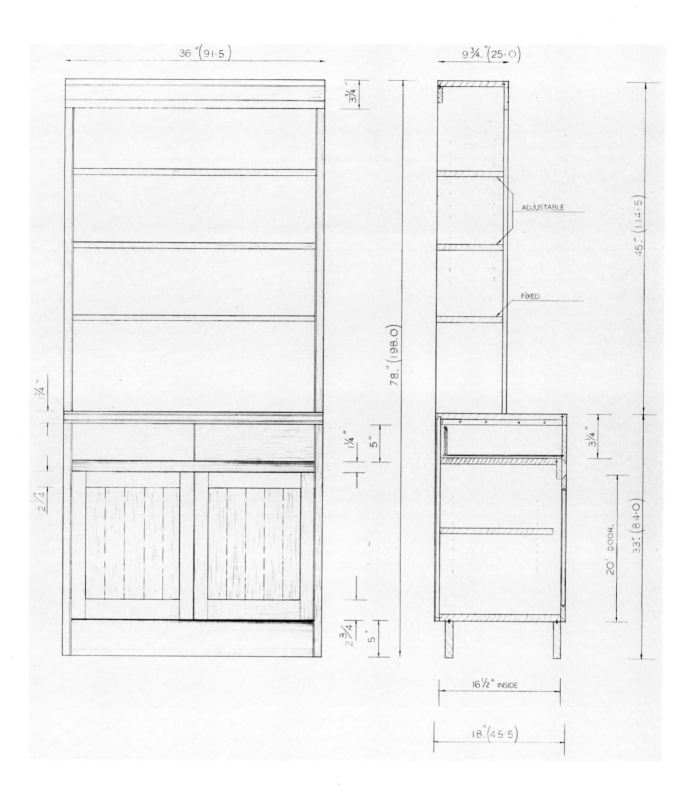

36 "(91·5)

9¾. "(25·0)

¾"

78."(198.0)

1¼"
5"

¾"
¼"

2¼

2¾
5"

ADJUSTABLE

FIXED

45". (114·5)

¾"

20' DOOR.

33." (84·0)

16½" INSIDE

18."(45·5)

169

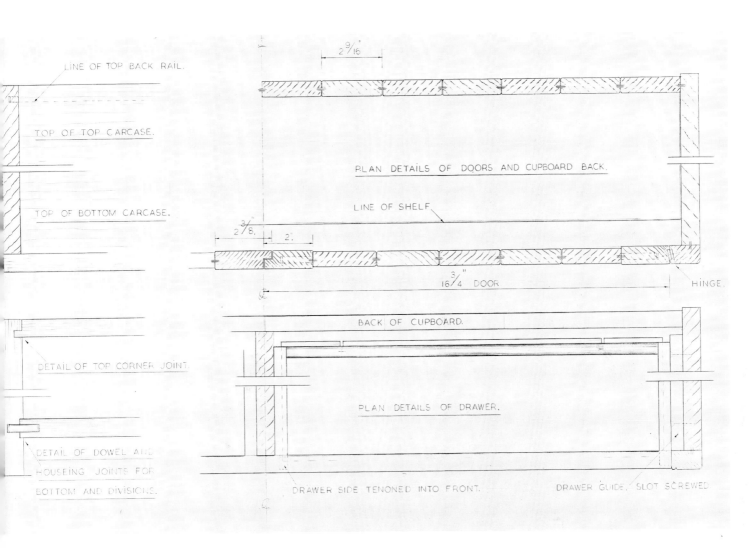

LINE OF TOP BACK RAIL.

TOP OF TOP CARCASE.

TOP OF BOTTOM CARCASE.

DETAIL OF TOP CORNER JOINT.

DETAIL OF DOWEL AND
HOUSEING JOINTS FOR
BOTTOM AND DIVISIONS.

2 9/16"

PLAN DETAILS OF DOORS AND CUPBOARD BACK.

LINE OF SHELF.

3/8" 2'.

16 3/4" DOOR   HINGE.

BACK OF CUPBOARD.

PLAN DETAILS OF DRAWER.

DRAWER SIDE TENONED INTO FRONT.   DRAWER GUIDE. SLOT SCREWED.

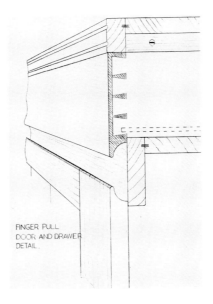

FINGER PULL
DOOR AND DRAWER
DETAIL.

Fig. 144 (a) Elevation.
Fig. 144 (b) Plan.
Fig. 144 (c) Detail perspective.

material and cutting list		dresser/bookshelf unit			
		FINISHED SIZES			
No.	**REQUIRED FOR**	**L.**	**W.**	**TH.**	**NOTES**
2	Ends	78″ 1980mm	9″ 228mm	¾″ 18mm	
2	Ends	33″ 838mm	8¼″ 210mm	″	
1	Top (top carcase)	35½″ 900mm	9″ 228mm	″	
1	Fixed shelf (top carcase)	″ ″	″ ″	″ ″	
1	Top (bottom carcase)	″ ″	17¼″ 440mm	″ ″	
1	Bottom	″ ″	16½″ 420mm	″ ″	If using through dovetailing and mortise & tenons, increase fixed horizontal members to 36″ or 915mm
1	Horizontal division (bottom carcase)	″ ″	15¾″ 400mm	″ ″	
2	Base rails	″ ″	5″ 127mm	″ ″	
1	Drawer rail (top carcase)	″ ″	3¼″ 83mm	″ ″	
1	Back rail (top carcase)	″ ″	″ ″	″ ″	
1	Cornice rail	36″ 915mm	3¾″ 95mm	″ ″	
1	Top front rail (bottom carcase)	36″ 915mm	1¾″ 45mm	″ ″	
2	Adjustable shelves (top carcase)	34″ 864mm	9″ 228mm	¾″ 18mm	
1	Adjustable shelf (bottom carcase)	″ ″	15½″ 394mm	″ ″	
2	Upright face pieces (top carcase)	41½″ 1054mm	1¼″ 32mm	″ ″	
2	Upright face pieces (bottom carcase)	31½″ 800mm	″ ″	″ ″	
1	Upright drawer division	6″ 153mm	16½″ 420mm	″ ″	
	Drawers				
1	Pair of fronts	33½″ 850mm	5″ 127mm	″ ″	Cut in one length
4	Sides	16½″ 420mm	4″ 102mm	½″ 12mm	
2	Backs	″ ″	3½″ 90mm	″ ″	
2	Bottoms	16″ 405mm	16¼″ 413mm	⅜″ 10mm	
4	Drawer guides	″ ″	1″ 25mm	½″ 12mm	
	Doors				
3	Stiles	20″ 508mm	2″ 50mm	¾″ 18mm	
1	Centre stile	″ ″	2½″ 63mm	″ ″	
1	Pair of top rails	32½″ 812mm	2¼″ 57mm	″ ″	Cut in one length
1	Pair of bottom rails	″ ″	2¾″ 70mm	″ ″	Cut in one length
10	Panel strips	16″ 405mm	2⁹⁄₁₆″ 65mm	⅝″ 15mm	Set in centre of door frames
	Backs				
14	Panel strips	27½″ 698mm	2⁹⁄₁₆″ 65mm	⅝″ 15mm	

5 DINING TABLE

This design has many advantages over both round and oval tops, since both of these require a lot of space around them and look odd if they are pushed up against a wall. In this design, the table can be pulled out for entertaining and can comfortably seat six people, but for most of its life it rests quite happily against a wall to be used by two to four people. It is a solid, chunky design with good stability, which is always a problem with centre pedestal tables, particularly when they are large enough to accommodate six diners.

Materials: The top is supported by only four rails and requires timber that is well seasoned and relatively stable. To ensure this it is advisable to join together several narrower boards, preferably quarter-sawn, with well-fitting plywood tongues. It is quite extravagant in its use of timber, and I therefore suggest inexpensive home-grown hardwoods, such as wych elm, Dutch elm, ash, chestnut, sycamore or, a little more expensive, light or brown oak.

Construction: *Centre column:* This 5″ (127mm) octagon is probably best made by gluing three pieces together ensuring that the joints, which should be tongued as well as glued, come on the apex of the octagon. (As drawing)

Fixing the Top: The top needs to be removable, and is screwed through from the extremities of the four rails, plus a series of twin glued buttons. (diag. 2) It is vital that the top is allowed to move by the use of slot screws across its width, the top being locked at the centre.

All the joints for the feet and top rails are standard and should be well fitting, with the base of the table being further strengthened by the inclusion of a 12″ × 1″ × ¼″ (305 × 25 × 6mm) thick metal cross inserted flush by router and screwed into place. This cross can quite easily be made up by the local blacksmith or metalworker.

Finishing: This is a no-nonsense, practical design utilizing all the advantages of inexpensive solid timber and the surface finish should reflect this. I suggest a scrubbed and washed top surface for sycamore, chestnut and light oak, and an oiled surface for elm, brown oak and olive ash. The underframe should be lightly sealed for the scrubbed surfaces and oiled for the others.

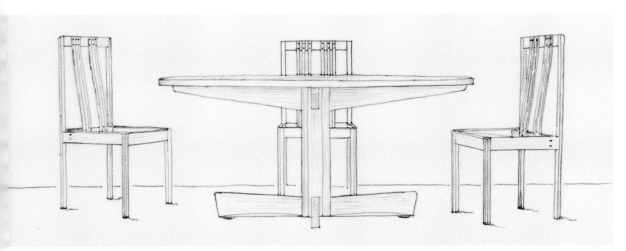

Fig. 145   Dining table perspective.

172

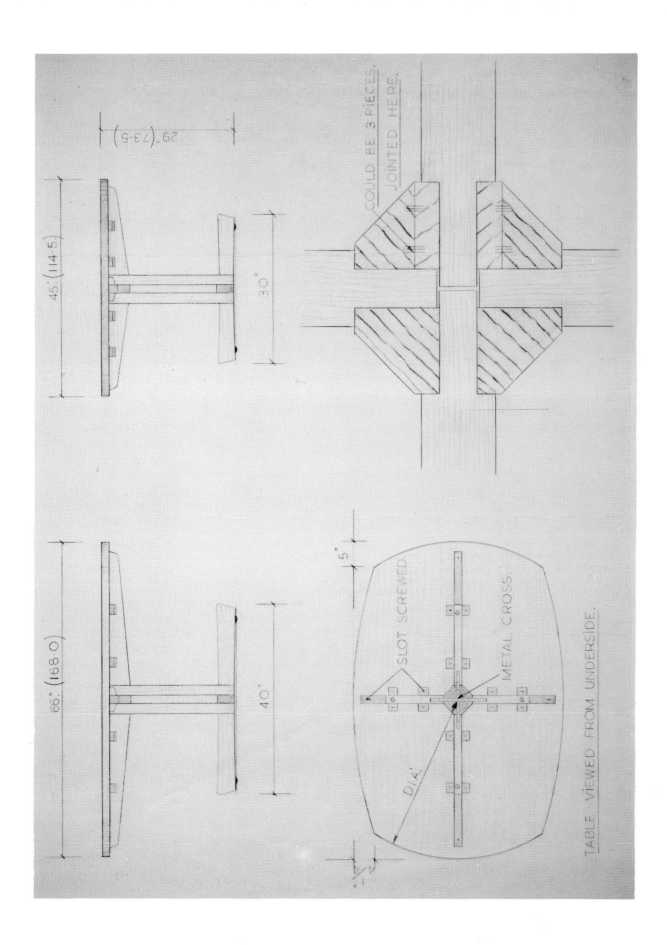

29" (73·5)

45" (114·5)

30"

COULD BE 3 PIECES. JOINTED HERE.

66" (168·0)

40"

5"

SLOT SCREWED.

METAL CROSS.

DIA.

TABLE VIEWED FROM UNDERSIDE.

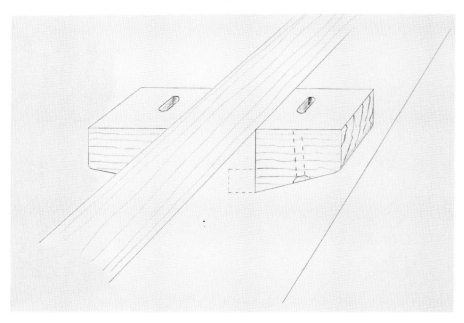

Fig. 146   Plan & elevation. (p. 172) and button detail.

material and cutting list		dining table			
		FINISHED SIZES			
No.	**REQUIRED FOR**	**L.**	**W.**	**TH.**	**NOTES**
1	Top	66″ 1675mm	45″ 1145mm	1¾″ 45mm	Mark out from template with appropriate joints
either					
1	Centre column finished octagon)	27″ 685mm	5½″ 140mm	5½″ 140mm	
Or					
1	Centre core	27″ 685mm	5½″ 140mm	2⅜″ 60mm	Made from 3 pieces tongued & glued together
&					
2	Outer faces	27″ 685mm	5½″ 140mm	1⁹/₁₆″ 40mm	
2	Top rails	31″ 787mm	5″ 127mm	2″ 50mm	Tapered as template
2	Top rails	21″ 535mm	5″ 127mm	2″ 50mm	For rails and feet, keep as close to 2″ or 50mm as the board will allow
2	Feet	20″ 510mm	5″ 127mm	2″ 50mm	
2	Feet	15″ 380mm	5″ 127mm	2″ 50mm	

6 DINING CHAIR

This chair with octagonal legs is designed to go with the dining table but would happily sit with many refectory style tables as well. It is very comfortable with or without a padded cushion, giving positive support to the back.

Materials:
The back slats and seat should be of straight grained white ash cut from the outside edges of the board and if possible from young trees. The back slats need to be cut oversize for width and trued up later after any subsequent movement. The rest of the chair will be in the same timber as the dining table, and the design is most successful when there is a strong visual contrast between the bold white ash slats and the timber of the legs, etc.

The long back legs are unsupported for much of their length, so you should be looking for stable timber here, or cutting oversize and truing up later.

Construction:
This design is ideal for jigging up for quantity production and is similar to one of my standard designs that has been made in considerable numbers. All joints are at 90 degrees and the back slats are simply held in tension to the shape required. A considerable amount of thought went into determining the position of the top and bottom rails that hold them as this is critical for comfort.

The grooves in the side rails for the seat slats are worked by router from a double-sided jig. This is essential even if only four chairs, i.e. eight side rails, are being made. All the joints are standard mortise and tenons from one setting of the mortiser and circular saw, with the exception of the wedged ones on the side rails. Similarly, all the holes in the back rails to hold the pins and back slats are standard and pre-bored using a jig before assembly. (see assembly of back slats.)

Assembly and Gluing:
The side frames have to be glued first ensuring that they are square and out of wind. Once finally set, the seat slats and whole chair can be assembled but not the back slats, which are best left until all the other parts of the chair are complete.

Fixing Upright Slats:
All the holes for the ebony (or other hardwood) pins will have been accurately pre-bored to a jig on the pillar drill on both top and bottom rails ensuring perfect location. Next experiment with one slat and G cramps to achieve the exact length required and the degree of curve. Once having determined this, all the remaining slats can be cross cut to length and accurately pre-bored for the pins and bottom screw. All the pins are cut to accurate length, thus ensuring that there will be no necessity for flushing off afterwards except for a mere scrape. Be careful and sparing with the glue and do not attempt more than two slats at a time on each chair, clamping back carefully with G cramps and leather covered blocks. All that should now remain is to remove any surplus glue and tidy up the slats at the pin positions.

Finishing:
Chairs, in my opinion, because of the complexity of surfaces, lend themselves to only two finishing techniques: either a brushed-on oiled finish or a sprayed lacquer, and the choice here will be determined by the finish used on the dining table.

Fig. 147   Dining chair perspective.

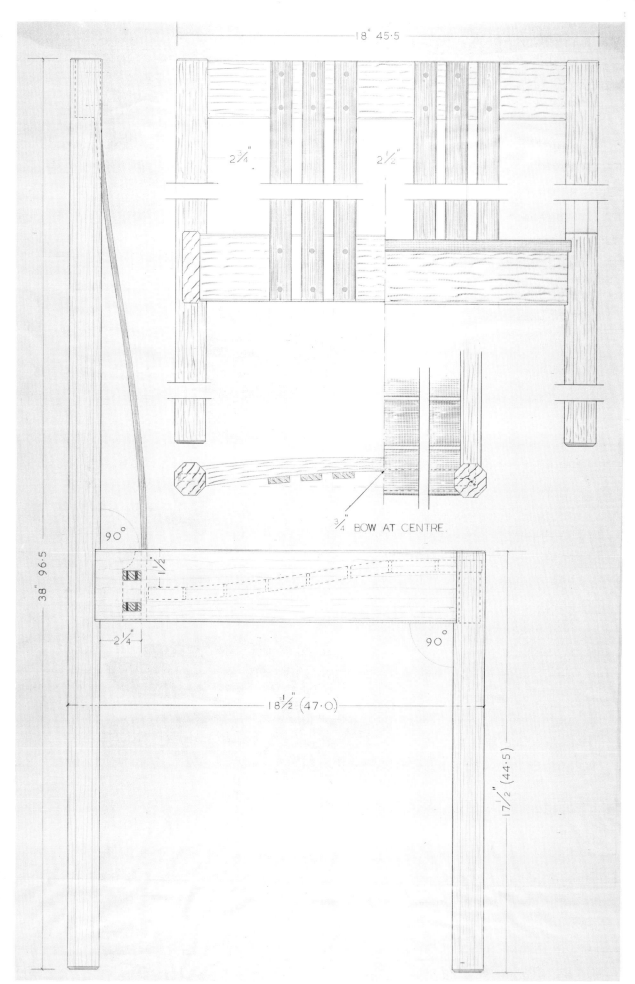

Fig. 148 Elevation & plan.

materials and cutting list   **dining chair**

No.	REQUIRED FOR	FINISHED SIZES			NOTES
		L.	W.	TH.	
2	Back legs	38″	1⅜″	1⅜″	
		965mm	35mm	35mm	
2	Front legs	17½″	″	″	
		445mm	″	″	
2	Side rails	17½″	3″	¾″	
		445mm	75mm	18mm	
1	Front rail	″	″	″	
		″	″	″	
1	Back rail	″	″	″	
		″	″	″	
1	Curved top rail	″	2½″	1¼″	Cut from template
		″	63mm	32mm	
6	Upright slats	23¼″	¹⁵⁄₁₆″	¼″	
		565mm	24mm	6mm	
6	Seat slats	16¾″	1⅝″	½″	
		425mm	42mm	12mm	
2	Seat slats	″	2″	″	
		″	50mm	″	

7 STUDENT'S DESK and 8 LOW BACKED CHAIR

7 STUDENT'S DESK

This piece has its origins in the traditional school desk and is an attempt to arrive at a purely functional design with no fuss and undue expense but which is, nevertheless, still a quality item of furniture with the hallmarks of the craftsman much in evidence. Its design also relates closely to the low-backed chair, a design that had already proved itself in other uses and which lent itself naturally to this new role of partnering the desk.

Construction: I resisted the temptation to include drawers, trays or partitions in favour of keeping the maximum area of uninterrupted space inside. The routered out recesses and compartments on the desk top accommodate correspondence, notepaper and envelopes, pens and pencils, when the writing surface is actually in use. The inside surface of the hinged flap could have a mirror or a pinboard, or indeed both, attached for occasional use as a dressing table.

Despite the apparent simplicity, it is not the easiest of pieces to construct and it is time-consuming as a one-off. Also, I do not see this piece as a design to be repeated in large numbers in batch production, but rather as a design to be made up in sets of 2, 3, or 4 as and when the need arises, either as pieces made up 'on spec' or as orders.

8 LOW BACKED CHAIR

The general concept of this design came in 1976 when I was designing inexpensive furniture for the Swiss Catholic Mission in Westminster, London. Later, in 1983, I came back to this basic piece and modified it, with the benefit of hindsight and an increased budget, for Penarth Church near Cardiff. The result here is a more comfortable chair, less severe in its appearance, lending itself to this new situation. The design has been warmly welcomed by members of the orthopaedic profession who see it as a positive aid to the reduction of back problems.

It is quite an expensive chair to produce as a one-off and like its original in 1976 it is ideal where quantities are required, and machinery and setting-up time can be fully utilised. But having said this, as no upholstering is involved, even as a one-off it compares very favourably in the time required in its making with a one-off traditional desk chair.

Construction: An essential item of equipment for this design is a tilting arbor circular saw fitted with a blade that will give a fine accurate cut which requires no further attention once off the machine. An accurate, full-size setting-out of the side elevation should be made from which all the angles of each segment and joint can be plotted. Each segment is numbered, grooved and finally glued together; but at this stage omit the short back, which needs to be glued up, shaped and finished before it is finally screwed and glued to the finished seat and chair.

Materials: It is essential that the timber should be thoroughly dry, for you do not want undue movement across the width of the seat owing to the restriction of the base rail. People have in the past questioned this construction, but in practice it has produced no problems whatsoever, and I have a chair from that original batch of 50 that has now withstood three exceptionally hot summers and numerous Devon monsoon winters. However, I do ensure that my timber is well seasoned and that the bottom mortise and tenon joints are pinned and glued with a PVA resin. I have successfully produced this design in ash, elm, English oak and yew; sycamore is another possibility, all in fact tough, robust timbers which are not likely to split easily.

Fig. 149   Student's desk and low backed chair.

180

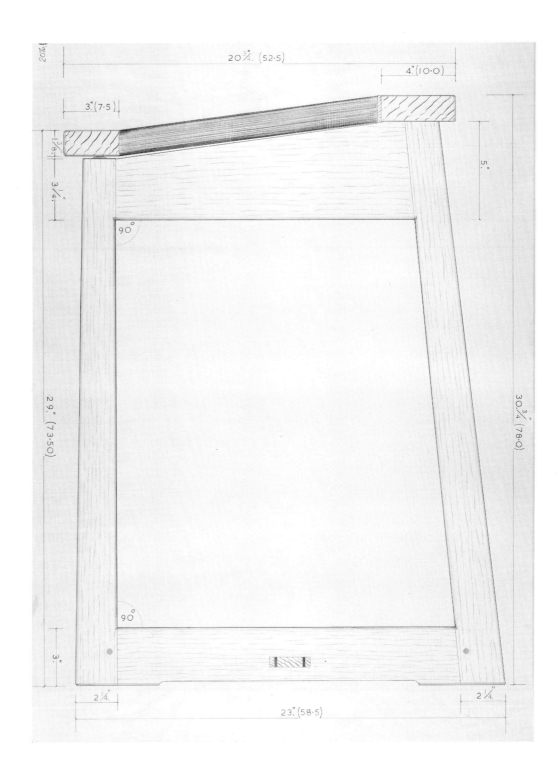

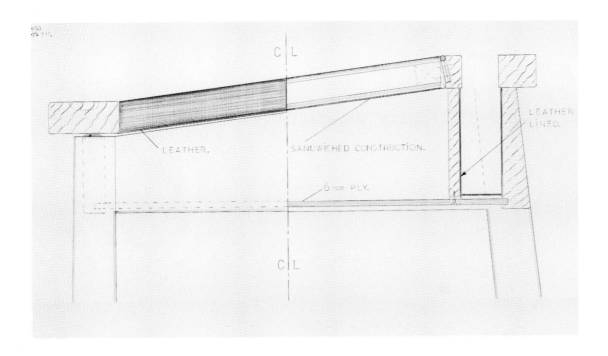

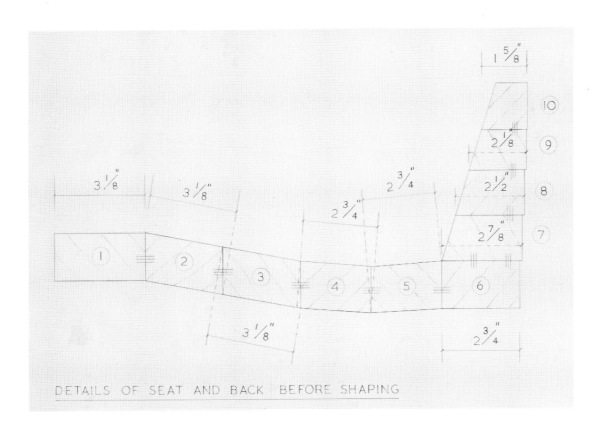

DETAILS OF SEAT AND BACK BEFORE SHAPING

Fig. 150   (a) Desk elevation.
              (b) Desk detail.
              (c) Chair detail.

182

(d) Chair elevation.
(e) Desk plan.

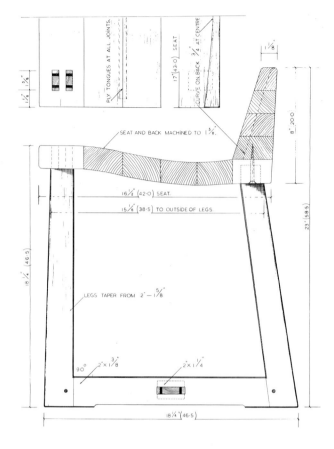

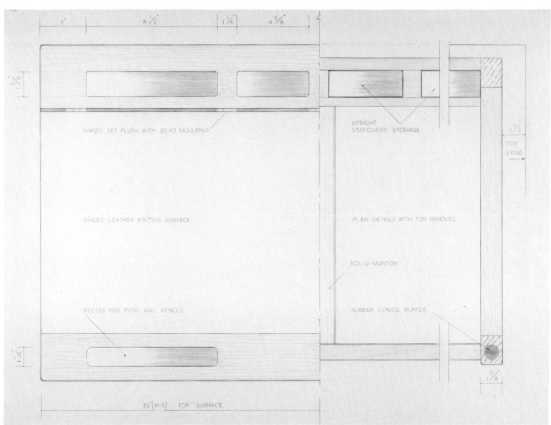

material and cutting list		student's desk			
		FINISHED SIZES			
No.	REQUIRED FOR	L.	W.	TH.	NOTES
2	Back legs	29¾″ 755mm	2¼″ 57mm	1⅜″ 35mm	Taper from 2¼″ to 1¾″ (57 to 45 mm)
2	Front legs	27½″ 698mm	″ ″	″ ″	
2	Base rails	22″ 560mm	3″ 75mm	″	
1	Foot rail	33″ 840mm	″ ″	1¼″ 32mm	
2	Top side rails	18¾″ 472mm	5″ 127mm	1⅜″ 35mm	
1	Back rail	32½″ 825mm	″ ″	1¼″ 32mm	
1	Front rail	″ ″	3¼″ 82mm	⅞″ 22mm	
1	Long partition rail	31″ 788mm	4⅝″ 118mm	½″ 12mm	
	Top				
1	Back rail	36″ 915mm	4″ 102mm	1⅜″ 35mm	
1	Front rail	″ ″	3″ 75mm	″ ″	
2	Top panel	36″ 915mm	14″ 315mm	¼″ 6mm	
1	Top core approx.	120″ 3m	1″ 25mm	1″ 25mm	For inner frame of ply sandwich construction
1	Centre munting	17¾″ 450mm	2″ 50mm	¾″ 18mm	
2	Bottom panels	14¾″ 375mm	17¾″ 400mm	¼″ 6mm	Cedar veneered ply

material and cutting list		low backed chair			
		FINISHED SIZES			
No.	REQUIRED FOR Seat & Back	L.	W.	TH.	NOTES
3	Nos. 1, 2, 3	17″ 430mm	3⅛″ 80mm	1⅝″ 40mm	These are squared up measurements before angles are cut. Advisable to cut out a little oversize.
1	No. 7	″ ″	2⅞″ 73mm	″ ″	
3	Nos. 4, 5, 6.	″ ″	2¾″ 70mm	″ ″	
1	No. 8	″ ″	2½″ 64mm	″ ″	
1	No. 10	″ ″	2⅛″ 54mm	″ ″	
2	Front legs	18¼″ 465mm	2⅛″ 54mm	1⅜″ 35mm	Tapering from 2⅛″ to 1⅝″ (54 to 40 mm)
2	Back legs	17½″ 445mm	2⅛″ 54mm	″ ″	
2	Base rails	17″ 430mm	2″ 50mm	″ ″	
1	Cross stretcher	15″ 380mm	″ ″	1¼″ 32mm	

9 DROP-LEAF TABLE

This is an ambitious piece which highlights the different approaches to design of the cabinetmaker and craftsman on the one hand and the fine artist and industrial designer, who are not so wedded to traditional skills, materials and values, on the other. This design has its roots firmly in tradition since the concept of the circular drop-leaf table has been around for many centuries, and nothing in it has been compromised to cost, efficiency or current fashions, and yet it still appears to me to be as appropriate to the needs of many in 1985 as it was in 1968 when I first designed it.

It is not a design for large scale production, as the necessity for careful grain and timber selection, so crucial for the success of the finished piece, and the hand skills necessary for its execution, make this definitely a craftsman's piece. Although a veneered chipboard top and laminated legs would still retain the overall visual concept, it would ruin what this particular table is about, which is solid timber being worked with a sensitive touch.

Materials: It is important to remember that although the floating leaves of this design have been around for many centuries, it is nevertheless structurally a very risky thing to do in solid timber, since that large unsupported area is very susceptible to cupping. So here we have to follow tradition and select the timber with utmost care both for moisture content, species and, equally important, its original position in the growing tree. This is why so many tables in the past were made from Cuban mahogany, the most stable of all timbers, but now unobtainable. Unfortunately, quarter sawn timber, which is preferable for its stability, does not usually display the most interesting grain pattern except in the case of oak, but at all costs avoid outside plain sawn boards and remember that narrower boards glued together are more likely to remain stable than wide ones. For the legs, select timber that naturally follows the curve of the full-size template you will have made.

This table is particularly successful and looks equally good but remarkably different in rich English walnut or brown oak on the one hand, and straight grained cherry, yew or light oak on the other. The light oak in particular gives the design a freshness that makes it far more appropriate for modern light interiors.

Construction: Keep the timber for the top as thick as possible from the planer at the outset. Glue up the leaves flat and out of wind. Once set, allow free air flow around them as though they were suspended on the table itself. Leave them for as long as possible whilst making the rest of the table, and then finally true up and thickness them before fitting.

Fig. 151 Drop-leaf table perspective.

186

Fig. 152   *(a)* *Plan.*
              (b) *Elevation.*
              (c) *Working detail.*

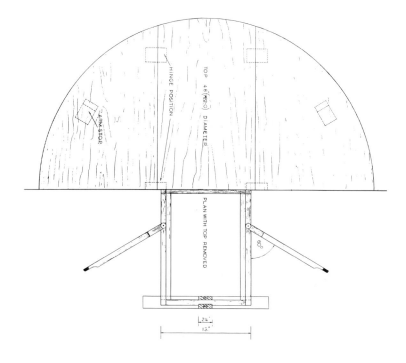

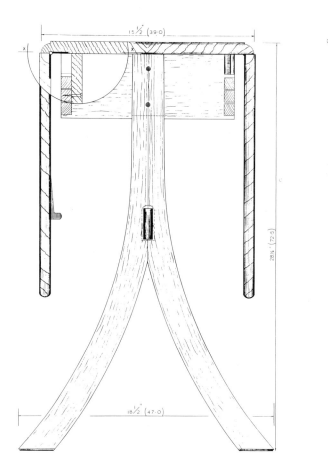

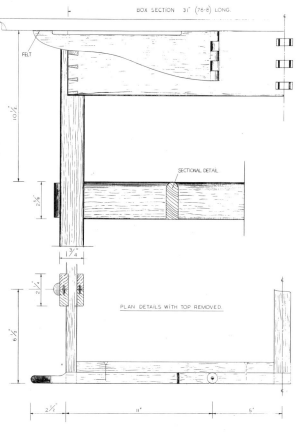

material cutting list		drop leaf table			
		FINISHED SIZES			
No.	REQUIRED FOR	L.	W.	TH.	NOTES
4	Legs (joined at centre)	29″ 737mm	5¼″ 133mm	1¾″ 45mm	To be cut to template following the natural curve of the timber and to avoid undue waste
2	End rails	12½″ 318mm	4½″ 115mm	¾″ 18mm	
2	Side rails	31″ 788mm	4½″ ″	″ ″	
2	Arms	13″ 330mm	3½″ 90mm	″ ″	
4	Inner strengtheners	14″ 355mm	4½″ 115mm	″	
1	Cross rail	12½″ 318mm	″ ″	1¼″ 32mm	
1	Rail	32½″ 825mm	2⅝″ 66mm	⅞″ 22mm	
	Top – to finish 48″ (1220mm) diameter				
1	Centre fixed section	48″ 1220mm	15½″ 395mm	¾″ 18mm	Mark out with aid of template to avoid undue waste
2	Leaves	46″ 1168mm	17″ 432mm	″ ″	

Index